NATIONS OF THE MODERN WORLD

ARGENTINA H. S. Ferns
Professor of Political Science,
University of Birmingham

AUSTRALIA O. H. K. Spate
Director, Research School of Pacific Studies

BELGIUM Vernon Mallinson
Professor of Comparative Education, University of
Reading

CEYLON S. A. Pakeman
Formerly Professor of Modern History, Ceylon
University College; Appointed Member, House of
Representatives, Ceylon, 1947–52

CYPRUS H. D. Purcell
Lecturer in English Literature,
Queen's University, Belfast

EAST David Childs
GERMANY *Lecturer in Politics, University of Nottingham*

MODERN EGYPT Tom Little
Managing Director and General Manager of
Regional News Services (Middle East), Ltd, London

ENGLAND John Bowle
Professor of Political Theory, Collège d'Europe,
Bruges

FINLAND W. R. Mead
Professor of Geography, University College, London;
Formerly Chairman, Anglo-Finnish Society

MODERN John Campbell
GREECE *Fellow of St Antony's College, Oxford*
Philip Sherrard
Assistant Director, British School of Archaeology,
Athens, 1958–62

MODERN INDIA	Sir Percival Griffiths
	President of the India, Pakistan and Burma Associations
MODERN IRAN	Peter Avery
	Lecturer in Persian and Fellow of King's College, Cambridge
ITALY	Muriel Grindrod
	Formerly Editor of International Affairs *and* The World Today
	Assistant Editor of The Annual Register
JAPAN	Sir Esler Dening
	H.M. Ambassador to Japan, 1952–57
KENYA	A. Marshall MacPhee
	Formerly Managing Editor of The East African Standard Group; *producer with British Broadcasting Corporation*
LIBYA	John Wright
	Formerly of the Sunday Ghibli, *Tripoli*
MALAYSIA	J. M. Gullick
	Formerly of the Malayan Civil Service
MOROCCO	Mark I. Cohen
	Director of Taxation, American Express
	Lorna Hahn
	Professor of African Studies, American University
NEW ZEALAND	James W. Rowe
	Director of New Zealand Institute of Economic Research, Inc.
	Margaret A. Rowe
	Tutor in English, Victoria University, Wellington
NIGERIA	Sir Rex Niven
	Colonial Service, Nigeria, 1921–59; Member of Northern House of Assembly, 1947–59
PAKISTAN	Ian Stephens
	Formerly Editor of The Statesman Calcutta and Delhi, *1942–51; Fellow of King's College, Cambridge, 1952–58*

PERU	Sir Robert Marett *H.M. Ambassador in Lima, 1963–67*
SOUTH AFRICA	John Cope *Formerly Editor-in-Chief of* The Forum; *South African Correspondent of* The Guardian
SPAIN	George Hills *Formerly Spanish Programme Organizer and Latin America correspondent, British Broadcasting Corporation*
SUDAN REPUBLIC	K. D. D. Henderson *Formerly of the Sudan Political Service; Governor of Darfur Province, 1949–53*
TURKEY	Geoffrey Lewis *Senior Lecturer on Islamic Studies, Oxford*
THE UNITED STATES OF AMERICA	H. C. Allen *Commonwealth Fund Professor of American History, University College, London*
WEST GERMANY	Michael Balfour *Reader in European History, University of East Anglia*
YUGOSLAVIA	Muriel Heppell and F. B. Singleton

BELGIUM

BELGIUM

By

VERNON MALLINSON

PRAEGER PUBLISHERS

New York · Washington

BOOKS THAT MATTER

Published in the United States of America in 1970
by Praeger Publishers, Inc.
111 Fourth Avenue, New York, N.Y. 10003

© 1970 in London, England, by Vernon Mallinson

All rights reserved

Library of Congress Catalog Card Number: 72-104772

Printed in Great Britain

For
Paul, Claire, Geneviève
and Bénicia

Preface

My CONNECTIONS with Belgium go back to the 1920s when it was just as cheap to spend a summer holiday on the Belgian coast as anywhere in Great Britain. I was then firmly reprimanded by the proprietor of a newspaper kiosk for my addiction to a number of trashy thrillers churned out by an unknown hack-writer – Georges Simenon! The same kindly Belgian lady proceeded to lend me 'respectable' Belgian authors from her own private library and so, unwittingly, started a chain of events which have drawn me closer and closer to the Belgian people in sympathy and understanding as the years have sped by. With the coming of the Second World War my expertise on Belgium (such as it then was) warranted my recruitment into S.O.E. and throughout those war years, and beyond, I became inextricably involved in Belgian affairs. I have never had cause to regret this involvement. It has brought me many friends in many walks of life, not all of whom by any means share my opinions, but all of whom respect them. And so it follows that, as I have been meditating on and writing this book over the last two years, I am tempted to suggest that Belgium is possibly the last true democracy to flourish in western Europe. All turns, of course, on how you define democracy. But I am not to be caught up in that argument.

For the earlier part of this history of the Belgian people I have drawn freely on Henri Pirenne's monumental study, to which he devoted the greater part of his life. My more detailed analysis of the contemporary scene is based partly on my own notebooks and diaries, partly on discussion with informed Belgians from various political groupings, partly on careful cross-checking in the relevant newspaper files, and partly on a mass of documentation readily procured for me by members of the staff of the Belgian Embassy in London. To them, and in particular to Mlle F. van Haelewyck, I am most grateful.

My manuscript was almost complete when it was announced that Marcel-Henri Jaspar had just published his memoirs (*Souvenirs sans Retouche*). I hastened to read what he had to say. My own account of the events 1939–45 differs in some respects from his, but I have seen no reason to change my opinions. Most recently Belgian friends have sent me cuttings from *Le Soir*, in which Paul-Henri Spaak has been serialising extracts from a promised two-volume account of his own stewardship. The first volume (*Combats Inachevés*) has already appeared. I have not read it, but the extracts I have read in *Le Soir*, while again differing in some points of detail, do not seem to justify any basic change in my approach to and interpretation of Leopold III's relations with his government and subsequent actions. It is rumoured that Albert de Vleeschauwer will now feel compelled to tell his side of the story. If and as it appears I shall read it with interest. But I shall be surprised indeed if his account forces me to abandon my view that Leopold III allowed himself to be manoeuvred into the position of becoming a politicians' scapegoat.

The House of Coburg, it seems to me, is worthy of support because its strengths outweigh any weaknesses anyone can unearth or conjure up. Without the House of Coburg Belgium could hardly have become a modern nation, prosperous and self-reliant. Without the single-minded and disinterested devotion to his country's cause of each single monarch she could not have hoped to survive to become what she is today. And without that continued single-mindedness of King Baudouin she cannot hope today to solve her internal problems centred on the complexities of federalism. As my story unfolds all this should become evident.

University of Reading,   VERNON MALLINSON
June 1969

Contents

Maps

List of Illustrations

(All are inserted between pages 112 and 113)

15

Acknowledgements

THE AUTHOR AND PUBLISHERS wish to record their grateful thanks to Monsieur William Ugeux and his staff at the Institut Belge d'Information et de Documentation, Brussels, who provided the majority of the photographs and located those not on their files.

Nos. 21, 24, and 30 are reproduced by permission of Agence Belga, Brussels.

Chapter 1

Introductory

MODERN BELGIUM IS SURROUNDED in the north by the Netherlands, in the east by Germany and the Grand Duchy of Luxembourg, and in the south by France. She has a coastline 42 miles in length along the North Sea, the main seaports being Ostend and Zeebrugge. The Scheldt estuary enables sea-going vessels to reach Antwerp which is about 50 miles inland and which, along with Rotterdam and Hamburg, is one of the three largest ports of northern Europe. The port of Ghent – the second largest in Belgium – is linked to the sea by canal. Antwerp itself is linked to the entire world by over 290 regular shipping lines and has the reputation of being the fastest 'turn-around' port in the world. In 1964 the freight handled amounted to 46.6 million tons, and important works in hand for the completion of a new sea-lock (1,650 feet long and so far the largest in the world) will permit the passage of ocean-going ships of 80,000 to 100,000 tons fully laden. In addition to all this 85 per cent of Belgium's total foreign trade passes through Antwerp. Latest figures available (1965) show that Belgium's own merchant fleet comprises one hundred ships with a total gross tonnage of 727,851 tons. It is one of the most modern fleets in the world, 41 per cent of the ships being little more than five years old. Internal navigable waterways extend for over 1,000 miles and link the great industrial regions to neighbouring countries and to the seaports. They are used by some 6,000 lighter craft carrying over 15 million tons of freight per annum.

Population

The population of Belgium in 1830 was less than 4 million, but within a hundred years it had risen to 8 million. By 1947 the figure stood at 8,510,000 and the latest census reveals an increase to 9,556,000 (120,000 attributable to immigration) living on 11,779 square miles of territory and thus making a population density of

19

roughly 810 inhabitants per square mile. This is slightly lower than that of the Netherlands but comparable to that of densely populated regions elsewhere in western Europe (the English industrial basin, the Ruhr, northern France, and the north of Italy). The growing prosperity of the country throughout the nineteenth century has led to the replacement of small townships by a concentration of the population in large urban areas, Brussels itself being an outstanding example with a population of over one million and yet being no great distance from other big cities. Antwerp is only 30 miles away and has a population of 700,000; Liège (60 miles distant) has 500,000; Charleroi (32 miles away) has 300,000; Ghent (also 32 miles away) has over 200,000; Bruges (60 miles away) houses 100,000 inhabitants.

Local Government

This phenomenon of concentration in the cities is still continuing. The poles of attraction, of course, vary in size according to the degree of industrialisation attained by the region concerned, but they spread all over the country with the sole exception of the Campine. Belgium divides itself into nine provinces and the population distribution province by province at the end of 1965 was as follows:

Antwerp	1,494,062
Brabant	2,108,296
	(includes the capital city, Brussels)
East Flanders	1,029,165
West Flanders	1,294,695
Hainaut	1,333,432
Liège	1,017,582
Limburg	624,446
Luxembourg	219,450
Namur	378,106

The fundamental duality of the Belgian nation has also to be reckoned with, for the language boundary marks the dividing-line between regions which are populated in very different ways. Greater Brussels itself (officially bilingual but with a French-speaking majority) accounts for 12 per cent of the population. The Flemish provinces account for 55 per cent of the total population figure and have a population density of 975 inhabitants to the square mile. In the south the density is only half as much: 473 inhabitants per square mile representing 33 per cent of the total population.

Each of the nine provinces is headed by a Provincial Council elected by universal suffrage. The Council in turn elects a Permanent Deputation whose task it is to deal with the day-to-day running of provincial affairs. Each province is divided into about forty administrative districts or *arrondissements*, each district being headed by a government commissioner who bears the title of District Commissioner. In overall control of a province is the Governor who is both appointed and dismissed by the King. Provincial Councils have far greater powers that an equivalent English County Council. In the first place they nominate about one-third of the members of the Senate. They receive financial grants from the state, but they also raise their own taxes (the bicycle tax, for example, which, in a country where cycling is almost as universal as in Holland and is also a popular national sport, proves to be a constant and sound source of revenue). They administer their own school systems and until recently fixed their own salary-scales for teachers, thus vying with one another to attract the most competent teachers, and boast of the most advanced educational programmes. They are responsible for a number of hospitals and similar institutions. They do their own policing (as opposed to the nationwide *Gendarmerie*) and are held responsible for the maintenance of all but the most important roads.

Each *arrondissement* comprises a number of *communes* or townships, and the *commune* in effect forms the basis of the entire civil administration of the country. There are some 2,660 in all, all jealously guarding their privileges and independence as handed down from the Middle Ages. Generically they are termed 'towns' though such a 'town' may be as small as Durbuy in the Ardennes (population 3,000) or as large as the important suburb of Brussels, Schaerbeek, with a population of more than a quarter of a million. Each such *commune* is administered by a Town Council consisting of the burgomaster, aldermen, and councillors. The burgomaster is appointed by the King on a recommendation from the Town Council, and is almost invariably already an alderman. In cities and industrial areas the burgomaster is most frequently of the professional class, often a lawyer, and he may also be a senator or an elected deputy for the constituency. In a smaller town he will be of some commercial or industrial importance, such as the owner of a factory. In a village community (such as Durbuy) he would be most commonly the local squire. Members of the Town Council are elected every six years and aldermen in turn are elected by the Town Council, their number being specified by law.

The Judiciary

The administration of justice is equally decentralised. The supreme legal authorities are the Assize Courts (one for each province), the Courts of Appeal centred on Brussels, Ghent, and Liège, and the *Cour de Cassation* which is the highest court of all and is established in Brussels. Below this level the country as a whole is divided into twenty-six legal districts, each of which has its own court for both civil and criminal offences. At the lowest level there exist 250 judicial *cantons* each of which has its own Justice of the Peace. There is no death penalty, the last execution (by guillotine) having been carried out as long ago as 1851. Other important legal bodies are the Conciliation Boards set up to arbitrate in disputes between employers and employees and the Council of State (established in 1946), whose important function is that of drafting laws and their decrees of implementation and to give its considered opinion on projects and bills submitted to its close scrutiny by the government.

The Constitution

The Belgian constitution, as first promulgated in 1831, has seen little change over the years and is still regarded today as a model of its kind because of the wide and tolerant outlook it reflects. It begins by recognising three authorities which though separate in law are in fact interdependent. These are the executive, the legislature, and the judiciary. The executive power is vested in the King and his Ministers. The legislative power is wielded collectively by the King and Parliament. In dealing with judicial power (the organisation of which we have just briefly analysed) the constitution charges its judges with the task of representing the justice of the nation as opposed to acting as mere agents of the executive.

Thus, though the King reigns and has considerable rights and responsibilities, he does not rule. His own person is inviolable. It is his prerogative to implement decisions of the legislative authority by means of Royal Decrees which may never run counter to the basic tenets of the law. No act by the King is effective unless it is countersigned by a Minister, and by the same token no ministerial decision can have legal force until countersigned by the King in the form of a Royal Decree. The underlying aim of this clause in the constitution is to provide for a stable form of authority and to safeguard the King's status as supreme arbiter. The King, however, may dissolve or prorogue Parliament. He appoints and dismisses his Ministers. He can (and often does) refuse to accept a Minister's resignation. When a particular government falls he tries to find a suitable Minister to form another government, it being necessary, of course, for that particular Minister and his team to obtain the support of a majority of members of both the House of Representatives and of the Senate. The King appoints civil servants, magistrates, and diplomatic representatives abroad. And he also confers rank in the armed forces of which he is the Commander-in-Chief, though not since 1949 actively so, it having then been clarified that his first duty must always be to act as supreme Head of State.

Legislative power resides with Parliament, which consists of two elected houses – the House of Representatives and the Senate. The Lower House and the Senate enjoy the same powers, so that draft laws and bills may be first presented equally well to either assembly. They do not become law, however, until they have been approved by both houses and promulgated by the King. Parliamentary elections generally take place every four years, it being usual to hold both these elections and those for the Provincial Councils on the same day. The age of eligibility for election to the Lower House is twenty-five and to the Senate forty. Election is on a basis of universal suffrage for both men and women over twenty-one years of age, but, granted that it is universal suffrage, it is incumbent on every qualified elector to present himself at the polling booth to record his vote. Failure to do so is a breach of the law and failing a medical certificate (or some such reasonable excuse) the errant elector will be fined. The method of election is by proportional representation. The Lower House comprises 212 members and the Senate 178, though only two-thirds of the senators are chosen by popular vote. The remaining one-third are nominated by the Provincial Councils and co-opted by the senators themselves. The Prince of Liège, as brother of the King, is himself a senator by right.

Political Parties

Political activity is today dominated by three main parties: the Christian Social Party (PSC), the Belgian Socialist Party (PSB), and the Party of Liberty and Progress (PLP). Communist representation is negligible. Within the last decade two more parties have steadily gathered support, though they are no way near representing a serious challenge to the three main parties. These are the *Volksunie* (Flemish Nationalists), who gained 20 seats in the Lower House at the 1968 elections, and the Walloon Federalists, who took 12 seats. The *Volksunie* originally came into existence to defend the cultural, political, economic, and social interests of the Flemish people. The Walloons have latterly felt it imperative to organise their own counterblast to these tendencies. As for the three main parties, the Social Christians have supporters in every class, since they represent in modern form the interests of Catholic voters. The great majority of the agricultural population votes for them and they share with the PLP the votes of the middle classes and those of the industrial leaders in the towns. The Belgian Socialist Party gets its main support from the working classes, though it shares with the PLP and the PSC votes from office-workers and civil servants. In agricultural areas and among the middle classes its influence is marginal. The PLP (the new name taken by the Liberals in 1961) is supported by a large section of the middle classes, civil servants, office-workers, industrialists, and members of the liberal professions. It obtains little support in country districts. Its present-day importance resides in the fact that, since the PSC and the PSB are often almost equally matched on election to Parliament, neither usually manages to command a sufficient majority in order to be able to govern alone. Thus the PLP acts as an effective mediating force and can always threaten to topple a government if its measures or attitudes seem to be moving the country towards ill-considered or ill-advised action. Unlike the Liberal Party in Great Britain it is also strong enough to form a coalition government with one or other of the main parties and to be able to provide Ministers of important cabinet rank.[1]

The Prosperity of Belgium

We have already discussed the importance to the economy of Belgium's ports and sea-carrying trade, and of its inland waterways. It is no exaggeration to add that wherever one looks in Belgium — from Flanders to the heart of the Ardennes — the presence and the work of man are everywhere visible. Belgium is a prosperous country, and it owes its prosperity, of course, to the fact that it is located at the very heart of western Europe at the crossroads of the Latin and

[1] At the 1968 elections the PSC claimed 69 seats in the Lower House, the PSB 59 seats, and the PLP 47 seats. The communists held 5 seats.

Germanic worlds. It is equally a particularly important crossroads for air travel, figures for 1964 showing that 170,000 civil aircraft belonging to over forty international airlines touched down at Belgian airports. The Belgian railway network, with a total length of 2,840 miles, is one of the densest in the world, and Ostend (as every traveller knows) is the starting-point for railroad penetration into the heart of Europe. In 1964 Belgian rail services transported over 66.5 million tons of freight and 275 million passengers. A million motor vehicles of all kinds travel on Belgian roads every year. Seven international motorways run right across Belgian territory, and its own network comprises over 14,700 miles of main roads and 6,430 miles of state highways. However, while it is true to stress that this prosperity is the result of being located at the hub of one of the main western European crossroads, with all the main international lines of communication either crossing Belgian territory or converging on it, and also of lying along the edge of the Meuse – Scheldt – Rhine delta, this is by no means the whole story. Belgium's present status as a top-ranking economic and industrial power is equally in part due to its once-rich deposits of coal and iron-ore, to the foresight and acumen of its leaders (from the King downwards) throughout the nineteenth century, and to the will to work in all fields of endeavour which has characterised the Belgian people through the centuries.

Figures from a 1966 census reveal the working population (excluding members of the armed forces and the Militia) to be 3,722,448, of which 31 per cent were women. The gross national product in 1964 amounted to 768.2 billion Belgian francs (572.3 billion in 1960 and 459.8 billion in 1958). During 1964 the national revenue *per capita* stood at 65,000 francs, or about half the corresponding figure for the United States. An estimate of the distribution of the working population by sector of economic activity runs as follows:

Agriculture	216,000
Industry: extractive	102,000
manufacturing	1,267,000
building and construction	276,000
transport and communications	245,000
Trade, banking, insurance, services	1,404,000
Unemployed	55,000

The working population continues to follow a trend which has become more marked in recent years but which is common to most countries with a highly developed economy: there is a marked drop in the number engaged in agriculture and a corresponding increase in the number of people employed in services, etc., while capital investment makes traditional industries less and less labour-intensive.

The following comparative table showing the distribution of the active population according to their work is very revealing:

	1890	1910	1947	1961
Agriculture, horticulture, etc.	22.1%	22.5%	12.6%	7.5%
Industry (including coal-mining, quarries, and sand-pits)	54.2%	45.0%	49.0%	47.7%
Trade, public services, and the liberal professions	23.7%	32.5%	38.4%	44.8%

The trend of the level of activity of the population as a whole is that of an industrialised country with increasing prosperity. Around the turn of the century some five out of ten Belgians were actively employed. Today this proportion is no more than four out of ten. Fewer women are at work (except in the professional classes), following an improvement in the overall standard of living.

Geographical distribution of those employed in industry

	1896		1961	
	Number	%	Number	%
Antwerp	101,743	9.2	241,155	15.9
W. Flanders	107,807	9.8	168,711	11.2
E. Flanders	166,721	15.1	211,470	14.0
Limburg	18,229	1.7	77,994	5.2
Total (Flemish)	394,500	35.8	699,330	46.3
Hainaut	264,705	24.0	213,391	14.1
Liège	188,854	17.2	195,350	12.9
Luxembourg	18,980	1.7	16,221	1.1
Namur	53,994	4.9	43,856	2.9
Total (Walloon)	526,533	47.8	468,818	31.0
Brabant	180,226	16.4	343,822	22.7

The shift of industry from the Walloon to the Flemish provinces is, as will be seen later, a fundamental cause of present acrimony, and is strikingly illustrated by the table on page 26.

Brabant, of course, includes the huge Brussels agglomeration. The most striking figures, however, are those concerning the province of Limburg. Scarcely half a century ago the Limburg province was a vast sandy waste, scattered with pine-trees and overrun with heather and broom. The white sand was used for the glass industry in the province of Namur and in the Borinage, but that was about all the inhabitants could wrest from their inheritance. The province was rightly dubbed the poorest in the country, and its inhabitants were considered to be the most wretched in Belgium, 'eating meat on only the four big church festivals of the year', as one writer, Georges Virrès, put it. The tables were turned overnight when it was found that there were rich coal deposits there. Mines were sunk and towns grew up round the pithead gear in regions which so far had existed only as barren wastes. The first coal was extracted in 1917 and there has been a steadily increasing output ever since, the mines of Genck, Winterslag, Zolder, and Zwartberg being among the most important in the country. Other industries have now followed, and Limburg today plays a vital role in the economic life of Belgium. Not surprisingly it currently has the highest birth-rate in the country. Its close-knit farming community, however, still dominates the scene and the province remains one of the most Catholic and conservative to be found anywhere in Belgium.

On the international plane Belgium has always championed free trade and within Belgium itself economic freedom is the golden rule. Anyone can establish a business enterprise or embark on some form of economic activity once purely administrative formalities have been complied with. Free competition is the keynote, and the exercise of these economic liberties is carefully safeguarded by a number of laws regulating abuses of economic power such as unfair competition, exclusive sales contracts, premium and clearance sales, hire-purchase sales, and loans.

Since the Second World War Belgian industry has steadily attracted foreign investment, and in 1967 the total contribution from the United States accounted for about 80 per cent of overall investment. American investments are mainly in the field of industry, though American firms show a lively interest in Belgium as an operational base for their own activities within the European Economic

Community. France takes second place, followed by the Netherlands, Italy, Great Britain, Germany, Switzerland, and Sweden. According to Belgian economists this could be the first indication of greater interpenetration in Belgium of certain industries having their principal place of business within the Common Market.

Belgium's share of world trade was in 1964 roughly 3.6 per cent. Yet she only accounts for 0.02 per cent of the total land surface of the globe and only 0.35 per cent of the total world population. In other words, Belgium's share of world trade is 175 times larger than her territorial area and ten times larger than her population figures. She exports 40 per cent of her total industrial output (mainly metals, machinery, machine-tools, glass, chemicals, diamonds). On the other hand, apart from coal, clay, sand, and stone, the country has no natural resources and must purchase her essential raw materials from abroad. The Belgian economy therefore depends to a very great extent on world markets and exports are vital to the country's subsistence.

Agriculture

Though the total area of farmland in Belgium is only just above 4 million acres, the industry is capable of supplying 80 per cent of the total requirements of the population, thanks to specialised intensive methods used by operators of small and medium-sized farms. Agriculture accounts for 6 per cent of the working population and its contribution to the national revenue amounts to about 7 per cent. It produces raw materials for a number of processing industries (flax, sugar-beet, hops, tobacco) and has made notable material progress in the field of both animal and vegetable selection. Horticulture and market-gardening are rapidly expanding enterprises and account for the bulk of exports in this field.

Coal-Mining

Coal is the basic asset of the Belgian economy and is mined in five basins: the Borinage, the Central Basin, Charleroi, Liège, and the Campine Basin, the latter possessing 70 per cent of total known reserves amounting to an estimated 4,500 million tons. In 1964 the total output stood at 21.3 million tons. Coking plants are the main outlet for soft coal and of the total annual output of over 7 million tons of coke about 9 per cent is exported. The gas industry is also a great coal consumer. Practically all the electricity used in Belgium is produced in thermal power-stations and the main raw material there used is low-grade coal.

The Steel Industry

Steel-making is one of the oldest of Belgian industries and is also one of the most important sectors of the Belgian economy. After Luxembourg, Belgium has the highest *per capita* steel production in the world – almost one ton. Two-thirds of her product is sold abroad. The industry grew up around the main coal-mining regions in the south; two large mills are located in the province of Luxembourg at the extreme northern limit of the Grand Duchy's iron-ore deposits; there is a mill in Brabant; and ever new and more modern plant is being set up, notably at Chertal (near Liège) and near Ghent. Today, of course, much of the iron-ore comes from overseas, but thanks to the port of Antwerp and the well-developed inland waterways transport costs are kept at a minimum. Constant experimentation goes on, and amongst the recent achievements must be numbered the development of the LD-AC process, the manufacture of electrolytical tinplate, the production of cold-rolled steel, and (for the first time in western Europe) the production of crystal-aligned steel for use in the manufacture of transformers.

The modern non-ferrous metals industry dates back to the beginning of the nineteenth century when a Liège chemist, Daniel Dony, succeeded in isolating and manufacturing zinc. Today Belgium ranks among the principal world exporters of non-ferrous metals and is among the leading five for cobalt, zinc, copper, germanium, and radium. She is the biggest producer in the world of germanium and radium, and is one of the few countries which export tantalum, niobium, and selenium.

Engineering

Mechanical engineering is the most important sector of industry in the country and alone supplies 20 per cent of the entire national production figure. It is a very ancient industry, going back to Roman times, and several existing firms are hundreds of years old, though extremely dynamic and well-equipped. It is also an industry remarkable for an extraordinary degree of specialisation, and apart from about twenty-five giant concerns employing almost one-third of the total manpower in the entire industry there are countless small firms manufacturing a very wide range of highly diversified products. The industry in fact produces anything from ordinary wire to complete industrial plant; from screwdrivers to locomotives for the Trans-Europe Express; from contact-breakers to hydro-electric power-stations; from nautical gear for sailing dinghies to refrigerator ships. Some of these manufactures have achieved a world-wide reputation – notably the Browning pistol and the FN light automatic rifle (adopted recently by several NATO armies) and both manufactured at the centuries-old small-arms factories in Liège. Also in Liège work is now progressing (under a joint programme with German, Italian, and Dutch manufacturers) for the supply of jet engines to the armed forces of the four countries involved. Other manufactures highly valued abroad include surgical instruments, sporting guns, diamond tools (especially bits for drilling oil-wells), electrical engineering equipment, electronic appliances, and telecommunications equipment.

The Chemical Industry

Since Ernest Solvay invented in 1863 the soda-manufacturing process which bears his name, the chemical industry has developed in many other directions extending from fertilisers to photographic film. Abundant supplies of coal have made possible an important nitrate production and the development of the distillation products of the benzol group. The pharmaceutical industry has of recent years made great strides. New branches have been added such as petrochemicals. The petroleum industry itself has undergone extraordinarily fast development (again due to the port of Antwerp), and from having started as a mere distributor of gasoline Belgium has today five refineries in Antwerp and one in Ghent with a production capacity of 14 million tons per annum. The 430 firms engaged in the chemical industry generally employ over 60,000 and have an annual turnover in excess of 40 billion francs; in tonnage of merchandise exported Belgium ranks among the ten principal chemical exporters, her exports for 1964 being valued at some 22.3 billion francs. The chemical industry, however, brings further renown to Belgium in that it not only exports its products but also its skills. More and more enterprises call on the knowledge and assistance of skilled Belgian personnel, and between 1958 and 1964 no fewer than seventy complete factories were planned and supervised in countries such as Bulgaria, Canada, the Netherlands, Hungary, Yugoslavia, the United States, the USSR, South Africa, Romania, Iran, Israel, Japan, and Mexico.

Textiles

The Belgian textile industry with its 135,000 workers and employees, mainly concentrated around Ghent and Verviers, occupies a very important place in world production. Apart from flax it imports all its raw materials. Based on a long tradition dating back to the Middle Ages, Belgian woollen and linen cloth enjoy a first-class reputation abroad, and in woollens and worsted Belgium ranks only second to France among the continental countries of the Common Market. One of the first countries in the world to manufacture rayon, Belgium now exports a complete range of rayon and staple fibre, nylon and acrylic products, for the most varied uses. Total Belgian exports of textiles in 1964 amounted to 15.5 per cent of the overall value of Belgian exports.

Glass-Making

Belgium has one of the biggest glass industries in the world, largely because it is able to procure abundant and pure supplies of the necessary raw materials within the country itself. Sand comes from the Campine; limestone and dolomite from the Sambre and Meuse valleys; and the chemical industry supplies the sodium salts, sulphates, and carbonates it needs. Belgium was the world pioneer in the switch from hand operation to mechanical drawing and has now led the industry for many years. More than 80 per cent of the flat glass produced is for export, the United States being Belgium's biggest customer. The total annual output of glass of all kinds is in excess of 800,000 tons; and Belgium alone exports more window-glass than West Germany, France, Great Britain, and Japan put together.

Diamonds

The Diamond industry is one of Belgium's greatest specialised sectors and by tradition it has remained centred on Antwerp. All kinds of precious stones can be cut in Antwerp, and in terms of value the industry's exports account for about 4.2 per cent of total Belgian exports, estimated at over 11 billion francs per annum. Belgium also imports cut diamonds and through its central exchange of diamond brokers finds a ready market both for these and for its own products. Antwerp still remains the world market centre for cut diamonds and has likewise gained a world-wide reputation both for industrial diamonds and for the manufacture of all kinds of tools associated with the diamond industry.

Secondary (Artistic) Pursuits

Secondary but by no means negligible industries are concerned with the manufacture of paper and with printing (including playing-cards); with processing leather and making footwear; with cabinet- and furniture-making; with building construction. Among what might be termed the art industries the *Cristalleries du Val-Saint-Lambert* are the most important, the traditional skill of the glassblower presumably dating back to the fifteenth century when Venetian craftsmen first set foot in Antwerp. The manufacture of ceramics has flourished since the early sixteenth century and today there are 250 firms at work, employing almost 20,000 people. The making of artistic brass, bronze, and pewter ware for either religious or domestic use has been centred on Dinant since the thirteenth century. Finally, what might be termed a luxury skill today – the making of tapestry – has been traditionally centred on Tournai, Bruges, and Oudenarde, and workshops in these towns have been dispatching their masterpieces throughout Europe since the fifteenth century. At the beginning of the sixteenth century the art tapestry workshops in Brussels alone employed more than 40,000 people. A central workshop for tapestry renovation was established in Tournai in 1930 and in 1954 the Belgian government was proud to present to the United Nations a piece of fine modern tapestry worked in Mechlin.

The Role of the Universities

The universities and the higher technical and technological institutes have, of course, a large part to play in the industrial development of Belgium, and technical training at all levels is highly developed, there being more than 200 technical schools and insti-tutes spread throughout the country. Again, industry values highly all the research possibilities these institutions can offer and remains in very close liaison, not only by being actively represented on governing bodies, but also by large financial grants and by gifts of specimens of the latest equipment available for the varying manufacturing processes. In 1928 the National Fund for Scientific Research was set up by the Belgian government and is an important source of scholarship funds for young scientists. Credits appropriated by the state for the year 1965, for example, to be devoted solely to scientific research amounted to 8 billion francs, or over one per cent of the gross national revenue. In its time the National Fund for Scientific Research has made possible the stratosphere exploration by Piccard and Cosyns (1931–2) of Brussels University; Belgian participation in the second International Polar Year (1932–3); the creation of a scientific station on the Jungfraujoch; the construction of Professor Piccard's bathyscape; the building of the second French deep-level bathyscape; and the design and construction in Antwerp (1955) of the first electronic calculating machine. Other important appropriations for furthering scientific research include the Franqui Foundation for awarding important prizes to scientists of exceptional distinction and for bringing foreign scientists to lecture in Belgian universities; funds for medical and cancer research; for research into the nuclear sciences; for research into aeronautics and agriculture.

In 1947 the Inter-University Institute of Nuclear Sciences was founded, and this was soon followed by the establishment at Mol (in the Campine, near Antwerp) of a Nuclear Energy Study Centre equipped with three large reactors. The centre is a private, non-profit-making institution whose board of directors comprises representatives of the state, the universities, and industry. Its principal object is to supply a national laboratory used for all kinds of nuclear research, and to train specialists in the various branches of nuclear science for the nuclear industry itself and for the universities. Excluding a large number of foreign research workers and trainees, Mol today has a working strength of some 1,200 personnel and makes Belgium the sixth nuclear power in the world, ranking immediately after the United States, the USSR, Great Britain, France, and Canada. Finally, to emphasise once again the importance attached to scientific research at all levels throughout Belgium, it is worthwhile recording that in the year 1965 no less than 31,536 people were engaged in such scientific work – 8.65 per cent of the scientific working population.

The People

And so to the Belgian people themselves. It is important to remember that Belgium has two distinct ethnic groups. In the northern part is the Flemish group, speaking Dutch, which is one of the Germanic languages; and in the south we find the Walloon group, speaking French, a Romance language. The nordic type is distinguished by a few common features which include tall stature, a somewhat elongated head, fair hair, and light eyes. The Walloon type is smaller of stature, thickset, round-headed, and with dark hair and eyes. Of course, there has been much intermingling over the centuries, and not a little addition of Spanish blood, and most of the population have their characteristics coming from both main types. The most recent census figures (1966) show that the Flemish provinces have a total of 5,308,299 inhabitants; the Walloon provinces 3,112,958; the German-speaking *Cantons de l'Est* in Liège province 60,537; and the Brussels area (predominantly French-speaking) 1,074,586. The Flemings are for the most part strong and sincere practising Catholics. The Walloons are more often than not nominally Catholic, much in the same way as many in England would profess adherence to the Church of England, though there are strong free-thinking groups, particularly in the industrial areas.

The Fleming is a slow but deep thinker, and, as I have tried to describe him elsewhere, a curious mixture of sensuality, paganism, and mysticism combined with a love of pomp and pageantry and the good things of life.[1] He has never been better depicted than in the paintings of Peter Bruegel or Jérôme Bosch. The modern artist James Ensor (1860–1949) also makes some telling revelations. Two important modern playwrights, Herwig Hensen (1917–) and Michel de Ghelderode (1898–1962), in their own highly individual way add further facets to the understanding of the Fleming; the former by his deep introspection and the latter by his tortured studies of the poles of duality – Catholic and pagan – in the various types of mediaeval farce he conjures up for us. As the late Paul Fierens, a distinguished art critic, was fond of repeating, 'there *is* a Flemish vision of the universe and he who would truly understand the Belgian people as a whole must first grasp this'. The poet Guido Gezelle (1830–99) best illustrates this vision in its most approachable form as he hymns the simple forms of Nature and invests them with symbols which repeatedly bring us back to a loved and loving Creator. Stijn Streuvels (1871–1969) gives us the reverse side of the coin with his novels depicting the primitive passions of the Flemish peasant; and Maurice Maeterlinck (1862–1949), in his plays in particular, the intellectual's blend of symbolism with mysticism.

Not that the French-speaking Walloons do not betray most of

[1] *Modern Belgian Literature (1830–1960)*, London, 1966.

the same characteristics. Their approach, however, is more lively, more mercurial, less intense if no less sincere. The Walloon is fluent, witty, and often caustic; he feels himself inescapably caught up in the mainstream of the French way of life and thought, and in consequence is understandably hurt at any condescension on the part of the French or any suggestion that he is too aggressive, too boastful or ostentatious, too unsubtle, or given to 'mauling' the French tongue. He can certainly be very stubborn as he can be most generous-minded. Two modern surrealist painters, Paul Delvaux 1897–) and René Magritte (1898–1967), best illustrate, with their perfectionist and academic compositions, the differences between Flemish and Walloon symbolism and mysticism in art. Fernand Crommelynck (1885–) writes with subtlety and gusto, producing farces that are reminiscent of Molière. Herman Closson (1901–) deals mainly with the personalities of history and contrives to put on the stage characters who are surprisingly human and whose contradictions are on that account more easily understood. The simple lyricism of Gezelle is matched by the deceptively simple nostalgia of Maurice Carême (1899–). And then there is Georges Simenon (1903–) whose detective stories are never just detective stories and whose novels also catch in various subtle ways that divisiveness in Man's nature.

Art and Literature

None will deny the importance of Belgian painting, particularly that of the so-called Flemish School, which reached a peak of achievement in the fifteenth and seventeenth centuries. The Flemish painter is essentially a chronicler. His work is carefully observed, close to reality, and then imaginatively transposed as his fantasy or his faith directs. He has a zest for colour and takes an almost sensuous delight in retailed pictorial representation. The altarpiece *The Adoration of the Lamb* (in the Cathedral of St Bavon at Ghent) is one of the most famous examples in the world and is the work of the brothers Hubert (*c.* 1370–1426) and Jan (*c.* 1390–1441) van Eyck. The best of the works of Hans Memling (*c.* 1435–94) are in one single collection in the Hospital of St John in Bruges. The purity of approach of Gerard David (*c.* 1460–1523) is counterbalanced by that of Jérôme Bosch (*c.* 1450–1516), who knew how to express both the terror and the ecstasy of life for the common people in the strife-torn Middle Ages. It was on Bosch that Peter

Bruegel the Elder (*c.* 1525–69) modelled himself, scorning the manorial backgrounds and scenic artificiality which had so far characterised religious painting and giving us instead a rich anthology of peasant lore set in the village and in the midst of rustic life. Peter Paul Rubens (1577–1640) dominates the sixteenth and seventeenth centuries, lesser but important names including Jacob Jordaens (1593–1678) and Adriaen Brouwer (1605–38). The present age is still dominated by James Ensor, though Constant Permeke (1886–1952) is claimed as one of the leaders of Flemish expressionism. Among sculptors he is matched by Rik Wouters (1882–1916), Georges Grard (1901–   ), and Charles Leplae (1903–61), who often gave rein to his fantasy through figures inspired by scenes of folklore. Georges Minne (1866–1941) is equally outstanding because of his detachment from time, his mystic feeling, and the melancholy which pervades all his figures. His work has had influence both in France and Germany. Finally, among surrealist painters who have achieved worldwide recognition, one again cannot ignore René Magritte (1898–1967), whose refined imaginary universe stems always from the material everyday world, and Paul Delvaux (1897–   ), who achieves his effects from a careful academic composition which uncannily emphasises the surrealist nature of his work.

A truly Belgian voice in the field of literature could not, of course, make itself heard until the kingdom had properly established itself. The Flemish writer Henri Conscience (1812–83) was first in the field with a series of novels in which he talked to the people at the people's level and made them proud of their race and language. What he did for the Flemish novel Guido Gezelle (1830–99) did for Flemish poetry. He thinks in song and maintains that the profound melancholy of living can only be assuaged by song:

> 'O Song, O Song,
> You help the pain
> When grief strikes, and disaster –
> O Song, the wounded heart again
> Grows whole when you are master . . .'

The work of these Flemish writers was paralleled by that of Charles de Coster (1827–79) who, in his masterpiece *Thyl Ulenspiegel* (1867), tells in legendary and deliberate archaic form the generous fury of the Belgians in revolt against the Spanish tyrant. In the 1880s two important literary magazines, one Flemish and one French, thrust Belgian literary effort onto the international scene. *Van Nu en Straks* (From Now On) launched the formidable Flemish critic and author Auguste Vermeylen (1872–1945) and gave us the novelists Stijn Streuvels (1871–1969) and Cyriel Buysse (1859–1932) – also a playwright of distinction who, in both novels and plays, treats of the struggles of a peasant class against the nobility of the countryside. Herman Teirlinck (1879–   ) is another important novelist of this group, obsessed by the mysterious forces which shape the lives and destinies of his often heedless and taciturn heroes. The one important poet, Karel van de Woestijne (1878–1929), makes articulate the anguish of modern man and depicts the haunting and melancholy beauty of city life:

> 'I only ask for rest: I do not ask for peace.
> Oh, tender evening-shine of lamps and faces
> when noble night rolls up along day's misty places,
> when will your pure glow make my worries cease?'

The French magazine *La Jeune Belgique* provided the impetus needed to launch such important names as Camille Lemonnier (1844–1913), with his startling naturalist novel *Un Mâle*; Georges Rodenbach (1855–98) and his evocative story of *Bruges-La-Morte*; the poet Emile Verhaeren (1855–1916), with his works in praise of the energy and beauty of life; Charles Van Lerberghe (1861–1907), who in one magnificent symbolic poem, *Chanson d 'Eve*, sought to describe the divine infancy of the world's first woman; Maurice Maeterlinck (1862–1949), the dramatist who never ceased to be a poet, the philosopher who gave us not only *Blue Bird* but also *The Life of the Bees*. In many ways in direct line of descent from the examples set by these early writers we now have the impressionistic and tortured novels of André Baillon (1875–1932); those of Charles Plisnier (1896–1952), the first foreigner to win the *Prix Goncourt* with his *Faux Passeports* (1938); those of Franz Hellens (1881–   ), who claims that the fantastic and the real are inseparable and that we may only reach for what is real through the fantastic; and those of Marie Gevers (1883–   ), a charming regional novelist who cleverly evokes the Campine region where she has always chosen to live. The younger novelists of today are dominated by female writers: Françoise Mallet-Joris and Dominique Rollin whose themes are the human passions; Maud Frère, the novelist of adolescence; Beatrice Beck, another Goncourt prizewinner. Among the

poets must be mentioned Henri Michaux (1899–   ), who seeks
constantly to escape the futility of modern living through his own
imaginary world; Marcel Thiry (1897–   ), who on the contrary
preaches acceptance of the modern world; Roger Bodart (1910–   ),
who hymns the natural pleasures of ordinary existence – the only
real and permanent things life has to offer. In addition to playwrights mentioned earlier we should note as well José-André Lacour
(1919–   ) whose *L'Année du Bac* (1958) subtly catches the modern
idiom of the post-war generations of adolescents, Charles Bertin
(1919–   ) whose play *Love in a Labyrinth* was performed in Birmingham, England, in 1950, and Jean Mogin (1912–   ) who argues
that if you deny the existence of the external world you do so at
your peril. Mogin is one of the most promising dramatists of the
moment.

The Flemish theatre has been dominated by the novelist Herman
Teirlinck, who in a famous play, *Slow-Motion Picture* (1922), first
borrowed for the stage the techniques of the cinema. Gaston Martens
(1883–   ) has given us *The Village of Miracles* and *Birds of Para-
dise*, the latter being adapted for the French stage and later turned
into films produced both in France and America. Herwig Hensen
(1917–   ), poet and mathematician, takes a classical theme such
as *Lady Godiva* to preach a philosophy of pride, provocation, and
rebellion if we are to keep the personality intact. The younger generation is led by Tone Brulin (1926–   ) and Hugo Claus (1929–   ),
both of whom have broken with tradition and are rapidly making
a name for themselves abroad. Paul Van Ostayen (1896–1928)
launched the expressionist movement in modern Flemish poetry,
and he has been followed by Richard Minne (1891–   ), Raymond
Herreman (1896–   ), and Bert Decorte (1915–   ), a virtuoso who
writes in Latin as well as in Flemish. Herreman claimed that:

> 'We have no banner
> over our heads unfurled.
> With no drawn sword
> do we tilt at windmills.'

Younger contemporary Flemish poets follow this lead and take
as their themes love, the family, the past history of Flanders, and
the queer characters it has managed and still manages to produce,
treating the whole with commonplace matter-of-factness. The
modern Flemish novel is dominated by Felix Timmermans (1886–

1947), Ernest Claes (1885–1968), and Willem Elsschot (1882–1960). Maurice Roelants (1895–) is the first to introduce the Flemish reader to the psychological novel, being in the same tradition as François Mauriac. Gerard Walschap (1898–) is almost by instinct the 'born' novelist whose works are dominated by the problem of happiness. In the present post-war period there are many novelists at work, the most important of whom are Johan Daisne (1912–), whose novel *The Man Who Had His Hair Cut Short* (1947) has recently been turned into a macabre film, and Louis-Paul Boon (1912–), a generous and violent writer who seeks to uphold the dignity of man by highlighting his present despair.

A Way of Life

Both Flemings and Walloons have a well-deserved reputation for honesty, for industry – the need to be actively employed at something or another is almost a national disease – and for enjoying to the full and unashamedly the good things and the good life their industry can procure for them. They spend freely though they are by no means spendthrift. They are cautious but they give generously once they know their help is needed. They are fundamentally kind-hearted and they make a great fuss of children without necessarily spoiling them. Despite the disintegrating influences of modern times the family is still of great importance and the Belgian is very much a family man, delighting in seeking his pleasures along with his wife and children. As for the wife, she is fanatically houseproud and most obviously ranks cleanliness as next to Godliness. She is the one who carefully watches over her children's progress through school, sees to it that they are confirmed and attend Mass regularly, keeps a wary eye on the family budget, and neglects no opportunity to further the interests of her brood (amongst which she ranks her husband).

The German Count Keyserling once described the Belgians as noisy, lovers of display and of parades. There is much truth in this, but it is a heartening sight to attend some village *kermesse* at which the local brass band proudly and efficiently performs; at which the parish priest has his own role to play (along with his choristers and other children) in some religious parade which forms an integral part of the feasting; and at which everyone unashamedly enjoys himself in much the same way as his forebears have done since the Middle Ages. In the towns, of course, there is much more sophistica-

tion but no less merriment. Alongside all this the Belgian is a great
sports 'fan', association football, basketball, and cycle racing being
the chief attractions. Pigeon fancying and rabbit breeding (for food)
are common preoccupations of the working class, while the well-to-
do and the bourgeoisie might easily indulge in game-shooting and
wild-boar hunting, the Ardennes providing such sport in abundance.

On the intellectual plane, while the average Belgian may be said
to distrust intellectualism as such, he is nonetheless a sincere patron
of the arts. He will buy a picture from perhaps a struggling artist
and pride himself on its possession and the investment he has made.
He will commission a bust of his wife or daughter from a sculptor
to celebrate some important family occasion. He is a fairly regular
theatregoer, so much so that, even with the counter-attraction of
television, theatres in provincial towns can flourish. He knows what
music he likes without claiming to be a connoisseur and is a faithful
concert-goer (this often a family occasion), proudly conscious of the
fact that the late Queen Elisabeth (grandmother of Baudouin I)
was the initiator and patron of what has now become an important
annual international musical festival and that Belgium was the first
country to attempt to draw children at an early age to the love of
good music through the *Jeunesse Musicale* (Children's Concerts)
movement. He is avidly curious about what is going on in the greater
world outside and is in consequence a ready subscriber to lectures
of all kinds on exploration or travel in exotic countries, or simply
(if he is a Catholic) on some aspect of the Church's work or teaching.

With all this he is no respecter of persons from the royal family
downwards. He judges a person on proven results. He has the courage of his convictions and obstinately holds to them. He values above
all else his comfort and his independence, but if he has to choose
between the two he will sacrifice everything for his independence.
Politics he leaves to the politicians, being only moved to anger and
action when their mismanagement (real or imagined) troubles his
own equanimity or peace of mind. Then, the heat is on, and with
a vengeance! Yet withal he is a friendly and dynamic person, warm
in his affections, good-natured and likeable, curiously given to self-
belittlement despite a certain ostentation, a mass of attractive contradictions. He is, of course, what his history has made him.

Chapter 2

Glorious Heritage

WHO WERE THE ORIGINAL *Belgae* about whom Caesar writes so eloquently is still a matter of dispute among historians. They must have been one of the outstanding Celtic tribes which settled between the Rhine and the North Sea from the seventh century B.C. onwards. They certainly resisted the Roman invasion of their territory for five long years, drawing reinforcements continually from England where, it is said, they had also settled and founded a capital at *Venta Belgarum*, the future city of Winchester, being governed there by King Cunobeline (the hero of Shakespeare's play *Cymbeline*). After the Roman pacification (52 B.C.) they enjoyed some 400 years of prosperity based on the great highways built by the Romans to open up the Mediterranean to the north; Christianity came to the country in the second century; and in the third century the Emperor Diocletian divided *Gallia Belgica* into three provinces, largely autonomous since they were governed from Rheims, Cologne, and Trèves. The Frankish invasion began in the third century, and when the Romans finally withdrew (A.D. 445) the country became a frontier province of the Merovingian empire. Clovis, King of the Franks, was baptised at Rheims in 496, so reconciling himself with the Christian hierarchy of the Belgo-Romans, and then went on to the unification of Greater Gaul, choosing Paris as his capital. The Merovingian dynasty ended in 751 when Pépin the Short packed off the then puppet monarch to a monastery, had himself crowned and anointed at Soissons (thus becoming king by Divine Right), and rewarded the Papacy for its support by establishing the Papal States (756).

Pépin died in 768, to be succeeded by his son Charles, born at Jupille (now a suburb of Liège) on one of his father's estates in 742 (?), and who was to construct his empire as the future Charlemagne with Belgium as its centre. Crowned as Holy Roman Emperor by the Pope at Rome in 800, he vowed the whole of his reign and his work to the cause of Christendom. He brought peace in some semblance to his empire, he introduced orderly government, and he founded systems of education. From the point of view of Belgium, however, the Carolingian dynasty forced her to cease to be a frontier outpost and made her the hub of European affairs. This position was still further accentuated when quarrels amongst the grandsons of Charlemagne, who died in 814, led to the Treaty of Verdun (843) by which the short-lived empire was divided. Put very briefly, the treaty created two compact blocs: France (*Francia occidentalis*) and Germany (*Francia orientalis*), with a convenient buffer state to separate them – Belgium (*Francia media*). So was Belgium's destiny as the cockpit of Europe decided.

It would be tedious and not very profitable for our purpose to cover the next 500 years of Belgium's history. Europe was torn by strife. It is important to note, however, that as imperial power completely collapsed between the eleventh and twelfth centuries so did various principalities assert their identity – the prince-bishopric of Liège, Flanders, Brabant, Hainaut, Namur, Luxembourg, etc. – each a rival of the others, each fiercely jealous of its independence in the face of French or German suzerainty, each by suitable marriages seeking to extend its power and political influence. Yet Belgium prospered and enjoyed sufficient periods of peace under sound rule for it to become the first great urban civilisation in mediaeval Europe. As early as A.D. 700 Flemish merchants were trading regularly with Venice, Syria, and Constantinople. In the ninth century they were shipping cloth and weapons to Scandinavia. By the tenth century Liège already enjoyed cultural and commercial relations with Poland. In the eleventh century Godfrey of Bouillon became one of the leaders of the First Crusade, entered Jerusalem triumphantly in 1099, and became its first king. The Crusades, indeed, gave a new impetus to industry and commerce. In Flanders textile-making became a major industry in the hands of the newly developed guilds. By the thirteenth century Russia had established trade relations with western Europe – particularly with Belgium – and was regularly importing cloth from Ypres, Bruges, Ghent, Poperinghe, Oudenarde, Dixmude, and Roeselare, while Flemish merchants imported Russian wax and furs. The commercial city became the focal point of political power and the new merchant bourgeoisie were not tardy in recognising and exploiting their strength. They won charters of privilege for their respective towns from the nobles and so reduced their power that in normal times and in most cases they were only able to levy such taxes as the cities themselves determined were just and reasonable. They established the system of *communal* autonomy allied to provincial autonomy (which sprang from the princes themselves) which is still the outstanding feature of administration in Belgium to this day.

This period of booming prosperity and self-assurance reached its apogée during what has come to be called the Golden Age of Belgium – the Burgundian period (1384–1555). The last of the Counts of Flanders, Louis de Male, had in 1369 married his only daughter Marguerite to Philip the Bold, first of the Dukes of Burgundy and brother of Charles V of France. Slowly Burgundian influence spread itself, and by means of skilful purchase, a few minor wars, and a calculated matrimonial policy the House of Burgundy succeeded in uniting practically all the Belgian principalities under its rule. Successive dukes governed firmly but wisely and their domain soon became the richest country in the Western world. The country lived in a happy balance between absolute sovereignty and representative government. Belgian merchants no longer travelled the world, for the world came to their doors and Bruges (Venice of the North) became one of the greatest ports in Europe and a world centre for trade and banking, to be superseded later by Antwerp as Bruges gradually silted up. Bruges, however, remained the capital of the northern provinces and the four dukes in turn (Philip the Bold, John the Fearless, Philip the Good, and Charles the Rash) matched their genius for diplomacy and their realism in maintaining well-equipped armies by love and patronage of the arts. Bruges became the 'Florence of the North', and the number of painters, architects, musicians, and writers grew constantly. This is the period of Van Eyck and Memling, of Gérard David and Jérôme Bosch, of Peter Bruegel the Elder; of the designing of the Palace of the Prince-Bishops in Liège and of the 'King's House' in Brussels; of the chroniclers Jean Froissart and Philippe de Commynes; of Erasmus who, although born in Rotterdam, lived most of his life in Brussels and Louvain; of the founding of the University of Louvain (1425); of Andreas Vesalius (Brussels-born), the founder of anatomy; of Mercator and Ortelius (of Antwerp), both to become widely known because of their geographical studies and map-making; of the establishment of his printing press in Antwerp by the Frenchman Plantin and the publication there of the famous Alcala polyglot Bible.

But for the ambitions of Charles the Rash who succeeded his

father, Philip the Good, in 1467, Burgundian possessions might have remained a great buffer state between France and Germany and so changed the whole course of European history. Charles, however, sought not only to carry on his father's policy of closing the door to foreign interference and making an alliance with England[1] to neutralise France, but was determined to create a firm political link between his eleven provinces and the Franche-Comté and Burgundy. This was too much for Louis XI of France, who, wily in the extreme, was more than a match diplomatically for the bluff Burgundian warrior. War resulted in which Charles, outmanoeuvred and abandoned by everybody, was miserably slain at Nancy in January 1477.

Charles was succeeded by his daughter, Mary of Burgundy, who married Maximilian of Habsburg, heir to the Emperor, and so assured the autonomy of the Belgian provinces by bringing them directly under the guarantee of the golden seal of the Holy Roman Empire. Their son, Philip the Fair, married the heiress to the throne of Spain, Joanna the Mad, and from this marriage was born in Ghent on 24 February 1500 a son whose destiny was to prove not dissimilar from that of Charlemagne. This boy, Charles, who received a thorough and intensive education directed by the future Pope Hadrian VI, became Prince of the Netherlands at the age of fifteen, King of Spain and of the Colonies of the New World at nineteen, and one year later Emperor of Austria, to be known henceforward as Charles V.[2] Despite the impossible burden of his far-reaching commitments and anxieties throughout Europe (which need not here concern us) Charles V remained deeply attached to the land of his birth and by appointing able regents to rule directly there for him promoted the wave of expansion begun under the Dukes of Burgundy. He saw the Burgundian territories (which now extended to seventeen provinces to include what is today Holland) as 'one indivisible and inalienable block' and by the Convention of Augsburg (1548) granted them the status of an independent sovereign state and incorporated them into the Holy Roman Empire under the title of the Circle of Burgundy.

---

[1] In 1468 he married Margaret of York, sister of Edward IV of England, and thus sided with the Yorkists during the Wars of the Roses. Louis XI sided with the Lancastrian cause.

[2] It was not until the accession to the throne of Leopold II in 1865 that Belgium would again be ruled by a native-born prince.

It was in Brussels in 1555 that Charles V finally decided to abdicate from all his responsibilities. He passed the Empire to his brother, Ferdinand, and his son Philip II inherited Spain together with the seventeen provinces. Philip II, however, was no Burgundian but a proud, haughty, austere, and bigoted Catholic – a Spaniard first and foremost – and neither he nor the Castilian dukes he sent to govern the provinces were ever popular. The situation was further complicated by the rapid spread of Protestantism and the way in which (particularly from 1560 onwards) numerous pockets of Calvinistic and egalitarian 'republics', each under the spiritual direction of its pastor and the pastors grouped into a consistory, had firmly established themselves, especially in the northern provinces. True, Charles V had himself started the Inquisition, but Philip II now vowed himself not only to rule all his possessions as an absolute monarch, bringing them all under Spanish influence, but also to stamp heresy out ruthlessly. Discontent against all these oppressive measures smouldered for several years. The cruel Duke of Alba was dispatched to the provinces to bring them to heel as civil war broke out in 1567. The following year Alba excelled himself by the number of executions and arrests he carried out. No fewer than nineteen high-ranking noblemen went to the scaffold on 1 June. Four days later he proceeded to override the charter of the Order of the Golden Fleece (by which its knights might be judged by none other than the King in person) by summarily executing the acknowledged ringleaders of the dissident group of nobles, Counts Egmont and Horne, in full view of the populace on the Grand' Place in Brussels.

This was the beginning of the end. The nobles now organised strong and underground resistance groups known popularly as the Beggars of the Sea and the Beggars of the Woods, and the Prince of Orange finally declared a war of liberation.[1] By 1579 the division of the country was an accomplished fact, the so-called Catholic Lowlands where the King of Spain managed to retain his authority being the territory later to become Belgium, and the United

---

[1] Charles de Coster's classic story *Thyl Eulenspiegel* movingly narrates all these events. Charles Reade's novel *The Cloister and the Hearth* is equally not without interest to the earlier period. But see also Pieter Geyl, *The Revolt of the Netherlands 1555–1609* (2nd edition, London, 1958); *The Netherlands in the Seventeenth Century*, Part I, *1609–48* (2nd edition, London, 1961); *The Netherlands in the Seventeenth Century*, Part II, *1648— 1715* (London, 1964).

Provinces in the north the country later to be known as the Netherlands or Holland. In 1598, both ill and wearied, Philip II handed
over his troublesome territories to his daughter Isabella, the wife of
the Archduke Albert of Austria, who had been a cardinal since the
age of eighteen and Archbishop of Toledo without ever having
been ordained a priest. The dislike of the Belgian provinces for
Philip II did not extend to Isabella, who indeed proved unusually
popular, but the death of the Archduke in 1621 ended a truce with
the Calvinist armies which had lasted twelve years, and war again
broke out with the United Provinces. With the death of Isabella
herself in 1633 the serious attempt Philip II had made to form a
national dynasty in the Lowlands failed since she died childless.
The country reverted once again to a system of appointed governors-
general established in Brussels as representatives of an absent king.

Meanwhile the United Provinces had become involved in the
Thirty Years' War (1618–48) and there now ensued for Belgium a
century of misfortune in which she became a battlefield for the
Habsburgs and the Bourbons. The Treaty of Munster (1648) laid
down the northern frontier of Belgium and closed the Scheldt to
her shipping. Louis XIV's resolve to establish the hegemony of
France throughout Europe and to give his country her so-called
natural frontiers brought further suffering which involved over
the years the siege of Namur, the Battle of Neerwinden, the fall of
Charleroi, the bombing of Brussels (from which resulted the Grand'
Place as we today know it), and important battles waged by Marl-
borough's armies at Oudenarde, Ramillies, and Malplaquet. Then
finally, as Louis XIV in turn wearied and gave up the unequal
struggle he had brought upon himself, the Treaties of Utrecht (1713)
and La Barrière (1715) imposed the southern frontier on Belgium
as it now exists and transferred the Catholic Low Countries from
the Spanish Habsburgs to the Austrian branch of the family, insisting that this was no matter of subjection but was to mark the
continued allegiance of the territory to the line of the Dukes of
Burgundy.

The beginnings of Austrian rule brought a short period of calm
and prosperity, the Emperor Charles VI dispatching a very able
governor, the Marquis de Prié, to act for him. De Prié fought hard,
but unsuccessfully, to overcome the Dutch closure of the Scheldt
to shipping to Antwerp and retaliated by developing the port of
Ostend on which he based a newly promoted 'Imperial and Royal

Company of the East and West Indies'. Belgian ships again set sail
for India and China. Trading posts were established, and so successful was the venture that London and Amsterdam became seriously
alarmed at the competition. The Emperor Charles VI, mainly to
placate the other powers in the vain hope that they would accept
his daughter's succession without trouble, closed the company down
in 1731 when it was at the peak of its trading activities.

The death of Charles VI and the accession of Maria Theresa provoked the so-called War of the Austrian Succession (1740–8) and
once again Belgium became a battlefield for the English, the French,
and the Austrians. There now followed a further forty years of peace
and prosperity for Belgium under the enlightened but firm rule of
Maria Theresa (1740–80) and her son Joseph II (1780–90). New
economic measures introduced by Maria Theresa brought a marked
material development in both industry and agriculture. By skilful
diplomacy she managed to keep both herself and Belgium out of
the Seven Years War (1756–63). She was a sincere patroness of both
scientists and artists and in 1772 founded the Royal Academy of
Science and Letters (today known as the Académie Royale). She
profited from the suppression of the Jesuits in 1773 to laicise and
modernise secondary education by creating her own colleges in
place of those formerly run by the Jesuits, and in 1777 set about the
formidable task of killing analphabetism among the teeming thousands of her subjects by elaborating an all-embracing plan for a
state system of primary education. It came to nothing.

Joseph II, a firm disciple of the Encyclopaedists, tried to do too
much too quickly and through his clumsiness and lack of tact soon
managed to set all Belgians unanimously against him. He wished
to free the Belgians from the powerful ascendancy of the Catholic
clergy. He sought to unify the administration of the provinces
on more modern and progressive lines. He visited Belgium (as
Maria Theresa had never done), but as an ordinary member of the
bourgeoisie without pomp, pageantry, and ceremony of any kind.
He had the pomp-loving Belgians genuinely puzzled, and particularly when he issued a decree (for the sake of tidiness and uniformity)
that all public *kermesses* (traditional feasts and junketings) should
be held on the same day throughout all the parishes. He reformed
the judiciary. He secured some attenuation of the Dutch blockade
of the Scheldt. He reopened the coastal ports to stimulate a growing
seaborne traffic. But he so bombarded and bewildered the Belgians

with his reforms that they could just take no more. Besides, revolution was by now in the air, seeping through insidiously from France.

In 1790 the States-General met in Brussels and founded the Confederation of the United Belgic States. The republic was short-lived, mainly because the leaders could not agree among themselves. The new Emperor, Leopold II (brother of Joseph II), quickly reasserted his authority for a short span of two years. Then the revolutionary armies of France invaded and by 1794 had annexed Belgium to France to make of it a simple French *département*. The Belgians, who had begun by hailing the French enthusiastically as genuine liberators, were soon disillusioned. They were treated as a conquered people. Priceless art treasures were whisked away to Paris. The whole economy of the country was geared to the French war machine. And French laws, imposed on the Belgians by military might, compelled a far more radical change in habits than Joseph II would ever have wished for. Anti-clericalism and the ruthless persecution of priests and nobles equally shocked the Belgian's healthy respect for his Burgundian traditional way of life. The introduction of conscription in 1798–9 provoked a Peasants' Revolt throughout the country. It was stamped out quickly and cruelly.

Once Napoleon had come to power life became more normal, though liberty as the Belgians understood it was out of the question. The French language was forcibly introduced throughout the Flemish provinces and an attempt was made to organise a state school system on the Napoleonic pattern. Liège found itself turning out the cannon and firearms Napoleon so badly needed. Verviers clothed his soldiers. The farmers grew food. And Antwerp, completely liberated since Holland was now also a part of the Empire, prospered (in Pitt the Younger's picturesque language) as part of the pistol aimed at England's head.

Napoleon's disastrous Russian campaign and the Battle of Leipzig (16–18 October 1813) marked the beginning of the end of French occupation. The Russians, Prussians, and Swedes entered Belgium from the north and east in January 1814 and by 1 February the Prussian general von Bülow had occupied Brussels. Meanwhile, the coalition powers, while still prosecuting the campaign against Napoleon, were already thinking about the future of Belgium, Pitt the Younger having urged as early as 1805 its amalgamation with Holland. A secret meeting of the allies called at Troyes-en-Champagne on 15 February 1814 confirmed the English plan;

a further secret meeting at Chaumont on 1 March ratified the arrangement; but by the Treaty of Paris (30 May 1814) Holland was simply and mysteriously promised an increase in her territorial possessions. Before the Congress of Vienna (22 September 1814 to 9 June 1815) could promulgate its final decisions Napoleon had escaped from Elba and landed at Antibes. Profiting from the general disarray into which the allies were now thrown by the tumultuous reception Napoleon was receiving throughout France, William of Holland anticipated the findings of the plenipotentiaries at Vienna by proclaiming himself King of the Low Countries on 16 March and then placing his new 'kingdom' in a state of military preparedness. The allies were too preoccupied other than to be thankful that William was on their side. The Belgians themselves were bewildered. And so it was that as the last battle against Napoleon was fought at Waterloo on Belgian soil, Belgians themselves were to be found fighting on both sides.

Waterloo, however, was of greater significance for the Belgians than could have been understood at the time. In the first place it was the last battle ever to be fought on Belgian soil for a century. Secondly, because it made inevitable the absorption of Belgium into the Kingdom of the United Netherlands, it redeemed her from too much preoccupation with her Burgundian past and thrust her into the mainstream of modern European politics. Once the separation of the United Provinces (Holland) from the Catholic Lowlands (Belgium) had become a fact in the sixteenth century, Belgium had followed Spain in her steady decline. Enlightened Austrian rule had later rejuvenated her. French occupation had proved a unifying factor for all her various principalities, even the notoriously independent prince-bishopric of Liège succumbing. Thirdly, and because of all these factors, she came to realise her own identity and her economic potential, and to grasp that she need never again be subject to the arbitrary whims of any other European power.

Chapter 3

Birth of a Kingdom

THE STORY OF HOW KING WILLIAM OF HOLLAND came to lose the Southern Province of his (so-called) United Netherlands and of how that Southern Province asserted its right to become a totally independent kingdom (Belgium) is one of the most fascinating and instructive in the whole history of modern western Europe, hinging as it does on the character and cultural and educational background of the Belgians themselves. Economic prosperity, due in the first place to Belgium's unique position at the crossroads of western Europe and allied to the tireless energy of its people, has not only brought the Belgians diverse and fruitful contacts with other peoples and given them a high standard of civilisation, but has also strengthened their feelings of self-sufficiency and their desire to see none hindered in the fulfilment of their lawful and private ambitions. Similarly, centuries of attempted absorption of both the Flemish and Walloon communities into the structural whole of some other European power have given rise among the Belgians, not so much to a positive patriotism stemming from a national ideal as to a stubborn insistence on the right of each individual to safeguard his own liberty, his own property, his religious beliefs, customs, traditions, folklore – in a word, his total cultural heritage. If he is an individualist, history has made him so. In the face of adversity he has learned to be serene, realist, and unshakeable in his devotion to what he has felt to be right and just. Accustomed through the centuries to the domination (not always harsh or intolerable) of this or that overlord, the Belgians have learned to group themselves into strong and independent *communes* to force from their temporal and spiritual rulers charters of independence and special privileges which thereafter they have sought jealously to preserve.[1] So tenacious and obstinate have they been in petitioning for *un redressement des*

[1] The earliest known charter is reputed to be that granted by Bishop Théoduin to the town of Huy in 1066.

griefs du peuple that they have usually managed for the most part to get their own way or at least to arrive at some workable compromise. When tempers have run too high on either side, then clashes have resulted and some hero has died a martyr's death for the people's passion for independence, for individual liberty and local autonomy, for the maintenance of a traditional way of life and the preservation of inherited customs and institutions.

It can be put baldly that William of Holland lost Belgium because of his failure to realise that he could not force reforms, however progressive and forward-looking, on a people whose entire cultural background had ill prepared them for accepting such reforms, and because of his inability to see behind and beyond contemporaneous difficulties arising primarily from the Congress of Vienna's determination to set about the reconstruction of the moral order of Europe. The annexation of Belgium to the French Republic in 1795 had been an economic necessity for the French, who had been quite cynical in speaking of Belgium as 'conquered territory to be milked with all speed'. William of Holland earnestly sought to redress the balance by conferring on Belgium all the benefits of firm but enlightened control he was bringing to his own country. The opening of the river Scheldt to Belgian shipping put an end to the long period of economic oppression the Dutch had brought to bear on Belgium since 1648, and Antwerp soon became a dangerous rival to the Dutch ports of Amsterdam and Rotterdam. Ghent quickly earned for herself a reputation as the 'Manchester' of the Low Countries. Brussels, from being the chief town of a French *département*, acquired a new life and a political vigour as the capital of the Southern Provinces. The drift of economic prosperity from Holland to Belgium was slow but certain. William paid much attention to the transport system of the country, set up schools of navigation at Ostend and Antwerp, established a School of Mines at Liège in 1825, and as early as 1817 was encouraging the English brothers James and John Cockerill in their new engineering enterprises at Seraing in the province of Liège.

If, however, prosperity came to the commercial and industrial middle classes, the lot of the unskilled labourer was no enviable one. Not all the hard-working characteristics of the Belgian, nor his opportunism, nor the undoubted manpower advantages accruing from high population figures, were going to be of much use in the new industrial order and given the keen competition for world markets that the nineteenth century heralded. On the very eve of the revolution the town of Ghent was petitioning the Ministry of the Interior for a grant of two million florins to ease the lot of its unemployed and find them work. Skilled operatives and skilled technicians were urgently required. The role of the enlightened monarch was clear: he must aim at a general raising of the educational standards, he must impose a system of tariffs and dues to bring order out of the present economic chaos, and he must rigorously combat the reactionary tendencies of the clergy and nobility who could not appreciate the needs of modern times. That meant that he would be supporting the strong liberal (and anti-Catholic) bourgeoisie who were intelligent enough to understand what William was about if not dynamic enough to take action themselves. From the Belgian's point of view, however, all William's actions represented a gross interference in matters which were not primarily his concern. And the situation was further aggravated by the undoubted hardship his economic measures of necessity at first imposed on the mass of the people. At the root of all the trouble, of course, lay the inescapable fact that neither the Dutch nor the Belgians welcomed with any enthusiasm the creation of an artificially United Netherlands.

Trouble started as early as 24 August 1815 when the publication of the Fundamental Law which decided the constitution of the United Netherlands made it clear that William had the sole right of regulating public education. It was fanned by the Belgian bishops who refused to swear fidelity to a clause of such dubious possibilities of interpretation and it was kept in a constant state of fermentation by William's insistence on imposing on the Belgians his own excellent system of schooling. Charges of duplicity and double-dealing on William's part (charges which were not without foundation) further undermined any confidence in any of his actions. The Belgians painstakingly listed their grievances one by one and demanded the traditional *redressement*. The Dutch monopolised most of the public offices and conducted the government in their own interests. Belgium, with twice the population of Holland, had only equal representation in Parliament with the Dutch. Belgium paid interest on the national debt equally with Holland, though the Dutch share should most obviously have been greater. The army was staffed by some 2,000 officers of whom only 288, however, were Belgian. In 1819 William had started a drive (with the best possible intentions as far as the Flemings were concerned) to banish French as the official language

in the purely Flemish provinces and so make Belgium constitute a
real barrier between France and Holland. This was followed up
by an 1823 ruling that henceforward Dutch would be the official
language for all administrative and legal purposes in these provinces.
An immediate protest was made, firstly by the Flemish bourgeoisie
whose whole cultural outlook was French and who traditionally
sent their children to be educated in the best French-speaking
schools in either France or Belgium, and secondly by the Catholic
clergy who feared that the first step was being taken towards infil-
tration of Belgium by the Dutch Protestant Church.

Thus, instead of winning any one faction, or group of factions,
to his side, William was alienating them all one by one and provok-
ing Flemings and Walloons, Catholics and Liberals, into a unison
of protest. He failed to see how all tied up with the national character; with the Fleming–Walloon question; with the Catholic–
Liberal controversies; with the sturdy independence of the *communes*. He needed to alienate as little as possible the Catholics,
whether Fleming or Walloon. In educational reform he needed
Liberal support against reactionary Catholic tendencies. He needed
at all costs the willing support of the *communes* who would have to
foot the bills for his reforms. Yet he drove all into an alliance against
him. And he made matters no better when, angered by the virulent
attacks and lampoons directed against him in the Belgian press, he
banished the most troublesome journalists (Louis de Potter, a
Liberal, and Jules Bartels, a Catholic) and placed restrictions both
on the freedom of the press and on freedom of association.

By 1828 the younger Liberals and Catholics had come to a working arrangement which would have been impossible for their elders
to achieve. Together they added up the score of William's duplicities
and decided the time had come once and for all to show a united
front, to call a halt to what seemed to them a persistent policy of
considering Belgium merely as an annexed province. By the end
of 1828 a national opposition campaign had been launched with
the Catholic and Liberal newspapers speaking as with one voice.
Petitions poured into the Lower House of the Dutch Parliament
(150 in all for the year 1829 and containing more than 360,000
signatures). Challenged for the very first time by a determined and
united opposition, William had to make concessions, and these concessions were fatal in that they strengthened the hand and the
importunity of the Belgians.

On 27 July 1830, Charles X of France prudently left Paris on a hunting trip and the Parisians profited from his absence by staging a three-day revolution, deposing him and bringing to the throne the bourgeois King, Louis-Philippe. French agents were active in Brussels and tempting invitations were issued to the Belgians to join in the revolutionary process. Belgian realism prevailed. It could scarcely profit the Belgians to throw off the Dutch yoke only to be absorbed by an even greater and more powerful nation. William sighed with relief and proceeded with his plans for special festivities which were to be held in Brussels on 25 August to mark the fifteenth anniversary of his accession to the joint thrones of Holland and Belgium. There were to be feastings, carnival processions, pomp and pageantry, and street illuminations on a vast scale. And William magnanimously requested that a mediocre operetta, Daniel Auber's *La Muette de Portici*, banned in July at the time of the French disturbance because of the outbursts of patriotism it had then provoked, should be back on the programme at the *Théâtre de la Monnaie*.

William's behaviour at this juncture can only be described as curious. Was it, as one historian (Pirenne) claims, that he found the situation so delicately poised that he felt he had at all costs to avoid incidents? Or was it (as Pierre Nothomb claims) that he was clumsily manoeuvring to bring matters to a head and so show the Belgians once and for all who was master? Whatever he intended, the outcome was certainly other than he expected, or had the right to expect, or what the bourgeoisie of Brussels expected. The winter of 1829–30 had been exceptionally severe. An economic crisis of unexpected proportions had swept the country. Factories had gone bankrupt and leading bankers had closed their doors. Poor relief could not meet the demands made for the simple necessities of life and hundreds of unemployed were aimlessly and dangerously roaming the streets of Brussels, Liège, Verviers, Antwerp, and Ghent. All this proposed pageantry in favour of a Dutch king was for them a mockery and an added provocation to insurrection. Posters appeared announcing: 'Monday, firework display; Tuesday, illuminations; Wednesday, revolution'.

And when Wednesday came, William inexplicably cancelled the entire programme of carnival processions and street illuminations on the pretext of heavy rain showers which were forecast but which did not materialise. He also issued instructions to the police and soldiery that no matter how high feelings might run they were on no account to make any display of strength or provoke any incident. With what were to have been the main attractions for the mass of the people thus cancelled, attention became focussed on the performance of *La Muette*. The theatre was packed. The bourgeoisie were there both to enjoy themselves and to applaud the patriotic sentiments in which the operetta abounded. Scores of young dandies forced their way into the crowded gangways, fully determined to enjoy themselves at everybody's expense. Crowds gathered and seethed outside the theatre. And inside, as the operetta unfolded its story, feelings grew more and more intense. By Act Two the whole audience was on its feet and cheering the tenor song:

> Sacred love of our fatherland
> Restore to us our daring and our pride!
> To my country I owe my life
> And through me it shall be free![1]

Out rushed the 'bloods' proclaiming liberty at last, whilst the populace, carried along on a wave of mass hysteria, rushed to pillage and loot and set fire to government buildings. The Dutch police and soldiery stood impotently by—under orders, seemingly—and resentfully allowed themselves to be disarmed. Not so the bourgeoisie. Appalled, and sensing what disaster could lie ahead, they met the emergency magnificently. Overnight they formed a civil defence committee and the next morning proceeded to the Town Hall where they declared a state of emergency, flew the Brabançon flag, and formed a civil guard to restore law and order. Within three days the situation was well under control and Brussels, to its extreme surprise, under its own military jurisdiction. News of the Brussels uprising quickly spread to the main provincial towns, and there similar incidents occurred which were handled in like manner. Thus, power slipped imperceptibly into the hands of the bourgeoisie throughout the whole of Belgium before William had even time to recover from his surprise or make anything like a display of military force. He was completely outmanoeuvred by events. A bourgeois separatist state had asserted its right to independence.

On 28 August a deputation left Brussels for The Hague to inform William of the serious nature of the situation and to exact con-

---

[1] 'Amour sacré de la Patrie,
Rends-nous l'audace et la fierté . . .'

cessions which could only lead eventually to separatism. William attempted to temporise while he sent armies under the Prince of Orange towards his dissident territory. This once popular prince was allowed to enter Brussels and to reach his palace with only a small escort, but he was left in no doubt as to the hostility that surrounded him. Meanwhile, volunteers from all parts of Belgium were flocking to Brussels to join the 'liberation army', and all hope of some compromise solution faded when William dispatched further Dutch troops to recapture his southern capital. A bloody battle raged for four days (23–27 September) and resulted in the defeat of the Dutch and, with their withdrawal, a further strengthening of Belgian national feeling, not only throughout Wallonia but also in such key Flemish towns as Ghent, Bruges, Ostend, and Antwerp which equally unceremoniously bundled out the Dutch occupying forces.

On 4 October a provisional government declared Belgium to be an independent state and called for the speedy election of a National Congress to hammer out a constitution. The elections were held on 3 November (one week after a particularly vicious 'river of fire and blood' Dutch reprisal bombardment of Antwerp had rendered impossible all further negotiations with William) and resulted in the nomination of 299 moderate-minded, traditionalist bourgeois delegates of whom roughly one-half represented Catholic interests and the other half Liberal aspirations. On 18 November the Congress reaffirmed the independence of Belgium. On 22 November it declared Belgium to be a hereditary monarchy, and two days later it excluded in perpetuity any member of the House of Nassau from succeeding to the throne. By 7 February 1831 the constitution had been finally settled – a constitution which has lasted down to the present and which (in broad outline) became the model for Spain, Portugal, Italy, Romania (and later even Holland) as these countries also moved towards a more democratic and representative form of monarchical government.

It was a remarkable achievement. Within rather less than six months the Belgians had not only had their revolution, effectively expelled the Dutch military forces, and shown to the whole world how responsible they were and intended to remain, but they had also built on the principle of a hereditary monarchy which, while maintaining the conception of a unified state, carefully safeguarded the people's traditional autonomy at a provincial and *communal* level. It was successful precisely because it heeded the essential character and spirit of the Belgians, as William of Holland had signally failed to do. Its success was secured by the greater powers of Europe who, at first dismayed at this upset to their carefully laid plans at the Congress of Vienna, were persuaded by Palmerston to accept the *fait accompli*, to help Belgium find its hereditary monarch, and to build in new safeguards centred on the new kingdom.

A conference of the greater powers assembled in London on 4 November 1830. Russia, Prussia, and Austria were all for the House of Nassau and immediate subjection of the 'intractable and mutinous Belgians'. The French, on the other hand, with Louis-Philippe still precariously perched on his throne, were ably represented by that wily statesman Talleyrand, now aged seventy-six, who sought only to serve the best interests of his country and prevent a European conflagration. A partition proposal he put forward was firmly rejected by Palmerston, and meanwhile the London Conference agreed that its immediate task was to secure an armistice between the Dutch and the Belgians. This became effective on 10 November. Russian and Prussian intransigence was then fortunately diverted by a Polish uprising of 29 November and Palmerston and Talleyrand were thus enabled to secure (by the protocol of 20 December) official recognition of the separation of Holland and Belgium. The independence of Belgium was formally ratified on 20 January 1831 and her neutrality was then guaranteed for all time. And now began the manoeuvrings to secure the so far elusive hereditary monarch.

The Belgians themselves were split into two factions, the one favouring the choice of the Duc de Nemours (the son of Louis-Philippe) and the other the candidature of the Duke of Leuchten-berg, son of the Prince Eugène de Beauharnais who had been viceroy of Italy under the Napoleonic régime. Leuchtenberg was suspect because of this and in the end the Congress elected the Duc de Nemours, only to be informed by Louis-Philippe (under firm pressure from Palmerston) that the House of Orleans could not accept the throne. Belgium was immediately plunged into a crisis of both indecision and intrigue, the Orangists (supporters of the candidature of the Prince of Orange, and many of whom were influential army officers) now gaining considerable ground in their campaign for their popular prince. On 24 February 1831 a Regent was elected (Erasme-Louis, Baron Surlet de Choquier). The Orangists attempted a *coup d'état* centred on Ghent and Mechlin which all but succeeded.

Insurrection spread to other major cities. Forced by circumstances to act decisively, the Regent dismissed his present advisers, a group of tired old men, and called on three vigorous patriots (Nothomb, Antoine Barthélémy, and Joseph Lebeau) to save the situation. Lebeau insisted on being placed in charge of foreign affairs, urged strongly the candidature for the throne of Prince Leopold of Saxe-Coburg, and dispatched an official delegation to London to sound out the prince.

Leopold was wary though not unresponsive, but he was certainly not going to compromise himself. He must be sure of the backing of the greater powers. Great Britain let it be known that, while she would not oppose the election of Leopold, she refused to put him forward as her candidate. France could do nothing but acquiesce. Congress met on 4 June and elected Leopold by an overwhelming majority (152 votes out of 196). They could not have chosen better, and they knew it. Born on 16 December 1790 in Coburg, Leopold had served with the Russian army, had strongly supported the Czar Alexander against Napoleon in 1813, and had distinguished himself in the subsequent military manoeuvres in Europe which brought about the downfall of Napoleon. When peace came he had settled in England and opted for British nationality. On 2 May 1816 he had married the Princess Charlotte, daughter of the Prince of Wales (later George IV) and heiress-apparent to the throne of England. Handsome, intelligent, discreet, gently ironic, he had quickly endeared himself to the English who looked forward with some relief to having a Prince Consort who, with Charlotte as Queen, would undoubtedly restore the tarnished name and reputation of the royal household. Their joy was short-lived. On 3 November 1817 Charlotte was delivered of a stillborn child and succumbed herself several hours later. At first inconsolable, Leopold came more and more to rely on his private secretary, the Baron Stockmar (the same who was later to counsel the young Queen Victoria), to lead the life of a typical English country gentleman, and to lavish his affections on 'Vicky', to whom he acted for some eleven years as guardian.[1]

[1] It is interesting to recall that Leopold's marriage to Charlotte started off a kind of chain reaction which was to involve the English monarchy in blood ties with all the principal royal houses of Europe. After the death of Charlotte the bachelor Duke of Kent was prevailed upon to marry Leopold's sister, Victoria, the future Queen Victoria being born a year later (24 May 1819). George III and the Duke of Kent both died in 1820. Leopold became a father-figure to 'Vicky' (she constantly referred to him when a child as

Leopold's initial caution over accepting the Belgian offer was due to a multiplicity of reasons, foremost among which was the fact that matters were in such a sordid political confusion in the English royal household that his chances of wielding real power there (for the common good) were far from negligible. Again, he had recently been offered the throne of Greece and had refused it (21 May 1830), partly because of a spate of invective this had provoked in English political circles (involving George IV), partly because of the confused political situation in Greece itself, but mainly because the Greeks could not (or would not) give the guarantees necessary to stabilise a monarchy there. He was now to prove equally intransigent towards the Belgians. Until the Belgian government had given him necessary guarantees of good faith by signing a peace treaty embodied in eighteen articles drawn up by the greater powers, he stayed where he was. Preliminary agreement was reached in London on 26 June 1831, but when the full text was made known to Congress angry debates ensued and it was not until 9 July that Lebeau secured approval by 126 votes to 70.

Leopold packed his bags and sailed in the royal yacht *Crusader* from Dover to Calais a week later. From the moment he set foot on Belgian soil near Veurne his reception became increasingly and joyously tumultuous. He insisted (against advice) on passing through Ghent, an Orangist stronghold, and succeeded in charming everyone there. And on 21 July he made his solemn entry to his capital, Brussels, took the constitutional oath in the Place Royale before a delirious crowd, and declared in ringing tones that: 'I have no other ambition than to see you all happy'.

'il mio secondo padre, il mio solo padre' – my second father, my only father). He was instrumental in securing her marriage to Prince Albert, and for the rest of his life both influenced and counselled her in all important decisions she was called upon to make.

Chapter 4

'Mr Go-Slowly' (1831–65)

THE EPITHET WAS NOT ENTIRELY UNDESERVED. Nor was it used in any disparaging sense. On the contrary, it epitomised Belgian admiration for Leopold's diplomatic skill and the astuteness with which he not only succeeded in convincing the world that the Belgians were a people to be taken seriously, in giving his country of adoption the firm foundations for a long period of peace and prosperity, but also in extending the influence of the House of Coburg throughout Europe. He firmly established a Belgian dynasty by his marriage in 1832 with Louise-Marie d'Orléans, the eldest daughter of the King of the French. He remained true to his own Protestant upbringing, but arranged that his children should be of the Catholic faith. And when news was rushed to him on 2 August 1831 to Liège, where he was playing his part in post-coronation ceremonial, that William of Holland had broken the armistice (he had never appended his signature to the eighteen-article peace treaty) and was at that very moment invading Belgium with strong forces led by the Prince of Orange, he refused to panic and handled the situation coolly and with characteristic Anglo-Saxon phlegm.

Of the courage of those who made up his Belgian volunteer army he had no doubt. He had equally no doubt that they could not be a match for the highly-trained professional soldiers whom William was now sending against them. Without any attempt, therefore, at consultation with his Ministers, Leopold immediately invoked the assistance of the greater powers. Great Britain responded by mobilising the fleet and France by dispatching an army of some 50,000 men to bolster Belgian resistance to the invader. It came none too soon. The Dutch were halted only at Wavre ten days later and there forced by the French general, Marshal Etienne-Maurice Gérard, to sign an armistice. European diplomacy once again took over. The French troops remained on Belgian soil until

60

30 September, and at a conference called in London on 14 October the original eighteen-article treaty was scrapped, to be replaced by a treaty of twenty-four articles which, at the insistence of Russia and Prussia, made considerable concessions to Holland to strengthen her as a defensive base against France and the terms of which were firmly declared 'final and irrevocable'.

The neutrality of Belgium was reaffirmed in terms which made it clear that she could have no real foreign policy of her own.[1] Belgium now lost to Holland all of the province of Limburg situated on the right bank of the Meuse. German-speaking Luxembourg became the property of the House of Nassau with the appellation of Grand Duchy, Belgium retaining only the French-speaking part (now the province of Luxembourg) and a German-speaking 'fringe' extending from Vielsalm to Arlon. Holland was to remain in undisputed control of the Scheldt estuary and thereby entitled to exact navigation dues on all Belgian shipping using the estuary to reach Antwerp. On the other hand, pilotage and dredging rights were to be freely accorded Belgium, and Holland had to maintain the lower reaches of the Scheldt in good order as well as to give Belgium free access to the interior waterways of Holland between the Scheldt and the Rhine, and similar land communication routes through Holland to Germany. It was finally made clear that Belgium must pay her share (just over fifty per cent) of the national debt of the former joint kingdom.

The treaty was harsh and a severe blow at the pride of the Belgians, who, though rightly considering themselves as victorious against William of Holland, were now being treated as mere pawns in the power game as played out by the greater nations. Stubbornly they resisted signing and were only finally brought to do so, on 1 November 1831, after a stormy debate in Parliament and much patient but unyielding persuasion on the part of Leopold. That William of Holland equally stubbornly now refused to append his signature gave them little comfort, for the Dutch were still in possession of the fort of Antwerp and therefore in total control of the Scheldt estuary. For all practical purposes the Belgians must consider them-

[1] It is interesting to record that this subservience of Belgium's foreign interests (as opposed to her colonial interests) to the wishes of the greater powers lasted in effect to 1936 when Leopold III had the courage to assert himself and enunciate his famous principle of 'independence-neutrality'. Similarly, Leopold II was only able to colonise Africa as a private individual launching a private business venture.

selves continuously at war with Holland until William thought fit
to abandon his attitude of passive resistance and could be brought
to the conference table.

Leopold could only adroitly manoeuvre towards this end. He
carefully 'arranged' his marriage with Louise-Marie d'Orléans.[1] He
immediately set about the task of turning his army into a
highly professional one by weeding out incompetent officers, buying
modern equipment and materials, and by engaging French and
Polish army instructors. He assured a stable government for domestic
affairs by firmly reminding Catholics and Liberals that, since the
independence of Belgium had been achieved through their 'uneasy'
alliance, it could only be guaranteed in the difficult years that lay
ahead through a prolongation of that alliance.

One immediate result was the decision taken by France and
Britain on 22 October 1832 that it was intolerable for William to
continue his occupation of Antwerp and that he must evacuate the
town by 2 November. William refused to budge. Immediately a joint
Franco-Britannic fleet blockaded the Dutch coast and on 15 November Marshal Gérard was again on Belgian soil to relieve Antwerp,
it being decided that Leopold's 'new' army (much to its disappointment) should not take part in the campaign so as not further to
worsen Belgian–Dutch relations. William's forces held out stubbornly and it was not until 23 December that the Dutch garrison
commander surrendered. William still sulked and it was only some
five years later when, amid increasing unpopularity in his own
country, he had to recognise that his chances of ever recovering his
lost provinces had completely faded and so suddenly announced
his intention to sign the peace treaty, on 14 March 1838. While all
the preliminaries dragged on (the treaty was not fully ratified until
19 April 1839), Leopold fought hard to retain Limburg and Luxembourg, first by threatening military intervention, only to be told
that in that case Austria would come to the help of Holland, and
finally by offering to buy from Holland the two provinces. It was
all to no avail. Belgium had to console herself with the thought that
she had acted energetically and responsibly and that her chosen
monarch, Leopold, had displayed both firmness and rare diplomatic
skill to leave the greater powers in no doubt as to the determination

[1] Not as cynical as it may sound. Leopold had known Louise-Marie for
many years and was genuinely fond of her, though he made it clear she
would never replace Charlotte in his affections.

of the Belgians to exercise their rights to the full to exist as a separate kingdom.

For the remainder of his reign Leopold's foreign policy consisted in affirming Belgium's neutrality and in realistically strengthening her defences. In 1835 Prussia had baulked an attempt to build a line of fortresses stretching from Antwerp to the German frontier, though, with British support, Leopold had succeeded in fortifying Diest. A convention of the greater powers called in 1831 had demanded the dismantling of part of the fortifications along the French frontier from the sea to the Sambre-et-Meuse. Leopold did nothing until 1860, when he dismantled the lot. In 1840 a European crisis provoked by rivalry between Egypt and Turkey, and which led to a coalition movement of the greater powers against France (who was backing Mehemet Ali, the viceroy of Egypt) gave Leopold his first opportunity to prove Belgium's neutrality. And as she stood firm even against threats of a French invasion, so she convinced the Dutch at long last of the hopelessness of the Orangist cause within Belgium and completely discredited that minority faction.

In 1845 the strength of the Belgian army was raised to 80,000 men, together with a reserve force of 50,000, and in 1853, in consequence of the danger presented by the rise to power of Napoleon III, the figure on the active list was raised to 100,000. An imaginative and grandiose plan to turn Antwerp into a vast fortified military zone was started in 1847 and, despite much resistance in the 1860s from pacifist-minded Flemings, brought to completion from 1859 onwards under the direction of the brilliant military engineer Henri Brialmont. In 1863, thanks to the more cordial ties now obtaining with Holland, it became possible to purchase from her the toll rights on the Scheldt and so turn Antwerp into one of the leading world ports. Skilfully, Leopold evaded all the pressures brought to bear on Belgium by King Frederick William IV of Prussia to join the *Zollverein* (the powerful German customs union) and in 1844 concluded instead a simple but advantageous commercial treaty. He concluded a similar treaty with France two years later, despite some considerable British opposition.

When the revolution of February 1848 unseated King Louis-Philippe it became Leopold's task to reassure his own government that such a happening was impossible in Belgium and to prove it at the famous rout of Risquons-Tout. On 29 March 1848 some two thousand Frenchworkers from the Lille area, fired with the revolutionary zeal then sweeping throughout France, invaded Belgium at this point (and also at Quiévrain), confident that the Belgian populace would rise in their support. Leopold's new army dispersed them, almost contemptuously – and the Belgian populace approved. Holland and Prussia were particularly impressed and sincere in their felicitations, and as the wave of revolution swept through Europe to reach Austria, Metternich himself found it prudent to seek safety and asylum for a time . . . in Belgium.

The *coup d'état* of Prince Louis-Napoleon Bonaparte and the establishment of the Second Empire in France in 1851 brought fresh difficulties which the marriage of the future Leopold II in 1853 to the great grand-daughter of Maria Theresa – the Archduchess Maria Henrietta of Austria – served only to aggravate. Belgium had given shelter and hospitality to a number of important French exiles (including Victor Hugo) and had made no attempt to curb adverse press reports on Bonaparte machinations in France. With Napoleon III firmly on his throne French attacks on the Liberal ministry of Charles Rogier in Belgium were launched with increasing virulence. A Concordat France made with Pope Pius IX in 1850, offering up in return the famous *Loi Falloux* whereby the Church in France was once again empowered to open its own schools as it wished, now became a subtle propaganda instrument with which to harry the Belgian Liberals, who were made to appear to be closing Catholic schools (via their 1850 School Law) at the very time that the 'enlightened' government of Napoleon III was encouraging Catholic education in every possible way. Charles Rogier had to tender his resignation to Leopold in September 1852.

The Crimean War (1854–5) gave Leopold still a further chance to prove his role as a buckler (his favourite expression) in defending the rights and integrity of his kingdom. The Anglo-French alliance urged him to 'twist' the neutrality clause by allowing volunteers to be recruited inside Belgium to fight a 'crusade' against the Russians. He refused. They then suggested that French troops garrisoned in the Papal States should be relieved by a Belgian force. This more subtle proposition was even more peremptorily rejected. The lesson was learned and the rebuff noted throughout Europe.

In home affairs Leopold was to prove himself equally competent and far-sighted. Stability and economic prosperity were interdependent and alike equally dependent on the Catholic–Liberal alliance (which had made the kingdom of Belgium a reality) being maintained for as long as possible. In the event it lasted only until 1839, but over those years a tremendous amount was achieved. In 1832 the Dutch florin was replaced by the Belgian franc. A law to regulate judicial procedure was passed in the same year and in 1836 came the *communal* and provincial laws, the former granting virtual self-government to all the large towns and the latter achieving a happy compromise between provincial yearning for independence and the necessity for some central governmental control.[1] The ancient Catholic University of Louvain was reopened (first at Mechlin) in 1834 and the 'free' university of Brussels created. The following year the universities of Ghent and Liège reopened as state universities, and in 1837 came the establishment of a College of Mining at Mons. All encouragement possible was given to industrial and commercial expansion. The English firm of John Cockerill opened new and modern metal works in Seraing. Established industrial and apprenticeship schools were given a new lease of life and new ones were created. Communication routes must also be speeded up, and here Leopold was bold and imaginative enough to force on the many sceptics about him the idea of developing George Stephenson's locomotive. Was not Belgium at the crossroads of European trade? Then if she jumped in first she could dominate all west–east railroad traffic. And so, after the usual stormy debates in Parliament, the money was voted and on 5 May 1835 Leopold solemnly inaugurated Belgium's first tiny stretch of railroad which ran between Brussels and Mechlin, the entire present network being completed under Leopold II in 1875 and coming under state control in 1900.

The Catholic–Liberal alliance, as we have already noted, cracked in 1839 once William of Holland had been brought to the peace table. Between 1840 and 1845 the moderate Catholic Pierre Nothomb, who enjoyed considerable prestige throughout Belgium for having fought side by side with the Liberals for independence, managed to prolong the alliance. His ministry was mainly responsible for passing, in 1842, the first School Law regulating primary

---

[1] The King had the right to nominate the burgomaster and aldermen to all independent townships, though in 1887 the nomination of aldermen was taken out of his hands for the electorate to decide. The King also nominates his provincial governors. Provinces manage their own financial affairs, may exact certain provincial taxes, run their own school systems, and generally decide their own destiny in so far as this does not run counter to national interests.

education. He reorganised teacher-training and created two new state-controlled colleges at Lier and Nivelles in 1843. About secondary education (still considered their prerogative by the Catholic Church) he could do nothing, but he did administer a sharp rebuff to certain *communes* which tried to hand over their secondary schools to the episcopal authorities with a view to off-loading expenses. He also instituted the system of the presentation to Parliament of triennial reports on the state of education throughout Belgium, to be considered as a basis on which to work for future reform and improvements.

When the 1845 elections left him with no effective majority support in Parliament he resigned, and Leopold, still reluctant to abandon the idea of coalition, struggled on for a further two years with a mainly Catholic-based government. This, in point of fact, gave the Liberals time to rally support to challenge Catholic pretensions and to prepare in 1846 an important manifesto outlining their main aims: the civil powers to be able to act independently of outside pressures and influence (i.e. Catholic influence); the ordinary clergy to be freed from arbitrary episcopal dictatorship in matters specifically non-religious; complete toleration for all religious beliefs; electoral reform; the lot of the poor and the working classes to be eased; belief in individual liberty as necessary to the well-being and healthy development of the whole community, the role of the state being reduced to that of 'watch-dog' to safeguard and cherish this *liberté sacrée*; free trade and free competition in all commercial, industrial, and consumer markets; educational reform.

At the 1847 elections the Liberals commanded a sweeping majority and for the first time forced the King into the position of being obliged to choose his Ministers, not completely according to the dictates of his own conscience or following his own predilections, but in close accord with changing party requirements. With Charles Rogier as their titular head the Liberals were to remain in power until 1852, to attempt faithfully to implement the promises made in their manifesto — and so sow the first seeds of anti-clericalism — and to set in motion a prosperity boom. In 1841 the first Chambers of Commerce were opened. Telegraphic communications were installed in 1846. Postal reforms (cheapening considerably the tariff on letters) came in 1849. The National Bank was opened a year later and was soon to make of Belgium an international banking centre. By 1851 the establishment of Belgian consulates in the leading trading countries had become imperative.

The two important pieces of legislation of Charles Rogier's government were the electoral reform law of 12 March 1848 and the law of 1 June 1850 regulating secondary education. By the former property qualifications were reduced to increase the electorate from 55,000 to 79,000; by the latter Rogier sought to relieve the Catholic Church of its monopolistic control of secondary education by the creation of an alternative state system. The Church was humiliated. Instead of the Church–State partnership established in principle by the 1842 law on primary education, here, so it seemed, was a deliberate attempt to deprive the clergy of their inalienable right to educate. True, provision was made for religious instruction in state secondary schools, but priests may only enter such schools by invitation. Belgian bishops were both indignant and inflammatory in their denunciations and even the Pope was moved to express his 'sorrow'. All Leopold's diplomatic skill was required to cool tempers. Between 1852, when Rogier resigned as he could no longer command a majority in Parliament, and 1857, Leopold ruled with a further coalition government in which Catholic influence was predominant. And in 1854, at the so-called Antwerp Convention, some of the sting was taken out of the School Law by a decision (in essence still in force today) that two hours must be set aside each week in all state schools, as part of the normal school timetable, for religious instruction. In return the bishops abandoned their claim to have some measure of control over the appointment of teachers to state schools.

This latest coalition government fell because of Catholic intransigence. A professor at the University of Ghent was accused of denying the divinity of Christ and immediate dismissal was demanded. Before the government could act the bishops of Ghent and Bruges excommunicated the whole university. The Prime Minister (himself a Catholic) had to heed Liberal denunciation of this action as an unworthy attempt to sway him in his decision, and, in consequence to refuse dismissal. A second and more serious crisis followed the celebrations held for the twenty-fifth anniversary of independence and turned rejoicing into insurrection. A law passed when Belgium was part of the French Republic had vested all control of charitable funds in the state. Catholics maintained that this law was not valid for the new kingdom of Belgium and that the express wishes of the donor should be observed – this in practice meaning that the Church in Belgium had since 1830 been accumulating substantial funds which they alone had the right to administer. Catholic members of the coalition government now unwisely tried to legalise their position by passing a law (dubbed by the angry Liberal bourgeoisie 'la loi des couvents') to enable a donor to state specifically by whom his gift should be administered. Angry and prolonged debates in Parliament gave rise to a mounting tension throughout the country. The Liberals argued that it was the duty of the government to protect the public from sectional (Catholic) interests, and that the passing of such a law constituted a serious challenge to all that Liberalism meant in Belgium. Insurrection broke out not only in Brussels but in all the large towns. The Papal Nuncio was booed; windows of religious houses were smashed; barricades appeared in the streets; and the civic guard was with the insurrectionists. There was nothing to do to save the ugly situation but dissolve the government, Leopold in person declaring the law null and void and appealing for moderation.

At the general election held in December 1857 the Belgians went to the polls determined to prove that the insurrectionists had meant business. There was to be no possibility of a return to the mediaeval conception of domination of the people by the clergy. Individual liberty, for which the Belgian had fought for centuries, was a sacred and inalienable right and was not to be jeopardised at this late hour by sectional Catholic interests. Seventy Liberals as against only thirty-eight Catholics were returned to the new Parliament. With Charles Rogier again as their titular head and Frère-Orban[1] as their effective spokesman the Liberals were now to enjoy thirteen years of undisputed influence in Belgian affairs.

The Catholics rallied themselves as best they could. They saw that they had lost the confidence of the voters because of the lack of

[1] Hubert-Joseph-Walter Frère-Orban (1812–96) was born in Liège, studied law in Paris, practised as a barrister in Liège, and was returned to Parliament in June 1847. He was soon afterwards appointed Minister of Public Works. From 1848 until 1852 he was Minister of Finance and founded the *Banque Nationale* and the *Caisse d'Epargne*. His work *La Mainmorte et la charité* (1854–7) was instrumental in bringing his party back to power in 1857, when he was again appointed Minister of Finance. He resigned in 1864, but soon returned to office. In 1868 he effectively became Prime Minister until 1870. In 1878 he became Prime Minister and Foreign Minister. After his overthrow in 1884 he continued active in politics until 1894, when he lost his parliamentary seat. He was author of several books and numerous pamphlets.

a clearly-defined political programme and an efficient press organisation, and that their right-wing clergy constituted as big a danger
to their political aspirations as did the Masonic Lodges to the
Liberal Party, which, now wedded to the positive philosophy of
Auguste Comte, claimed (with full Masonic blessing) that theo-
logical and metaphysical philosophies had failed and that the renovation of society could only come about through the application of
the same scientific spirit found effective in other departments of
human knowledge. The new drive and determination of the younger
Liberals, with the shrewd and ruthless Frère-Orban as their chosen
leader, had to be matched by similar tactics, and just as Charles
Rogier had been brushed aside as being an idealist, a democrat, and
a patriot rather than a party politician, so must the Catholics now
disavow their own ultramontane right wing. Five years' careful
preparation led to the calling of a huge Catholic Congress in
Mechlin in 1863 and there a new party programme was elaborated
which, while reaffirming in the strongest terms the Catholics' belief
in the 'free' school system, roundly denounced both clergy and con-
gregations who could not or would not face up to the political
realities of changing times and circumstances.

The following year Frère-Orban could only command a majority
of two at the general elections and felt bound to resign. Leopold
appealed to a moderate Catholic, Adolphe Dechamps, to try to form
a government, and though Dechamps did his best to implement the
findings of the Mechlin Congress, seeking his mandate on a democratic and decentralising basis, he failed to convince the mass of
Catholics who were suspicious of such new liberalising tendencies.
The ailing Leopold was equally chary of this sudden 'popular'
gesture and also afraid of possible Catholic anti-militaristic tendencies sabotaging his plans for the fortification of Antwerp. He therefore made what was to be the last determined stand of his long reign
by repudiating Dechamps and insisting that Frère-Orban remain in
office. Leopold died on 10 December 1865.

Throughout Europe the press was fulsome in its praise of this first
King of the Belgians, if not uncritical of the way in which he had
astutely managed to spread the influence of the House of Coburg
not only in Europe but even to Latin America,[1] and not a little

---

[1] His daughter Charlotte (1840-1927) had married in 1857 the Archduke
Maximilian of Austria who in 1864 became the ill-fated Emperor of Mexico
– shot during the republican uprising three years later.

envious of the way in which his go-slow tactics had always placed him in full control of any situation, and always to the advantage of his adopted country. His honesty and devotion to the cause of Belgium were never called in question, *The Times* shrewdly pointing out that 'instead of aspiring to a preponderant influence in the councils of Europe he had contented himself with developing the immense riches of those [Belgian] towns which were the glory of the empire of Charles V and which no power has ever succeeded in ruling except by bowing to their whims'. The Berlin newspaper *Kreuzzeitung* stressed that 'even his political adversaries must admit that the late King was endowed with the most outstanding qualities and the House of Coburg loses in him a leader whose political acumen is almost without parallel in modern history'.

As for the Belgians themselves, they were for once under no illusions as to their great good fortune in having had Leopold to rule over them. Nor were they unprepared for the end. The death of Queen Louise-Marie in 1850 had proved to be almost as bitter a blow to Leopold as had been that of Charlotte in England some thirty-three years earlier. For the last fifteen years of his life Leopold had withdrawn himself, while in no sense neglecting either his normal duties or what he took to be his obligations. Thus, though not himself well, he had journeyed to Osborne at the end of 1861 to console the widowed Queen Victoria and there his first attack of stone had declared itself. From that point onwards, and visibly to all, his health steadily deteriorated. Yet he would not spare himself. Much to the annoyance of Charles Rogier, who was now Minister for Foreign Affairs, he insisted on playing his customary vital role in Belgium's international dealings, fearing in particular the machinations of Napoleon III, and in 1864 carried out a programme of consultations which would have taxed even a much younger and more healthy man. At the beginning of 1865 he had a slight stroke, but this did not prevent him from again journeying to England to help Victoria who was distraught over the aberrations of Edward, Prince of Wales. He returned with dropsy and it was at last obvious that he was dying.

The state funeral was fixed for 16 December, the day on which Leopold would have attained his seventy-five years. All the reigning monarchs of Europe, or their representative princes, attended. The ceremony lasted the whole of Saturday, and grey skies and a steady drizzle of rain matched the pensive mood of the silent crowds who packed the long processional route from the palace in Brussels to the hastily erected mausoleum at Laeken.

On Sunday 17 December 1865 Leopold II slipped quietly into his capital city. The period of consolidation was over. A second and equally important period of expansion was about to begin.

Chapter 5

Leopold II (1865-1909)

LEOPOLD II WAS THIRTY YEARS OLD when he came to the throne and, although he was greeted enthusiastically as *Belge de coeur et d'âme* – the first truly national king the Belgians were to have, he was very much an unknown quantity. Nor did his somewhat cold exterior and natural aloofness help matters. It was of course known that he had travelled widely as Duke of Brabant, going as far afield as North Africa, India, Asia Minor, and the Far East, and that on his return from a visit to Greece in 1860 he had pointedly presented to Frère-Orban a piece of white marble taken from the Acropolis and on which he had had engraved the words: 'Il faut à la Belgique une colonie' (Belgium needs a colony).[1] At the end of the same year, and again in 1861, in speeches to the Senate he had not been afraid to voice his convictions and to announce that 'I think the time has arrived for us to extend our influence abroad. I believe we must lose no time over this, otherwise we shall see the best territories, already rare, successively occupied by more enterprising nations than our own'.

That these repeated hints largely fell on deaf ears is not surprising for the times. Once Europe had settled down after the 1848 revolutions (which in no way affected Belgium) there followed for Belgium a period of ever-increasing prosperity on a basis of strongly developed capitalist production and rapidly improved technical and commercial procedures. More and more markets were being secured abroad, new inventions were being tried out, new industrial enterprises begun. Important public works were also undertaken at home, and Belgium's future as a mainly industrial and urban country was finally decided. In 1860 France had been wooed by the Manchester

---

[1] This historic gift is now on view in the Colonial Museum at Tervueren, near Brussels.

school of economists, headed by Richard Cobden, to the principle of Free Trade and had signed the Chevalier-Cobden Treaty.[1] This was speedily followed by a similar treaty with Belgium in 1861, and the Belgians were quick to thrust home their advantages and to conclude during the years 1862–3 similar treaties with Great Britain, Prussia, the *Zollverein*, Spain, and Italy. The agreement with Holland in 1863, fully opening the Scheldt to Belgian shipping, brought greater prosperity to Antwerp than she had ever known since the sixteenth century, and Belgium once again became, as the Belgian historian Pirenne picturesquely puts it,

'what she had been during the Middle Ages and the Renaissance — a factory and an *entrepôt* situated at the crossroads of Europe and at last capable of profiting from the exceptional situation with which nature had endowed her but the use of which political machinations extending over three hundred years had denied her.'

Nor had the government neglected its important farming communities. Much uncultivated land was put under plough and new and intensive methods of agriculture were taught and practised. A decline in sheep-rearing was offset by a special drive in horticulture, and in 1870 as in 1840 Belgium was still the most advanced horticultural country in Europe. Mechanisation was brought to the land and the sugar-beet industry in particular made impressive strides forward. The government had equally realised that all this rapid and extended industrial and agricultural development could not be catered for by existing banking facilities and had therefore created in 1850 the *Banque Nationale* charged with regulating credit and backing all state financial operations without itself being empowered either to borrow or to indulge on its own account in commercial or industrial speculation.

All this prodigious effort was the work of the bourgeoisie, the new self-made men who had come to power with the creation of the new kingdom of Belgium. Economic liberalism and the production of wealth was the order of the day. Belgium was enjoying her first long period of external peace since the Burgundian rule of the fifteenth century. She must make fullest use of the opportunities

---

[1] Full details will be found in the author's unpublished thesis lodged in the library of the University of Leeds and entitled: *Le Traité Chevalier-Cobden de 1860 et sa contribution à la chute de Napoléon III.*

afforded her and these opportunities lay in western Europe. Thus the growing prosperity of the country was counterbalanced by an equally growing spirit of selfishness and by a narrow-mindedness which Leopold II, persistently and obstinately, and autocratically using the powers he could wrest from the ambiguous wording that governed his constitutional rights, did his utmost to overcome. It was the selfishness of the bourgeoisie which caused it to concentrate on its electoral interests and its party quarrels; to ignore repeatedly the insistent demands of the working class, whom it was educating to fit into the bourgeois hierarchy, for proper electoral representation; to oppose any protective intervention by the state in social and economic life; and so further to incense the workers to form their own radical Socialist Party. It was its narrow-mindedness which would not allow it either to heed Leopold's plea to prepare and arm the country adequately against an already worsening European situation or to appreciate his bold and imaginative personal swoop on Africa to carve out there a territory which he was later to bequeath to a still unwilling nation.

From the point of view of the bourgeoisie his first job was to ensure the continuation of the dynasty. This had been achieved by his arranged marriage in 1853 with the Archduchess Maria Henrietta of Austria in the hope that future princes of Belgium might be able to trace their line, not only to Philip the Good, but also to Maria Theresa.[1] His second job was to keep the wheels of constitutional government smoothly oiled and allow them to get on with the money-making. That he proved in the long run to be more far-sighted than they were and also a more astute and competent businessman was something they were later to find very hard to swallow. For the moment, however, Leopold could only patiently bide his time and hope in the long run to prevail. And the European situation as he came to the throne, given the short-sightedness of his Ministers, claimed all his attention.

After the victory of Sadowa in 1866 whereby Bismarck had virtually accomplished the unification of Germany, there were serious moves to placate Napoleon III of France by allowing him

[1] In point of fact he had only one son and three daughters. The son (Leopold) died in 1869 at the age of ten. Thus his younger brother, Philip, Count of Flanders, became the heir apparent. Philip's elder son, Baudouin, died in 1891 leaving Prince Albert (born 1875) next in line. With the death of the Count of Flanders in 1905 Prince Albert's succession to the throne was assured.

to annex Belgium, and a cunning attempt by the then French ambassador in Berlin, Vincent Benedetti, to get Prussian troops to back the annexation should another power come to the defence of Belgium in strict accord with the neutrality clause that had accompanied the establishment of the kingdom. Fortunately for Belgium, Great Britain had her own sources of information on this attempt further to upset the balance of power and forced Napoleon III to proclaim complete ignorance of what was supposed to be afoot. Leopold now begged his Ministers to look to the proper defences of Belgium, but he was only heeded after it was seen that Napoleon III, having bought up the railway system of the Grand Duchy of Luxembourg (with a view to annexing *that* country), was also trying to negotiate for a controlling interest in the Belgian railway network. A spanner was again thrown in Napoleon's machinations by the calling of an international conference in London on 11 May 1867 which unequivocally declared Luxembourg, as Belgium, to be neutral territory. The following year Leopold had the satisfaction of seeing the fortifications of Antwerp completed and of passing a law calling 12,000 men annually to the colours for varying periods of service, ranging between two and four years. It was a beginning.

The Franco-Prussian War of 1870 spared Belgium simply because Great Britain made it clear to both sides that the neutrality of Belgium must be respected. Nonetheless, great battles were fought perilously near the Belgian frontiers at Metz and Sedan, and it was considered prudent to mobilise some 83,000 men, the wisdom of this move being shown when they had to be used to disarm straggling and beaten French soldiers at frontier posts and so effectively to prevent any possible excuse for the violation of Belgian territory by the Prussians. Even now, however, all Leopold's persistence and powers of persuasion were necessary on 14 June 1887 to get monies voted to construct fortifications along the Meuse between Liège and Namur. The budget was exceeded. Parliament stubbornly refused to complete the construction of a fort at Lixhe (near Visé) and it was at this very point that the Germans broke through in August 1914.

On 14 July 1887 a bill to introduce universal conscription was defeated by 69 votes to 62 and Leopold II made his displeasure known in no uncertain terms. Some fifteen years' wrangling ensued, the Flemings stubbornly resisting any idea of compulsory military service, until on 21 March 1902 the effective strength of the armed forces was raised from 130,000 to 187,000 men and a compromise bill passed whereby the extra personnel required were to be conscripted by the drawing of lots – the unlucky 'volunteer' being always in a position to find a replacement.

In January 1904 Leopold paid an official visit to Berlin, where his most gloomy fears were more than justified. Ostensibly the visit was to discuss colonial problems, but the Kaiser confounded Leopold by first reminding him of the past glories of Belgium under Burgundian rule and then suggesting he might care to revive those glories by acquiring (through military collaboration with Germany) French Flanders, the French part of the Ardennes, and the French province of Artois. Leopold coldly and firmly rejected the proposition, only to be warned that if Belgium were not with the Kaiser, then strategical considerations only would in the future be taken into consideration by him. Leopold II was wearing his uniform as honorary colonel-in-chief of the Prussian dragoons, and so put out was he that his own astonished entourage witnessed their King driving in state to board the train to Brussels wearing his Prussian helmet back to front.

Still the Belgian bourgeoisie backed the right-wing Flemings with their own militant slogan of 'Nobody a soldier under duress'. On 21 July 1905 Leopold seized the occasion of the seventy-fifth anniversary of the founding of his kingdom to plead that 'actions are needed as well as words. I sincerely hope that you will no longer oppose the wishes of your King.' On 24 January 1906 Parliament voted 100 million francs to strengthen the defences of Antwerp and to build twenty forts along 105 kilometres of the Dutch frontier. By 1908 the Minister for War had to admit that the present lottery system of conscription, together with voluntary recruitment, was far from meeting manpower requirements. Cabinet changes in the same year made François Schollaert Prime Minister, and his successful piloting of the bill through Parliament (by 83 votes to 54) whereby Belgium assumed responsibility for the Congo gave him sufficient prestige to try to satisfy the dying King's last request— universal conscription. On 14 December 1909 Leopold signed his last document: military service was made compulsory for fifteen months on the basis of the conscription of one son per family, in principle the eldest son. 'The King is content,' murmured Leopold. Three days later he was dead.

In home affairs Leopold II's reign was largely dominated by the quarrel over the schools between Liberals and Catholics.[1] He had inherited the Liberal government of Frère-Orban, whose hold on power was considerably strengthened by the upsurge of national feeling which greeted the accession to the throne of the first truly Belgian King. Frère-Orban energetically opposed any extension of the franchise or the granting of more autonomy to the *communes* on the grounds that the influence of the bourgeoisie would thereby be seriously affected. More and more he identified the Liberal Party with anti-clericalism and let it be seen that he was basing government on the interests of the strong industrial class. An economic crisis in 1867 which led to strikes, insurrection, and some bloodshed caused the radical left wing of his party to agitate for an extension of the franchise in common cause with the Catholics. Sensing danger, Frère-Orban introduced a new electoral law which his left wing loyally backed, to find that the franchise was in practice to be extended only at a provincial and *communal* level. As Bismarck moved against France the Catholics vehemently attacked the costly military preparations of the government, talked in more moderate and conciliatory tones of even universal suffrage, exploited their advantages with considerable skill, and, on 14 June 1870, with the support of the exasperated left-wing radicals overthrew the Liberal government.

Throughout the critical period of the Franco-Prussian War this new Catholic government of the Baron Jules-Joseph d'Anethan hung on precariously in the shadow of Leopold's displeasure, he being, however, not so much anti-Catholic as alarmed and incensed by the refusal of the Catholics to appreciate the menace Germany constituted and to prepare the country to defend itself. In December 1871 Leopold was quick to seize the opportunity to rid himself of this interim government (on the pretext that it could no longer maintain law and order) and to replace it by a stronger and more right-wing Catholic group headed by Jules Malou. Malou remained in office for seven years, riding the tide of a period of economic prosperity which followed the Franco-Prussian War, and, in effect, giving the Liberals a breathing-space to rally themselves, to woo back some of their dissident radical-minded members, and to exploit the domestic situation to the full.

[1] See below, Chapter 14.

Between 1870 and 1878 passions reached an unprecedented degree of political invective. The proclamation of the infallibility of the Pope in July 1870 made the Liberals once again aware of the threat this constituted to state-controlled education, and they began to campaign actively for absolute and immediate separation of Church and state, complete secularisation of public education, and a revision of the 1842 School Law on primary education. On their side the Catholics displayed a new and irritating ultramontane attitude which laid them open to charges of wishing to undermine the constitution. Ardently political Liberals found it increasingly difficult to remain as heretofore within the bosom of the Church, though Frère-Orban was wise enough to proclaim his respect for the Church and its doctrines – in their proper place. In 1871 a further revision of the electoral law widened the franchise still more to give the Catholics control of the administration of the smaller towns, particularly in the Flemish provinces. A new linguistic law of 1873[1] was seen as a deliberate attempt to win Flemish-speaking Belgians to the Catholic cause and proved to be still another aggravation. In 1876 the Liberals might have won the elections had they been able to curb their militant left wing. Two years later, with a majority of nineteen in the Lower House and six in the Senate, Frère-Orban returned to power fully backed by all shades of opinion within his party and with a clear mandate to preserve their cherished national institutions from all taint of clericalism.

One of the first moves of the new Liberal government was a still further revision of the electoral law which, though politically justifiable in that it reduced considerably the number of privileged qualified voters, in effect deprived some 8,000 of the franchise. These were mainly clergy and Catholic-minded peasant farmers.[2] The creation of a state Ministry of Education speedily followed, and Frère-Orban made a tactical error in nominating as his first Minister for Education Pierre Van Humbeek, a leading Freemason who was well-known for his intransigent anti-Catholic sentiments. When the new Parliament assembled on 12 November 1878, Van Humbeek immediately gave notice that he would table a drastic revision of the 1842 School Law on primary education, and what came to be aptly dubbed the *loi de malheur* (the disastrous law) became effective

[1] See below, Chapter 13.
[2] More than 2,000 of these were *cultivateurs* and rather more than 1,500 in holy orders.

in June 1879[1] and unleashed on the Belgian people a schools' war which was to rage with unabated vigour down to 1914.[2]

This was not the time to match one form of extremism (Catholic ultramontanism) with another. Caution and compromise were necessary, particularly when it is remembered that the radical bourgeois group (the anti-Catholics), headed by Van Humbeek, were in a definite minority and could never hope to carry the mass of the Belgian people with them all the way. The Catholics fought back with spirit and effectively sabotaged the proper implementation of Van Humbeek's law by insisting that Catholic parents (under pain of excommunication) should boycott the state system and attend only the Catholic free-school system. Frère-Orban somewhat foolishly tried to involve the Pope by a speech in Parliament which set out to show that Leo XIII, if not with him, was equally not in favour of the extremist attitude adopted by the Belgian clergy. The Pope was too wily to fall into that trap and retaliated by saying that while the Belgian constitution was, from the Church's point of view, not an ideal constitution (being man-made) it was one in which the Catholics enjoyed real freedom and liberty of expression and they owed it as a duty not to attack the constitution but to *defend it whenever the very real liberty of the individual was in danger.* The Catholic Party in Belgium eagerly exploited this polemical statement. Were not the Liberals threatening personal liberty? Were they not trying to impose on the people what the people would not have? Thus, overnight almost, Belgian Catholics found themselves abandoning their former ultramontane attitude and standing as staunch and very real defenders of the Belgian constitution. Frère-Orban now yielded to increasing pressure from his left-wing supporters and broke off diplomatic relations with the Vatican on 5 June 1880. The Catholics retorted by comparing the various measures of Frère-Orban's government with those taken by William of Holland some fifty years earlier: the very people who were posing as apostles of enlightenment were seeking nothing more than the enslavement of the rest of the population.

And so, unfortunately for Frère-Orban, did the position also appear to the left-wing members of his party. To claim, as Frère-Orban

[1] There were 67 votes for and 60 against the law in the lower chamber. In the Senate the vote of an ailing senator secured a bare majority. He died the next day, this being hailed by the faithful as a judgement from Heaven.

[2] See below, Chapter 14.

claimed, that the Liberal Party represented the higher interests of the state; that there could be no liberty except by law; that there was no liberty of the citizen against the state; and that it was the duty of the state to prepare each embryonic citizen to be a citizen of such a state – all this was anathema equally to Catholics and radicals. The radicals had pressed again and again for electoral reforms. Again and again they had been cheated. Frère-Orban's government had reduced the franchise, not extended it. If the radicals had backed Frère-Orban earlier it had been to strike a blow at the Church. The Church had been taught its lesson. Nothing but universal suffrage would now satisfy the radicals. In vain Frère-Orban urged that at this time universal suffrage could only lead to church domination of the people. In vain he tried to compromise by a new electoral law of 1883, giving the vote to certain recognised professions and to all those who had satisfactorily completed their primary-school education.[1] The radicals shrugged this off and formed in the same year their separatist Liberal League. With this defection, the growing strength of the socialist movement, and an economic crisis on his hands, Frère-Orban could not long survive. At the elections of 1884 the Catholics returned to power with a majority of thirty-six.

Amid all this turmoil Leopold II had had as his main preoccupations the opening-up of the Congo and the military preparedness of Belgium. Increasingly he was coming to be viewed as a cold and aloof autocrat who put his own personal life (and pleasures), his own business interests (the Congo), and his military preoccupation first. This party strife and internecine warfare apparently meant nothing to him since he refused to be drawn into it or allow his own position to be in the least compromised. In point of fact, of course, he deplored the pettiness and bickering and was saddened by the evidence it gave that his people lacked the vision both to safeguard and to extend their country's interests. But this they could not understand even when, as Jules Malou returned to power, he pointedly reminded him that 'after 1878 the Liberals behaved as though there were no more Catholics in Belgium. It is now in Catholic interest not to forget that their country contains a large number of Liberals.'[2]

This advice went unheeded. The Catholics rushed through the

[1] State schools only. Ex-pupils of Catholic schools needed a special certificate of competence to be issued by the government.

[2] As we shall see later, this state of affairs (in a different context and in a different idiom) was to be paralleled during the reign of Leopold III.

1884 School Law, abolished the Ministry of Education (thus bringing all state education once again under the control of the Minister
for the Interior), and resumed diplomatic relations with the Vatican.
An immediate effect of the implementation of the law was the
abrupt dismissal of state teachers in Catholic-dominated *communes*,
a decrease in the salaries of such teachers as were retained, and
widespread uncertainty and discontent leading to some insurrection
in Brussels. Leopold II immediately pounced and demanded the
resignation of the two militant Catholic leaders, Victor Jacobs and
Charles Woeste. Jules Malou could do no other than resign as well
and Leopold was now in a position to nominate a moderate Catholic
leader, Auguste Beernaert, who was skilful enough never personally
to become identified with the cause of Catholic ideology, who gave
the country a ministry flexible enough to deal with pressing questions
of social reform, who enabled the King to push forward his colonial
enterprises, and who in consequence remained in power for ten full
years.

From 1886 onwards – the year in which a fresh economic crisis
reached its peak – Beernaert's government was preoccupied with repeated outbursts of civil unrest, the demands of the *Parti Ouvrier
Belge* (founded on 5 April 1885 at an historic meeting at the *Café
du Cygne* in the Grand' Place of Brussels) for a revision of the constitution leading to universal suffrage, and with how best to tackle
the more urgent social questions of the day. A *Commission du
Travail* was established, enunciated the important principle that
henceforward the government must make the lot of the working
class its concern, and introduced several important measures regulating the working hours of women and children, the housing
of workers, insurance benefits, and pension schemes. In 1890 the
Catholic Flemish Peasants' League (*Boerenbond*) was formed. Publication of the papal encyclical *Rerum Novarum* in the same year on
the condition of the working classes, and intended as a sharp reply
to the communist Manifesto, strengthened Beernaert's position. As a
rejoinder to the non-Catholic and socialist *Parti Ouvrier Belge* he
created the Catholics' own workers' association *La Ligue Démo-
cratique Belge*, and by the same token gave official recognition to the
existence of trade union movements. The impetus thus given to
reform by this moderate, patriotic, and high-minded politician led,
after he had left office, to the creation of the Ministry of Labour in
1895, to important workshop and factory rules to protect the worker

and minimise accidents in 1896, to the compulsory inspection of coal mines in 1897, to the conferment on professionally organised trade unions of full legal status in 1898, to compensation to workers for accidents in 1903, and to Sunday being declared an official day of rest in 1905. Beernaert also found time to represent Belgium at several important international conferences on disarmament, and the crowning point of his career came with the award of the Nobel Peace Prize in 1909.

It was in effect the *Parti Ouvrier Belge* which drove him from office in 1894. Now growing rapidly both in numbers and in solidarity, the movement insisted on immediate universal suffrage and threatened general strikes if it were not heeded. Serious strikes did break out in 1892, and a general strike followed by serious rioting in 1893 made Beernaert realise that he could no longer delay a decision even if he were to lose the support of his right-wing Catholic colleagues. The vote was given to all males over twenty-five years of age who had resided for at least one year in the same *commune*, but, in order to counterbalance any possibility of extreme radicalism, a plural extra vote was instituted for all heads of families, tenant owners, taxpayers, those in some recognised professional or public office, and those holding the secondary-school leaving certificate. In no circumstances, however, could any one elector accumulate more than three votes. It was also made compulsory for each elector to use his vote – a legal obligation which still remains in force. The new electoral law of 7 September 1893 immediately increased the electorate from a mere 137,000 to 1,381,000.

His work done, Beernaert resigned and Parliament was dissolved. All parties anxiously awaited the results of the new elections held in October 1894. The Liberals, who had for so long represented the interests of the well-to-do bourgeoisie and of the industrialist with marked radical and anti-Catholic tendencies, met their nemesis and returned only twenty members. The socialist *Parti Ouvrier Belge* exceeded all expectations by claiming twenty-eight seats. The Catholics found themselves with an overwhelming majority by taking the remaining 114 seats. Progressive Catholics of an earlier generation who had then urged universal suffrage had at last been proved right: the Flemish provinces – landowners, farmers, and farm labourers – had voted *en masse* for the Catholic Party. And, ironically, it had been the radicals and the industrial working classes who had forced the issue on an unwilling Catholic government.

The new Prime Minister, Jules de Burlet, lost no time in initiating desirable social reforms to ease the lot of the worker, to bring the worker as closely as possible within the Catholic orbit, and to reward the loyal Flemings by heeding their linguistic grievances. He also felt the time had come to implement more firmly the School Law of 1884 and so counter in particular any extension of the socialist hold on the children of the working class. There resulted the new School Law of 15 September 1895, piloted through Parliament by the Minister of the Interior, François Schollaert, a brilliant professor from the University of Louvain, a sincere and high-minded Catholic who did his best within his terms of reference to tighten up and generally modernise the instruction.

The next parliamentary elections of 1898 increased the Catholic majority by a further two votes and made it quite clear that the Catholics were now drawing their main support from the Flemish provinces, and the Liberals and socialists from the industrial areas of Wallonia. To have the country permanently divided in this way was not healthy. The socialists were also chafing over the undemocratic nature of the plural vote and once again threatening strike action. Some further electoral reform was needed, but which? After much hesitation, and with none of the three parties being particularly in favour, the system of proportional representation which had already been tried out fairly successfully at *communal* elections was adopted in 1899. New elections on this basis took place in 1900, and only 85 Catholics as against 33 socialists and 31 Liberals were returned. The Catholic majority had fallen from 72 to 20. It now became clear to the Liberals that they had to make common cause with the socialists if they were to come anywhere near achieving their joint educational aims. They also came out with a definite programme of their own which, while naturally putting compulsory state education to the fore, also called for a strengthening of the armed forces and the abolition of the prevalent practice of buying oneself out of military service. At the 1908 elections they secured 46 places in Parliament and reduced the Catholic majority to only eight. With victory almost within their grasp after so many years of persistent effort they became impatient and so intensified once again the schools struggle. François Schollaert, however, who had now become Prime Minister, manoeuvred carefully and saved the day for the Catholic Party. As we have already noted, he adroitly steered through Parliament a bill to annex the Congo on 20 August 1908 and he gratified the dying Leopold II also by the conscription bill which became law on 14 December 1909.

This Congo adventure of Leopold's is outstanding among his many remarkable achievements on behalf of his country and a signal example of his tenacity of purpose, in the face of all opprobrium, in pursuing his own undeviating course once he was convinced of the rightness of his policies. There can be little doubt that his dreams of colonial expansion were fostered by Leopold I who could not have failed to discuss with his son and heir his own unfulfilled aspirations and his own private, and unsuccessful, attempts at creating Belgian bases in Central America, in Brazil, in the Solomon Islands, in Abyssinia. It is certain that he encouraged the young prince's desire to travel and that from these early travels came the determination to seize the opportunity to be bolder than his father could have been.

Accession to the throne of Belgium in no way restricted Leopold II from both travelling extensively and interesting himself in a wide variety of geographical explorations. He returned from a long voyage to Egypt and India in 1876, and judged the European situation now sufficiently settled to address letters to various European powers inviting them to Brussels to discuss, among other things, the opening-up of Central Africa, the abolition of slavery, and the best means of conferring on the natives the benefits of modern civilisation. The conference was a personal triumph for Leopold. From its deliberations there resulted the creation of the *Association Internationale pour l'exploration et la civilisation de l'Afrique Centrale,* and Leopold was elected president of the whole enterprise. He devoted himself with vigour to the task and also saw to it that his own national sub-committee was fully active. Between 1877 and 1884 he launched five separate expeditions along the shores of Lake Tanganyika which, though they yielded no spectacular results, were indirectly important in establishing Belgium's right to recognition there by the other powers in Africa.

The turning-point came when Stanley succeeded in crossing Central Africa by discovering and following the course of the Congo river. An enthusiastic telegram which Stanley sent to London on 17 October 1877 evoked as little response in England as it would have done at that time in Belgium. Leopold, however, recognised Stanley's worth. In 1878 he summoned him privately to his palace at Laeken, introduced him to several influential Belgian businessmen, declared with them the formation of a *Comité d'Etudes du Haut Congo*, and dispatched Stanley as their accredited representative on a five-year voyage of further exploration. Stanley did a marvellous job and soon staked a claim for Leopold's company to colonisation rights in the Upper Congo. As the news leaked, other powers in the same area were stimulated to further exploratory activity. Leopold now cunningly and prudently stressed the international aspect of his *Comité d'Etudes* and his own peaceful intentions in the area. At the same time, in 1881, he created the town of Leopoldville.

Three years later, Bismarck judged it prudent to call an international conference in Berlin to attempt to settle the whole future of the Congo basin. By the time the delegates met, however, Leopold had already obtained America's full support for his company and official recognition of his company's flag. He was therefore in an extremely strong position in Berlin – yet lacking the support of his own government which was jealous of the brilliant outcome of his manoeuvres as it was apprehensive of the success he had had in rallying to his support some of the most able and most adventurous of the young army officers. The Belgian government was even more annoyed when, as the conference ended on 26 February 1885, all the delegates showed willingness to accept the Belgian flag rather than the flag of a private company. It brusquely declined all responsibility for Leopold's private venture, and on his return home from the conference Leopold had all his work cut out to obtain permission to rule at one and the same time as a constitutional monarch in Belgium and as an absolute (private merchant) monarch over the Congo.

Nonetheless, the new state came into official existence on 1 July 1885, and for the next twenty years Leopold was kept busy bringing order and pacification among his subject peoples, developing the natural resources and potential of his territory, and recruiting competent and devoted personnel to carry out the many and delicate tasks involved. On the other hand, it cannot be denied that Leopold deployed his powers as an absolute monarch to the full. Rival businessmen were both perplexed and angry at this state business enterprise run by a commercially-minded king who daily grew more ambitious and more successful. Leopold came to be increasingly attacked from abroad on the grounds that, while in theory slavery was abolished throughout his territories, the Congolese were so exploited as to be in a condition at least approaching slavery.

He was attacked from within Belgium by the socialists for the same reasons, and by politicians generally because of the increasing demands he made for government aid to develop his enterprises still further. Yet in fairness to Leopold it must be stated that he was behaving only as other industrial and capitalist bosses were behaving in Africa. The Congo was far from being the only place in which the workers could be said to be exploited. Leopold's real crime (in their eyes) was that he happened to be a king as well as an astute businessman. And the remedy, after all, lay with his own government to relieve him of his responsibilities. This, as we have noted, it finally and still reluctantly did by the law of 18 October 1908. But not before Leopold's business acumen and realism had at last made the Congo begin to yield appreciable dividends; not before he had considerably increased the size of his holdings by astutely playing off the greater powers one against the other. Leopold bore all the odium of opening up the Congo. The Belgian government and people reaped the harvest.

The charter Leopold secured from his government for the Belgian Congo was, for the times, both forward-looking and progressive. The Congo was made to constitute a legal entity, distinct from the mother-country and having its own laws, treasury, and monetary system. The Congolese were to continue living according to their own customs and under the direct authority of their clans and tribal chiefs, though they were placed under the protection of a Governor-General appointed by the King and responsible to the Belgian government. The whole colony was divided into four provinces, each under the authority of its own Governor, and these provinces were again divided into districts and then into territories under the control of district commissioners and territorial administrators. No business enterprise might be established without sanction at, at least, the provincial level and without giving proper safeguards regarding the employment and treatment of the African population. Adequate educational provision must be made for both the native and the white population.

This last clause on the development of educational facilities was an indirect tribute to and acknowledgement of what Leopold had so far achieved in this direction. From the beginning he had made an appeal to Belgian missionaries to take up work in the Congo and he had met with a ready response. To the missionaries he had assigned the task of providing instruction for the mass of the population, while he himself had become responsible for the training of suitable African personnel for the civil service and for work in European-organised enterprises. Following the explorations and the campaign against slave-traders he had gathered together large numbers of abandoned children in government posts. In 1890 he assumed official guardianship for such children and created school colonies for them, at Boma and New Antwerp, to house, feed, and clothe them and to provide basic instruction. In 1892 he empowered the missionaries to do likewise, and they in their turn created agricultural and vocational colonies, and extended their influence through their colonies as far afield as possible. The children themselves were wild and intractable, while parents were blinded by prejudices of all kinds and could see no object in sending their children to school. Children and parents alike needed a long and protracted period of indoctrination. The missionaries, by the very nature of their work and the kind of contact they had with the Africans, were eminently suited to their task and performed it most efficiently. By 1905 there were already in existence 59 fixed and 29 movable Catholic missionary posts served by 384 men and women. There were also 40 principal Protestant missions and 192 subsidiary ones served by 283 pastors.

In 1906 three important developments helped considerably to clarify the general situation. At home interest was steadily growing in the possibilities the Congo offered, and the necessity for securing specially trained personnel there was emphasised by the creation of the National School of Tropical Medicine which today covers all tropical requirements from the training of medical practitioners down to providing appropriate courses for sanitary workers, workers in hospitals, and missionaries. In the Congo itself Leopold established a school to train promising natives as commercial assistants. At the same time he created three vocational schools, situated at Boma, Leopoldville, and Stanleyville, and attached to government workshops designed to admit young men between the ages of twelve and twenty and to give them initial training as fitters, coppersmiths, blacksmiths, masons, carpenters, assistant telegraph operators, and prospective mechanics. Numbers were limited to thirty at a time for any given course at Boma and Leopoldville, and to twenty at Stanleyville. A highly successful elementary-school course was necessary for entry, and in addition to their special vocational studies pupils were given further compulsory education in reading, writing, and arithmetic.

Lastly, Leopold came to a firm and wise understanding with the Holy See over the recruitment and deployment of missionaries whom he wished to use over a wide area for the education of the Congolese from the lowest to the highest levels. Each missionary establishment sent to the Congo had to create a school, the size of the school being proportionate to the number of staff available. Programmes of studies in such schools had to be drawn up in agreement with the Governor-General. Instruction in either Dutch or French was obligatory, and courses in agriculture, forestry, and semi-skilled manual trades had to be available for all who could profit from such courses. The Governor-General was to receive periodic reports on the work of each school and the schools were to be open to government inspection at any time. In return, mission posts creating schools received free concessions of land varying between 100 and 250 hectares according to the importance of the post and the range of educational facilities provided.

Such was the nature of Leopold II's legacy to his people. The story of the early colonisation of the Belgian Congo remains one of the miracles of diplomacy. And the Belgians signally failed to appreciate the drama of the situation. They equally failed to realise that in all his undertakings he was giving Belgium the status and influence of one of the more important economic powers. He obtained markets for Belgian industry as far afield as China and South America. In every sphere his reign was one of expansion and important works – including those of military preparedness. While Leopold I had guided the nation through a period of foreign hostility, Leopold II gave her a long period of external peace and prosperity. Belatedly the Belgians have recognised this, giving him the label of 'great' and looking back somewhat nostalgically to his era as the English have looked back on the Victorian age. He died, however, a lonely and misunderstood old man; and as his coffin, drawn by eight black horses, headed a slow and ponderous procession through the streets of Brussels, catcalls and whistles were to be heard mingled with the mocking laughter of those who had bought and were reading various scurrilous broadsheets which purported to recount some of the late King's most titillating amorous adventures.

Chapter 6

Albert I (1909-34)

As the second son and fourth child of the Count and Countess of Flanders Albert had led an austere but sheltered and peaceful life until the unexpected death of his elder brother in 1891, when he himself was only fifteen, had made him sole heir to Leopold II. Nine years later he married in Munich Elisabeth of Bavaria, and throughout the turbulent years of Albert's reign, sharing as she did his own deep interest in social and economic questions, his concern for and patronage of the arts, letters, and science, she made an ideal companion. They had three children – Leopold (1901), Charles (1903), and Marie-José (1906). During these early years Prince Albert travelled throughout Belgium to study at first hand the economic and industrial progress of the country and to urge that Belgium's whole future depended on constant modernisation and still more and more highly-skilled manpower. He visited America and England to study industrial and economic methods there. He was made Lieutenant-General of the Belgian armed forces by Leopold II in 1907, initiated thenceforward by his uncle to the intricacies of the peculiar form monarchical government took in Belgium (as seen by Leopold II), and was finally despatched by him on an intensive tour of the Congo in April 1909. Conscientiously, Albert spent four full months there and had hardly hurried back to present his report to Leopold II than that old autocrat had died and left a still somewhat bewildered and timid young man to succeed him.

He was also at first equally bewildered, then delighted, and finally fortified in his various resolves by the enthusiasm with which the Belgian people greeted both Queen Elisabeth and himself. Of Leopold II they had had more than enough. A new and more exciting future for Belgium now dawned and Albert and Elisabeth, already, had proved themselves by showing themselves to be in the vanguard of progress and democratisation. The speech from the throne on Albert's accession also added support to this belief. 'Belgium', he said,

'in the course of her existence of three-quarters of a century, has not only realised but surpassed the most optimistic forecasts of her potential. She is happy and rich. But wealth creates obligations ... and a nation prospers only on the basis of its moral and intellectual strength ... A Sovereign must constantly heed the will of his people and at the same time care for the poor and the humble; he is the servant of the law and the mainstay of social peace and security.'

In the latter part of his speech, indeed, he showed deep concern with the fact that, while the period from about 1895 to 1914 was one of rapid economic expansion during which Belgium was boldly extending her influence throughout the world,[1] the plight of the working classes was not an enviable one and they were already becoming vociferous. In this they were in some measure aided and abetted by the Liberals (in particular their left wing) who felt increasingly frustrated by the way in which the Catholics were clinging to power despite rapidly diminishing majorities at each general election, and who in consequence joined with the workers' solidarity movements in clamouring for universal suffrage. The situation was further complicated by the fact that at the turn of the century it was possible to distinguish two important workers' movements: the Christian Democrats whose origins sprang from the founding by the Catholic Party in 1891 of the *Ligue Democratique Belge*, with the avowed aim of raising the moral and material situation of the worker, and who were strongest (as might be expected) in Flanders and the rural areas; and the Social Democrats who drew their main support from the industrial areas and from Wallonia. Thus, the language question at the workers' level was already posing problems.

Albert had almost immediately to contend with trouble in home affairs when at the 1910 elections the Catholic majority fell from eight to six and socialists and Liberals together redoubled their protests, which hinged on universal compulsory education and universal

[1] Her engineers and technicians were in demand everywhere. Antwerp had come into its own as the big carrying port of the world. The Congo was yielding its own rich harvest. Capital from abroad (particularly from Germany) was being invested in Belgian industry. The discovery in 1902 of a rich coal-field in the Campine raised still further the industrial potential of the country. The estimated wealth of Belgium had increased by two-thirds and the average income per inhabitant had risen from 510 to 850 francs.

suffrage. The Prime Minister, Schollaert, tabled a bill early in 1911 calculated on the one hand to placate the socialists and the Liberals and on the other to meet criticism from his own party that compulsory education would deal a severe blow at the firm hold on the schools they now had. He offered state-enforced compulsory education, but at the same time proposed an ingenious system by which state subsidies for education would be allotted to state and Catholic schools in proportion to the number of pupils they had registered on their rolls. This proposal, which would have inflamed the antagonisms centred on state- versus Catholic-controlled education, was contemptuously rejected by the socialists and Liberals, and members of Schollaert's own party took their revenge on him for the tactics by which he had made conscription to the armed forces compulsory in 1909 by also opposing the bill and therefore bringing down the government. Amid an atmosphere of tension and near-rioting in the large towns King Albert wisely accepted Schollaert's resignation and replaced him by Charles de Broqueville, who was to remain in office until the close of the First World War.

Charles de Broqueville was a capable and shrewd manipulator. He dropped the Schollaert bill on education, gave apparently little heed to a new coalition move on the part of left-wing Liberals and socialists, waited until their anti-clerical posturing and combative attitudes had had time to affect adversely the thinking of the moderate elements in all parties, and then blithely announced a general election on the pretext that Parliament was no longer truly representative in view of a sharp rise in population figures. His tactics resulted in the Catholics being returned with an overall majority of eighteen. Smarting at being so outwitted, the left-wing intellectuals fomented uprisings which had to be quelled with some severity. The question of universal suffrage was firmly proposed by the socialists in Parliament on 7 February 1913 and was rejected by 99 votes to 83. This time the socialists were sufficiently incensed to call a general strike which lasted for some ten days and it was only when a promise had been given that a parliamentary commission would be forthwith established to examine the whole question that the strike ended. Meanwhile de Broqueville was able to placate the Liberals and the *Ligue de l'Enseignement* (the State Teachers' Association) by passing on 19 May 1914 the *Loi Poullet* which made education compulsory to the age of fourteen, established the principle of equality between state- and Church-controlled education, insisted on the employment of properly certificated teachers for a school to enjoy a state subsidy, and made the central Ministry of Education responsible for outlining the general programmes of instruction. Nonetheless, at the June elections of 1914 the Catholic majority fell once again to a meagre eight. It was obvious to all as war broke out that the question of universal suffrage would soon have to be resolved and that the Catholic hold on office was now being menaced not so much by the Liberals as by a determined socialist caucus.

Amid all this domestic unrest King Albert had to cope with increasing menaces and threats from Germany, and though he was thankful that Leopold II had managed through sheer persistence to overcome the complacency of his government and sign on his death-bed a law requiring all Belgian males of eighteen years of age to do a period of military service, he realised how little time he had left fully to equip and train an army to meet any emergency that could arise. In 1911 occurred the Agadir incident when Germany, after several months of negotiation, finally agreed to France's protectorate rights in Morocco but took in exchange a strip of French Equatorial Africa which bordered the Belgian Congo. Then came the Balkan War of 1912–13 and Kaiser Wilhelm's arrogant intervention and dispatch of a German general as Inspector-General of the Turkish armies. On 29 May 1913 Albert had the satisfaction of seeing de Broqueville steer through Parliament a new conscription bill to make military service compulsory for all males for periods of fifteen to twenty-four months on active service and thirteen years in reserve, thus providing at once an annual intake of some 30,000. And he was more than glad that this had been done when, on a state visit to Germany in November 1913, the Kaiser informed him that war between France and Germany was inevitable and Count von Moltke boasted that the German armies were invincible. This was blackmail and Albert immediately informed both the French and his own government of what lay in store.

So much has already been written on almost every phase and aspect of the First World War that it would be tedious to attempt to cover all the ground yet once again. On 2 August 1914 Germany dispatched an ultimatum to Belgium demanding free access for her troops for an assault upon France, the pretext being that France herself was preparing to march on the Meuse by way of Givet and Namur. The whole of Belgium rallied behind Albert in his contemptuous rejection of the note. The Germans crossed the frontier on 4 August. A heroic stand made at Liège could not hold out for long. Brussels was occupied on 20 August and the armies then retreated to the defence of Antwerp. By October Antwerp had fallen and only the left bank of the river Yser now remained in Belgian hands. For the duration of the war King Albert and Queen Elisabeth stayed on these few square miles of unoccupied Belgian soil, Albert leading and encouraging his troops, and along with the allies making famous the names of Ypres, Dixmude, Passchendaele. The heroic stand of 'gallant little Belgium' became legendary.

Throughout occupied Belgium morale remained high, though suffering was great if not as brutal as in the Second World War. The shooting of Nurse Edith Cavell in 1915 for espionage was unwise, though legally justifiable. By neutral countries it was seen as nothing better than 'judicial murder' and it helped to tip the United States into the war. Leading Belgian citizens were not afraid publicly to condemn the severity of German repressive measures, the censorship of the press, forced labour, and the deportation of more than 120,000 persons, many of them women, to work for the German war effort. Adolphe Max, burgomaster of Brussels, was arrested as early as 26 September 1914 for his outspoken patriotism and open incitement to the citizens to refuse collaboration in any shape or form. The Primate of Belgium, Cardinal Désiré Mercier, soon to be proclaimed as 'the conscience of the world', repeatedly refused to be intimidated and to withdraw anything from his famous pastoral letter which he ordered to be read in all churches on 1 January 1915. 'The powers claimed [by the Germans] have no legal sanction. Thus you owe the occupant neither esteem, nor attachment, nor obedience. The only legitimate authority throughout Belgium is that of the King, his government, and your chosen representatives. The King alone has a claim on our affection and on our submission.' Brave words. Repeatedly the Germans sought to trap him. Repeatedly he refused to offer the German Governor-General a seat when he called upon him, merely listened to what he had to say, and then coldly called a servant to show 'monsieur' to the door. He finally offered him a seat and shook him by the hand when the German armies were beaten and in full flight. 'You are now my guest,' he said, 'and I receive you according to the laws of Belgian hospitality.'[1]

[1] Consult Jeanne Cappe, *Le Très Grand Cardinal*, Brussels (no date), pp. 72–90.

On 27 September 1918, the day following the second battle of the Marne, the Belgians who had so tenaciously held the important Yser front for all these weary years were at last able to move over to the offensive. Inspired by Albert they carried all before them and had liberated Bruges and Ostend by 17 October. There they paused to await the result of the British onslaught on the Scheldt, but before the second phase of their offensive could carry them to Brussels the armistice had been signed. On 22 November the King and Queen, accompanied by their children, rode on horseback at the head of the returning and victorious army through the streets of Brussels amid scenes of unparalleled and delirious rejoicing.

And now came the reckoning. Fifty-two months of German occupation and the heroic sacrifices demanded of the Belgian people were of more profound significance than was at first realised. On the debit side there was the sad loss in manpower (46,000 killed and 50,000 seriously wounded) and the complete collapse of the internal economy of the country. Rolling-stock was almost non-existent and the Germans had systematically destroyed all heavy industrial plant in an attempt to kill any serious post-war competition. The fine library of the University of Louvain was razed to the ground; 100,000 buildings were destroyed; 15,000 works of art had perished; and 100,000 hectares of arable land were either spoiled or flooded. Hard work was now needed to put the country back on its feet, and though in theory the Germans were going to foot the bill it soon became evident that any such hopes were illusory. The government had no alternative but to borrow money, to increase the national debt beyond all controllable proportions, and to see Belgium (along with greater and more powerful countries) plunge from one financial crisis to another. Fortunately, and thanks to the foresight of Leopold II, she possessed the Congo. She was also fortunate in the tenacity of purpose of her people and their determined will to triumph over adversity.

Indeed, the conduct of the working classes during the period of German occupation and the attitude adopted by the whole country to the aggressor won unstinted admiration throughout the world. When the real trial of strength came for the very first time to the new kingdom of Belgium, both military-wise and domestically, the Belgians had without any doubt proved themselves to be a unified nation. The working-class movement had become more assured, responsible, and authoritative. While King Albert had remained with his troops to hold on to what bit of Belgium the Germans could not wrest from him, his government had evacuated itself to Le Havre. There they had realistically dropped all party politics and created a Government of National Union which gave full recognition to the growing influence of the Socialist Party by the co-option of the veteran socialist leader Emile Vandervelde.

Belgium had fully earned the respect of all the greater nations and with it the right to sit at the conference table at Versailles where the final peace treaty terms were hammered out. And Emile Vandervelde was one of the Belgian delegates. From the terms of the Treaty of Versailles, ratified on 10 January 1920, Belgium regained the cantons of Eupen, Malmédy, and Saint-Vith, of which she had been dispossessed in 1815. France declared herself to have no further interests (military or otherwise) in the Grand Duchy of Luxembourg, and an economic union was established with the Grand Duchy on 25 July 1921 to last for fifty years.[1] A commission was set up (including French and English delegates) to discuss with Holland the best methods of jointly making fullest commercial use of the rivers Scheldt and Meuse. Certain works of art which at one time or another had been pilfered by Germany or Austria were returned, amongst them six panels of the Van Eyck brothers' priceless painting *The Adoration of the Lamb*, now on permanent view in the Cathedral of Saint-Bavon in Ghent.[2]

Finally, and most important from the point of view of Belgium's future in European affairs, not only was she granted a mandate by the League of Nations in 1924 over the former German African territories of Ruanda-Urundi, but the treaties of 1831 and 1839 whereby she had been condemned to an artificial form of neutrality were rescinded. Henceforward she was free to determine her own foreign policy and choose her allies as she felt inclined. Belgium quickly seized the opportunities that this afforded by becoming one of the first signatories of the League of Nations and by making a number of pacts with several European powers. The First World War had ended for ever the old, comfortable doctrine of Balance of Power

---

[1] The first full details of this economic union were worked out on 6 March 1922, but, as we shall later see, it was extended after the Second World War to form Benelux, and Benelux itself has been swept within the Common Market.

[2] This unfortunate work of art was again removed by the Germans in the Second World War and restored to the Cathedral of Ghent in 1945 by the American forces.

and this was now gradually being replaced by the principle of collective security. The security of Belgium depended in fact on only three countries: Great Britain, France, and Germany, and it was only her eastern neighbour that she still had reason to fear. In 1926 she became a signatory of the Locarno Pact by which the Belgian, French, and German frontiers were to be mutually guaranteed. She was a supporter of the Briand–Kellogg Pact of 1928 which condemned any recourse to arms to settle differences of opinion, but which left a given nation open to use force in its own legitimate defence. And in 1930, primarily to strengthen her economic position, she turned to northern Europe. By the Treaty of Oslo, signed on 22 December 1930, preferential customs arrangements were agreed upon between the Scandinavian countries, Holland, Belgium, and Luxembourg. The following year at Ouchy near Lausanne the Dutch and Belgians met to thrash out preferential arrangements which would be to their own immediate and mutual advantage.[1]

In his speech from the throne following his triumphant entry into Brussels King Albert had paid touching tribute to the ordinary Belgian soldier who had fought so valiantly behind the Yser and he had made it quite clear that new elections must be held as soon as possible and on a basis of universal male suffrage. Parliament wisely decided that the constitutional requirement of a two-thirds majority to pass a bill giving the vote to all males over the age of twenty-one, and with a six months' residential qualification, should be waived, and the elections were duly held on 16 November 1919. As was only to be expected, the composition of the Lower House was changed out of all recognition. The Catholics lost their overall majority and their representation fell from 99 to 73 seats. The Liberals were reduced from 45 to 34, and the socialists took 70 seats – a gain of 30. In the Senate, where universal suffrage did not apply, the Catholic majority was naturally maintained. It was clear that just as the old order was changing everywhere else in Europe, so was the balance of power shifting inside Belgium. The Liberals of the old school had had their day. And so now had the Catholics.

The only possible solution was to form a coalition government and to set about restructuring and modernising parliamentary representation. The two chambers met as a kind of constituent assembly and worked together for two years to carry out this necessary exercise. Left-wing members (somewhat surprisingly) rejected

[1] In effect this was the first tentative move towards Benelux.

the granting of the vote to women, except at the *communal* level. It was decided that representation in the Lower House should be double that in the Senate and that *députés* must be at least twenty-five years of age and senators forty. Provincial councils should continue to elect senators, but the Senate should henceforward be empowered to co-opt up to twenty extra senators. The life of both houses was fixed at four years.

In the meantime it is interesting to note that the coalition government contained several prominent socialists, among whom was Jules Destrée, who was entrusted with the Ministry of Education. He was the first non-Catholic to hold this vital post since 1884. For thirty years and upwards he had championed the rights of the working class. He initiated the implementation of the postponed 1914 *Loi Poullet* on education and saw to it that the salaries of primary-school teachers were immediately and substantially raised. When he left the Ministry in 1921 he was succeeded by a number of other like-minded men, and Belgium had to wait until after the Second World War before another Catholic took office as Minister of Education. All this has meant the end of the bitter school struggle between Catholics and non-Catholics, and every party has since tried to work together in greater harmony and to take a sensible and non-partisan view of problems as they arise.

In the next general election, held on 20 November 1921, the Catholics gained nine seats, the socialists losing two and the Liberals one. The socialists were now campaigning for a reduction in the period of military service to six months, and as a protest refused to enter the new government. King Albert in consequence had no other alternative but to call upon the Catholic Georges Theunis to form a Catholic–Liberal coalition. Unwittingly the pattern had now been set for the form of government Belgium was to continue to have right down to the present: a series of coalition governments, with only very occasionally one political party (*not* the Liberals) in sufficient strength to govern for a short spell on its own. It arose, ironically, from the fact that universal suffrage had been granted to a people who, however difficult they might make the existence of any government in office, are fundamentally conservative and traditionalist and will always vote for *their* party at a general election. Given the fact that the Liberals had lost their left-wing members to the more attractive and dynamic Socialist Party it meant that the Catholics and socialists were to remain almost evenly balanced, and that the Liberals, henceforward, were to be called upon to play the often unrewarding and frustrating but important role of mediating to hold the balance if either party rushed to some foolish policy of extremes. In a word, without Liberal support neither Catholics nor socialists could be sure to remain for long in office.

The elections of April 1925 gave the socialists ten extra seats at the expense of the Liberals, who lost ten, and the Catholics, who lost four. And, for the first time, two communist *députés* were returned. It would be tedious to attempt to discuss separately the efforts made by successive governments between 1921 and 1934 (there were seven in all) to deal with the various economic and financial crises through which Belgium had now to pass. A serious financial crisis in 1926, when Belgium faced bankruptcy, was successfully weathered thanks to the skill and draconian measures brought to bear on the problem by the financier Emile Francqui who, among other things, nationalised the Belgian railway system. By the end of 1926 the franc had been stabilised at 175 to the pound sterling and Belgium was favourably placed to profit to the full from a new world boom in trade and speculation. Important public works were now undertaken to improve the port of Antwerp, to complete the maritime port of Ghent, and to dig what was to be called the Albert Canal.

And then, as Belgium was celebrating the centenary of her independence, the Wall Street crash of October 1929 plunged the Western world into the greatest financial crisis of its whole history and naturally engulfed Belgium. The banks did what they could but once Great Britain had gone off the gold standard, on 21 September 1931, near panic resulted. Every country in Europe hastily erected customs barriers and Belgian exports suffered accordingly, so that by 1932 they were half of what they had been in 1929. Widespread unemployment rocketed the cost to the state of unemployment pay from 40 million francs in 1930 to more than a milliard francs in 1932. Hardship was particularly severe in the coalmining areas of Hainaut and ugly strikes succeeded one another throughout the whole summer of that year. The general election of November 1932 brought no significant change in parliamentary representation, and in despair almost, though mindful that the same men had performed something of a miracle in 1926, the country once again called on the services of Charles de Broqueville, Henri Jaspar, the veteran Catholic patriot of the First World War, and Paul-Emile Janson, the Liberal leader. All they could do was to apply draconian measures similar to those imposed by Francqui, balance somehow the budget, and hope that in time Belgium would weather the storm, particularly as there were now signs that the worst was over elsewhere in Europe.

Such was the situation which troubled the last years of King Albert's life and which Leopold III was to inherit. On the other hand, much had been quietly achieved since 1919 in the field of social welfare and reform. The Vandervelde Law of 1919 severely restricted the sale of alcohol and quickly put an end to scenes of public drunkenness and consequent misery among many working-class families. Death duties on private fortunes were introduced as well as a progressive income-tax scale. Funds were made available for the construction of modern but cheap housing for the working class, and within ten years 40,000 such dwellings had been completed. The law of 31 August 1920 introduced old-age pensions from the age of sixty-five. The law of 14 June 1921 brought an eight-hour working-day and a forty-eight-hour working-week. Obligatory old-age insurance became law on 10 December 1924. Security of tenancy for a rented dwelling became law on 20 June 1930. And the socialists were particularly gratified at the cancellation of Article 310 of the Penal Code, which had made punishable any attempt at picketing or otherwise persuading workers from pursuing their jobs, and its replacement by a law of 24 May 1921 which permitted full and free association of workers at any time and at any place.

On the evening of 17 February 1934 King Albert was due to preside at an important sports meeting in a large Brussels stadium. All his life a keen and enthusiastic rock climber, he suddenly decided in the afternoon of the same day to get some exercise by making a relatively simple climb at Marche-les-Dames near Dinant. He drove there with only one equerry and climbed alone. What actually happened has never been fully ascertained. In the sports stadium in Brussels puzzlement regarding his unaccustomed unpunctuality gave way to perplexity and then anxiety. Meanwhile, an increasingly worried equerry, anxious not to disturb Albert in pursuit of his favourite relaxation but conscious that time was getting short if the Brussels appointment were to be kept, reluctantly went in search of the King. He found him lying dead at the bottom of a rock face.

This people's King was given a war hero's funeral before a million men, women, and children who flocked to Brussels from the remotest corners of Belgium. His simple tastes were their simple tastes. His life had been their life. Something vital and extremely personal to each and every Belgian had been removed. It was much more than the end of an era. And with the equally tragic death of Queen Astrid only some eighteen months later it seemed that a blight had settled on the country, already in serious economic straits, already plagued by its Rexists and Flemish Nationalists, much perturbed by what was now going on across its eastern frontiers in Germany. That robust self-assurance, so vital to and so characteristic of the Belgian, was not fully to return until he had again been proved in war and until Baudouin I had been firmly seated on the throne.

Chapter 7

Political Disarray

KING ALBERT HAD MOST CAREFULLY PREPARED Leopold against the day when he must succeed to the throne; and if Albert failed in some measure it was primarily because he lacked an imaginative conception of his own role and secondly because he could do little (even had he wished to) to dispel the legend that had grown up around his own personage and that of 'gallant little Belgium' during the First World War. Leopold spent those war years at Eton, returning to visit America with his parents in 1919 and the following year to enter the *Ecole Militaire*. He visited Brazil (again with his parents) in 1921, Egypt with Queen Elisabeth in 1923, and then finally toured the Belgian Congo alone in 1925. His first major pronouncement came as a result of this tour when he warned the nation unequivocally that 'we must not blind ourselves to the fact that, side by side with the immense advantages we bring the Congolese and of which they are fully aware, our arrival has disturbed their age-old customs and traditions, and also their general physical well-being'.

In November 1926 he was most happily married to Princess Astrid of Sweden and the nation enthusiastically rejoiced with him. Josephine-Charlotte was born the following October, Baudouin in September 1930, and Albert in June 1934. In 1932 Leopold again visited the Congo, this time on an official mission to study problems of agriculture and methods of raising the living standards of the Congolese. The outcome was a government decree of 5 December 1933 regulating the sale of harvests primarily to benefit the cultivator and passing important measures to improve the agricultural education of the native population. And Leopold, immediately on his succession to the throne, followed this up with his personal creation of the *Institut National pour l'Etude Agricole du Congo Belge* (INEAC) on 24 March 1934.

Leopold III took the traditional constitutional oath on 23 February 1934, and it is significant that for the first time in the history of Belgium it was considered important that he should repeat it in Flemish. No monarch could have been called upon to assume office at a more difficult and treacherous moment. Though the Belgians acclaimed him and the increasingly popular Queen Astrid most warmly and sympathetically, it was the acclaim of a stunned, bewildered, and mesmerised nation. They still clung to the legend of Albert the Good, Albert the Patriot, and they could not grasp that King Albert, living perhaps too much on his legend, had failed in the last years of his life to be as decisive as he should have been in face of a steadily worsening political, economic, and international scene. It became Leopold III's unenviable and inescapable task to awaken the Belgians to the realities of the situation. That he did not flinch from it can be attributed to the careful schooling he had been given by his father. That he sometimes proved too inflexible and lacking in imaginative flair must equally be attributed to his upbringing. There was no legend to sustain Leopold III. And it can be argued that it was an unfortunate combination of all these circumstances that finally alienated the Belgian people from him.

The Royal Question, as it came to be called, was in reality the final episode in a long developing dispute over conflicting interpretations of the role of the monarchy. Leopold I and Leopold II had been autocrats and had exercised to the full the powers accorded them in the constitution. Albert had acquiesced in the pre-eminence of the legislature. He had promised universal manhood suffrage in 1919. By the early 1920s the socialists had risen to prominence as a major party. The Liberals in consequence came increasingly to play second fiddle, and the Catholics had to re-organise themselves to allow their working-class element a share in the organisation and management of the party. As the socialists became more politically conscious, so they rejected the idea of a strong monarchy and hankered after limiting the powers of the Crown to the right to be consulted, the right to encourage, and the right to warn – as in England. They failed, however, to recognise or to admit the essential differences between the two monarchies: monarchy in Belgium is indispensable to national unity in that the King stands above conflict, so that through him alone can Fleming and Walloon, Catholic and anti-clerical, identify himself as Belgian; monarchy in Great Britain is the result of homogeneity and not a necessary prerequisite to it. A subtle distinction but an important one. Nor did Albert himself help matters by discontinuing several seemingly unimportant practices such as his New Year's Day reception, his palace addresses, personal speeches to be delivered on important occasions, and the holding of political banquets.

Leopold III inherited in fact not only a confused political situation but also one in which Flemish–Walloon antipathies had been rekindled and one in which a disturbing Fascist movement (the Rexists), headed by Léon Degrelle, fished in the troubled waters and, on the pretext of purifying the Catholic religion from a sordid connection with politics and government finance, delighted in unearthing, exploiting, and exaggerating several so-called scandals and in gathering an army of malcontents to its Fascist meetings. It must also be remembered that within months of Leopold's accession to the throne, Hitler had succeeded Hindenburg in Germany as Head of State on 2 August 1934; that in March 1935, in defiance of Articles 178 and 193 of the Treaty of Versailles, he announced his intention of introducing conscription; and that the following March he triumphantly reoccupied the Rhineland. To add to all this Belgium was plunged into an economic crisis in which industry was slowing down and running even at a loss; in which unemployment was contributing to the growing misery and disaffection of the working class; and one from which there seemed small hope of emerging as tariff barriers went up throughout Europe and the Scandinavian countries and Holland failed in consequence to implement the agreements of the Conventions of Oslo and Ouchy.

Though it was immediately obvious to Leopold that Broqueville's coalition government of Catholics and Liberals was becoming increasingly incapable of coping with the worsening situation, he nevertheless tried hard to bolster it up as he knew his father would have done. In June 1934 he felt bound to interfere and strengthen the government from outside, but the policy of deflation then advocated by the Minister of Finance, Gustave Sap, bit too slowly and industry took fright. The inevitable collapse of the government came in November and Leopold now called upon an able trio of financiers to work in unison to try to stop the rot. Mockingly dubbed the 'Trinity of the Banks' by the socialists (Theunis, the Father; Francqui, the Son; Gutt, the Holy Ghost) they did their best. But as Camille Gutt sagely remarked, a parliamentary majority is never sufficient if the people have lost confidence. Fearing a devaluation of the franc the public rushed to the banks to withdraw their savings. In January 1935 Leopold received an angry deputation of the unemployed and urged on Theunis immediate reforms to alleviate their lot. And the Queen broke all precedent by addressing a moving appeal to the whole nation to come to the help of the unemployed by all the means in their power. The government collapsed on 19 March.

This time Leopold decided on much more drastic and personal intervention and nominated Paul van Zeeland as Prime Minister. It was a happy choice, and it came at the right moment when economic affairs throughout the world were beginning to take a turn for the better. Van Zeeland was a distinguished economist with no political affiliations of any kind. He was vice-governor of the National Bank and commanded authority in virtue of his position as Professor of Economics in the University of Louvain. He had no axe to grind and was listened to with respect by economists throughout the world. His first act was to perform the necessary surgical operation as quickly and as painlessly as possible by a devaluation of the franc by 28 per cent. Leopold gave him all the backing he could, strove hard himself to associate Belgium with the new world economic development, and at the opening of the highly successful World Exhibition held in Brussels that year spelled out his message very clearly: 'Peoples, no more than individuals, cannot live healthily with closed doors and windows. The return to prosperity depends on a much freer circulation of merchandise. World economy is in urgent need of a breath of fresh air.' With the Brussels Exhibition already a success Leopold and Queen Astrid left for a much deserved holiday, which was to end so tragically and abruptly with the death of the Queen in a motoring accident near Lucerne on 29 August.

Meanwhile, though the economic position of the country was slowly improving, the political situation worsened and Paul van Zeeland found the task of reconciling the position taken up by the three parties almost impossible. By March 1936 he was ready to throw in his hand, but Leopold, because of the delicate situation caused by Hitler's reoccupation of the Rhineland, persuaded him to stay on until at least the May elections. The results of these came as a further bombshell. The new Rexist Party claimed no fewer than 21 seats in the chamber – almost as many as the Liberals. The Catholic bloc lost 16 seats, mainly to the Rexists; the socialists ceded six seats to the communists; and the Flemish Nationalists doubled their representation to 16. All that Leopold could now do was to summon Vandervelde and Paul-Henri Spaak (as representing the socialists), Hubert Pierlot and Philippe van Isaker (Catholics), Adolphe Max and Léon Dens (Liberals), and to warn them in the strongest possible terms of the imminent danger of putting party before country. The crisis was finally resolved by the end of June with Paul van Zeeland for the second time heading a coalition government and determined to push through many fiscal, commercial, and industrial reforms.

That his projects came to nothing was due of course to the now rapidly worsening international situation, and equally to the virulence with which the Rexists exploited their new strength. These Leopold boldly attacked in a speech delivered on 7 November 1936 and did not hesitate to accuse them of wishing to sabotage the nation: 'The political climate of Belgium,' he said, 'is against all forms of violence. . . . Like my predecessors I intend scrupulously to observe the rule which places the King above all party strife. But I have the right and the duty to draw the attention of my compatriots to the perils which must result from this kind of prolonged disorder.' His warning was heeded. In April 1937 a Rexist *député* had to resign and all three main political parties called a truce among themselves and begged Paul van Zeeland, as a trial of strength, to contest the seat against Léon Degrelle. The Primate of Belgium, Cardinal Joseph van Roey, gave support by explicitly condemning both the doctrine and methods of Rexism. Paul van Zeeland polled a grand total of 276,000 votes against a meagre 69,258 for the Rexist leader. The triumph, however, was short-lived in that the politicians resumed once again their internal wranglings and in that Degrelle sought his revenge by unearthing a number of unorthodox practices at the National Bank, and so involved Paul van Zeeland that on 25 October 1937 he had to resign in order adequately to defend himself.

On 26 August 1936, Hitler boldly raised the period of conscription for military service throughout Germany to two years. Paul van Zeeland, fresh from a meeting in London with Eden, Flandin, and Grandi, had gloomily to report that the Italians were obviously unwilling to call Germany to task in view of their own successful Ethiopian campaign of six months earlier; that Flandin represented a bewildered and divided French government ill-prepared to go to war; that Eden would not undertake any action to expel the Germans from their 'historic' soil; that he had had to agree with the greater powers and follow their initiative in trying to open negotiations with Germany for a new Rhine pact; and that all he had personally obtained was a promise of military aid in the event of further German hostility. In simple terms all this meant that Belgium was now exposed beyond her strength. Her eastern frontiers were wide open to German attack; she was committed by the Locarno military agreements to support France, Great Britain, and Italy in the case of any aggression; and that aggression could only come from Germany since she felt herself no longer bound by the Locarno Pact.

Paul-Henri Spaak reacted vigorously in his capacity as Foreign Minister, though he was under no illusions that he might be able to carry the country as a whole with him. Nor did the outbreak of the Spanish Civil War on 16 July 1936 help matters for him with the socialist and communist members of Parliament. True, the armed forces of the country had been considerably strengthened from 1932 onwards by the introduction of more sophisticated weapons, by the mechanisation of the artillery and cavalry, and by the creation in 1934 of a crack frontier force, the *Chasseurs Ardennais*. The Catholics, however, had stoutly resisted an increase in the period of conscription, had rejected a programme for national defence placed before them by the General Staff and fully approved by Leopold, and even now their militant Flemish element backed the internationalists in the Socialist Party by refusing to vote funds for military expansion unless Belgium maintained her international obligations, especially towards the moribund League of Nations. Thus the obvious policy of rearming at home while allowing France and Great Britain to pursue negotiations was precluded. The solution lay in an entirely new foreign policy, one that came to be dubbed that of 'independence-neutrality', and one which critics of Leopold have claimed was foisted by him on an unwilling government.

The truth is that Spaak had mooted the necessity for a realignment of Belgium's interests as early as April 1936. At a foreign Press Corps banquet held on 20 July he elaborated on this idea and drew specific attention to the inadequacy of both the League of Nations and Locarno. 'I want only one thing,' he said, 'a policy that will be exclusively and totally Belgian.' Vacillation still continued, however, primarily because the government feared for its popularity, and it was left to Leopold to summon his Ministers on 14 October to deplore the government's failure to implement the recommendations of the General Staff and to stress his support of Spaak's utterance.

'The reoccupation of the Rhineland,' he affirmed,

'has completely set at nought the terms of the Locarno Pact and placed us once again almost in the position we found ourselves in before the war. Our geographical situation demands that we maintain a military force strong enough to dissuade any of our neighbours from encroaching on our territory to attack another country. In doing this Belgium will be collaborating in no uncertain way to the maintenance of peace throughout western Europe; and by so doing she has a right to call (as need be) for the help of every country which is interested in preserving peace.'

He concluded by urging that public opinion be alerted to the situation and be intelligently informed.

Spaak and Emile Vandervelde, the veteran socialist leader, enthusiastically welcomed this pronouncement and begged Leopold, in the name of the Cabinet, to release his speech to the national press. The result was an overwhelming victory for the government on 28 October when the chamber decisively supported, by 126 votes to 42, the policy of independence-neutrality and made provision for the necessary military disposition to mobilise 600,000 men with a minimum of delay. 'I wish to repeat,' said Spaak during the course of the debate, 'that our foreign policy does not mean a return to neutrality; we designate our foreign policy as one of independence.' The trouble was that neither this government, nor any successive one, ever attempted to spell out in what ways the policy of independence-neutrality was different from neutrality *tout court*. What is certain is that the policy, though introduced by Leopold and therefore identified with him, was accepted without question by each successive government down to May 1940.

The greater powers were at first nonplussed and bewildered by this apparent *volte-face* on the part of the Belgians, though England and France soon realised the logic of the situation from the Belgian point of view and by a joint declaration of 24 April 1937 relieved Belgium of all her obligations under the Locarno Pact and promised to come to her assistance should she be invaded. Belgium in return undertook to strengthen her armed forces, to defend her own territory in case of aggression, and to close her territory to any troops engaged in any aggressive war should they wish to use Belgium as a freeway or as a base for operational action. Germany was predictably more reluctant to come to such an agreement and it was not until 13 October that Hitler signed a similar declaration. Spaak then felt it imperative to spell out the Belgian position as clearly as possible for the whole world to take note: 'Belgium has no interests of any kind beyond her own frontiers; she has no ambition to be other than what she is; she is searching for nothing and she asks for nothing—other than peace.'

The fall of Paul van Zeeland's government led to the formation of another tripartite ministry under the Liberal leader, Paul-Emile Janson, which struggled on unhappily from 24 November 1937 until 15 May 1938 when Janson had to resign because he had no Cabinet to back him through his inability to solve the economic problems. The economic situation was again worsening, largely owing to the devaluation of the French franc and to the international tension caused by Hitler's entry into Austria on 13 March 1938. Production and exports fell rapidly, not only at home but also in the Congo, and the number of unemployed had increased by 38 per cent. Spaak now took over at Leopold's invitation, and his prestige was such that he was able to manoeuvre Belgium safely through the sorry charade of Hitler's first bite of the cherry in Czechoslovakia and the successive humiliations of France and England at Berchtesgaden, at Godesberg – and at Munich. By partial mobilisation and by placing twelve divisions on stand-by he demonstrated Belgium's firm determination to implement her policy of independence-neutrality. The country remained calm and confident – so much so that when Spaak somewhat sanguinely tried to strengthen his government in January 1939 by favouring the Catholics at the expense of the Liberals the latter retaliated by criticising the appointment to the Flemish Academy of Medicine of a certain Dr Maertens who had (unfortunately) been a noted Flemish 'activist' during the First World War. Petty political bickering took no heed of Belgium's serious position vis-à-vis the international situation and the whole incident was deliberately and selfishly exploited.

This time Leopold could not restrain his anger. He summoned his Ministers and warned them unequivocally that

'all semblance of responsibility is lost. We are facing a crisis of authority, of disorder, of confusion, sometimes of demagogy, and at a time when danger is on the increase and when the country's situation demands the firmest of governments, the highest economic endeavour, and manifest evidence of an ordered and disciplined public life. Gentlemen, the fault does not lie in our institutions: the fault resides in the shortcomings of those who are entrusted with governing the nation.'

He did not save Spaak, who handed in his resignation on 9 February 1939. And he himself was later not to be forgiven for his outspokenness.

Henri Jaspar now attempted to form a government and failed. Pierlot tried a Catholic–Liberal coalition – the Shrove Tuesday government – which lasted exactly a week. Leopold could now do nothing but dissolve Parliament on 6 March 1939; but he took the opportunity of addressing a letter to Pierlot in which he appealed once again to the good sense of the Belgians. This time he stresses shortcomings in constitutional procedure (a legacy from King Albert); he must have time to study and form his own opinion on decrees submitted to him for signature; he recalls that Article 65 of the constitution lays down that the King nominates and dismisses his Ministers, taking careful note of public opinion; he insists that once nominated his Ministers are neither delegates of a political party nor representatives of a given geographical region: they are exclusively servants of the executive; relations between the King and his Ministers must be strictly confidential and the King's personal opinions must never be published; nor must his Ministers publish decrees before submission to him, nor say in publishing them that they have already been sent to the King for signature. And then the final cut: political advancement must be seen to be a reward for merit and not as a favour granted to a friend. There must be national unity and a government capable of obtaining respect and maintaining the moral prestige of Belgium, who must, more urgently than before, be looking beyond her own frontiers.

Within a week of this sincere plea for national unity Slovakia had proclaimed her independence and Hungarian troops were penetrating into sub-Carpathian Ukraine. The German armies of the Third Reich occupied Prague, and Lithuania ceded the port of Klaipeda-Memel to Germany. It was no longer possible to harbour any illusions. The country went to the polls in a calm but determined frame of mind and, not surprisingly, betrayed a strictly conservative temper. The Catholics obtained 73 seats (a gain of 10), the Liberals

33 seats (also a gain of 10), the socialists 64 seats (a loss of 6) . . . and the Rexists were routed by securing only 4 seats (a loss of 17). The communists managed to retain their 9 seats and the Flemish Nationalists increased their representation by one seat, bringing their total to 17. Pierlot, however, still found some considerable difficulty in reconciling contradictory views and Leopold did not hesitate once again to summon the main political leaders and speak his mind.

'The future of our régime depends on the restoration, in all its independence and with full capacity for action, of a truly responsible executive who can really govern without being hampered at every turn by the dictates of party policy, by decisions taken by political groups and sub-groups, or by electoral preoccupations. The most important reform of all to be realised is a change in the mental attitude of you who are to govern . . .'

Once again Leopold had placed his finger firmly on the sore spot and he was again not lightly to be forgiven.

The immediate result was that Pierlot was able to form a government on 17 April, on the basis of a Catholic–Liberal coalition, and in the only too short a time that lay ahead was at any rate able to see Belgium prepared and the economy soundly based. Industrial output rose significantly. That able Minister of Finance Camille Gutt prepared a perfectly balanced budget and had the satisfaction of attracting back to the country 5 milliard francs-worth of gold that had been lost in 1938. Since the military reoccupation of the Rhineland by Germany, the National Bank had kept a minimum of gold reserves in the country and it now laid plans for successful and speedy removal of all its reserves as the necessity arose. As early as 1931 Lieutenant-General Giron had been charged with the task of co-ordinating all mobilisation services. There were stocks of petroleum, and the arms factory at Herstal was prudently transferred to Bruges. The cost of mobilisation was covered by the issue of security stocks. Plans for food rationing were well in hand, and on 1 May 1939 a special department was created to deal as necessary with rationing problems, though its immediate concern was to ensure adequate stocks of grain which, together with the promised harvest for 1940 and the grain still on the high seas on its way to the port of Antwerp, ought to supply sufficient food for up to six months of 'siege'. The Albert Canal, begun in 1930 and promised for 1941,

was so far advanced that the government was able to speed up the
final operations to have it functional by the end of 1939.

Events now moved rapidly. Learning early in August that Molotov
and von Ribbentrop had initiated discussions, the Belgian government urgently mustered certain special reserve forces. By 19 August,
when the German–Russian pact was published, general mobilisation
was under way and by 10 May 1940 a grand total of 650,000 men
had been called to the colours. On 23 August 1939 Leopold summoned a meeting of the Foreign Ministers of the Oslo Pact and in
the name of the various Heads of State (Belgium, Denmark, Finland,
Luxembourg, Norway, Holland, Sweden) made an anguished appeal
to world public opinion for peace and respect for the rights of all
nations, for European agreement and understanding: 'Our continent
is on the brink of committing suicide in a frightful war which will
have neither victor nor vanquished and in which all the spiritual
and material values of so many centuries of civilisation will be sub-
merged.' Pope Pius XII and President Franklin D. Roosevelt joined
their efforts to those of Leopold. On 28 August Leopold and Queen
Wilhelmina of Holland offered themselves as intermediaries in a
last-minute attempt to avert the crisis. On 1 September the German
armies invaded Poland. On 3 September Great Britain and France
declared war. Leopold immediately persuaded Pierlot to widen his
ministry by taking in five socialists, thus making it possible to give
the control of foreign affairs to Spaak. Belgium issued her declaration of neutrality in strict conformity with the agreements made with
Britain, France, and Germany in 1937. On 4 September Leopold
announced (in conformity with Article 68 of the constitution) that
he had taken supreme command of all the armed forces of Belgium.

In the lull period that followed it became increasingly clear that
Belgium's neutrality policy gave both Britain and France breathing
time. She refused Paul Reynaud's misplaced request to open her
frontiers to the Allied troops and contented herself with the manning
of some 250 kilometres of frontier lines, thus sparing French troops
to take up vital defensive positions on French soil. Prudently, however, the High Command entered into technical discussions with
their opposite French and English counterparts to make certain
that the Allies, if the worst occurred, were in a position to come
to Belgium's assistance should she invite them to do so. On 27 October Leopold made a broadcast appeal to the American people in
which he stressed Belgium's earnest desire for peace, spoke movingly

of his father's heroic and successful resistance in the First World War, left no doubt in anyone's mind that if attacked the Belgian people as a whole would stoutly resist, and expressed the hope that 'the American nation, so close to us in aspirations and institutions, may help and support us in the attitude we have taken to maintain peace and preserve our civilisation'.

Towards the end of October Queen Wilhelmina of Holland was prevailed upon by her Ministers to make another urgent appeal to the belligerents to come to terms and she invited Leopold to join her in this effort. Leopold left for Holland on 6 November and a joint telegram was sent by them the following day to the Heads of State of Germany, Great Britain, and France, again offering their services to bring about some settlement. Nothing resulted. All hope was finally gone when on 10 January 1940 a German plane on its way to Cologne got lost in the fog and came down on Belgian territory. The pilot was interned, but not before secret documents he was carrying and which he attempted unsuccessfully to destroy had been seized and their significance determined. There was no longer any doubt that a major German offensive was impending against the Allies and that the Germans intended to strike boldly through Belgium to achieve their objective.

The continued policy of independence-neutrality was again approved in the Senate on 16 April 1940 by a total of 131 votes against 3 communist votes, and with only 2 abstentions. Yet even at this critical stage a further government crisis could not be averted. On 25 April the Liberals refused to accept the educational budget in a confused wrangle over the linguistic position. Pierlot felt he must resign. Leopold stood firm and refused the resignation, arguing that 'this is not the time to provoke a ministerial crisis on internal and domestic matters'. And at dawn on 10 May, without any ultimatum or any formal declaration of war, the Fourth and Sixth German armies launched a formidable assault which immediately resulted in the destruction of over half the Belgian air striking-force and also gave them possession of key fortress positions on the frontiers. Immediately the Belgian government appealed to the Allies to come to their assistance and Leopold went directly to his own headquarters at Breendonck, near Antwerp, and issued a proclamation:

'For the second time in a quarter of a century Belgium – loyal and neutral – has been attacked by the German empire despite

1 Spinning frames in a Verviers textile mill. The Belgian textile
   industry has an important place in world production

2 An Oil Refinery in the port of Antwerp. The Belgian oil
   industry continues to make steady progress

4 Kalmthout Natural Briar Park in the Campine, Antwerp Province

3 A Belgian-manufactured reaper and thresher on a farm at Melden, East Flanders

6 BR2 experimental areas at the Nuclear Research Centre, Mol, Antwerp Province

5 A coalmine at Genck, Limburg Province. Coal is the Belgian economy's most important resource

7   The Hôtel de Ville in the Grand' Place, Brussels: a fifteenth-
century Gothic façade, with the tower dating from 1455

8   Aerial view of Louvain University Library and its surrounds.
The University dates from 1425

9   The Headquarters of the Common Market, Euratom, and the
European Coal and Steel Community in the Rue de la Loi,
Brussels

10 Frahan on the river Semois in the Ardennes

11 The tower of the Church of Our Lady and the Gruuthuuse Museum, Bruges

12 'The Beggars', a realistic painting of lepers by Peter Bruegel the Elder

13 The scene outside the *Théâtre de la Monnaie*, Brussels, on 25 August 1830

16 King Leopold I

17 Charles Rogier's statue in Liège

18 King Leopold II

19 Cardinal Désiré-Joseph Mercier

[*Opposite*] 14 King Albert and Queen Elisabeth enter Brussels,
22 November 1918

[*Opposite*] 15 King Leopold III and Queen Astrid

20   The Belgian government-in-exile in London. *From right to left in full view:* De Schrijver, Spaak, Gutt, Pierlot

21   Charleroi, April 1944. Léon Degrelle (*left*) and Sepp Dietrich (*right*) inspect Degrelle's collaborationist SS *Brigade Wallonie*

22 Paul van Zeeland

23 Achille Van Acker

24 A demonstration against the return of Leopold III, 1950

25   Paul-Henri Spaak

27 Queen Fabiola

28 Paul Vanden Boeynants

29 Gaston Eyskens

30 Police and Flemish students clash in Louvain during the disturbances of early 1968, which led to the fall of the Vanden Boeynants government

the most solemn engagements contracted before the whole world. The Belgians, deeply pacifist in intention, have done all they could to avoid this conflict. And now, needing to choose between self-sacrifice and dishonour, the Belgian of 1940 will be as resolute as he was in 1914.... France and England have promised their support. Already their troops are on the move to join ours. The struggle will be a hard one. Sacrifice and privation will be considerable, but none can doubt of the ultimate outcome. I intend to remain faithful to my constitutional oath to maintain the independence and integrity of our territory. As my father did in 1914, I have placed myself at the head of our army with the same faith and the same conscience. Belgium's cause is pure. With the help of God she will triumph.'

Chapter 8

German Occupation

IT WAS ALL OVER IN EIGHTEEN DAYS. The fort of Ebenemael, which was thought impregnable, fell in the first hours, thanks to the enemy's treachery and fifth column activities. The defensive position along the Albert Canal was nonetheless held for some thirty-six hours pending the arrival of Allied forces. In the meantime the Dutch were being equally hard pressed and had to surrender unconditionally on 15 May – at the very moment that the 14th and 15th German Panzer divisions were hacking to pieces the Ninth French army, breaching Sedan, and streaming towards Amiens and Abbeville. The Belgian armies had now fallen back to prepared positions along the Antwerp–Namur line, but this again became impossible to hold once the Dutch had surrendered and the thrust had taken place through Sedan. Confusion reigned – such a *Blitzkrieg* had been undreamed of – and the confusion was aggravated by a railway strike and by the thousands of Belgian refugees streaming along the highways to the relative safety of France and who were joined (on government instructions) by all able-bodied men between the ages of eighteen and thirty-five not yet mobilised.

On 12 May a conference of Allied leaders was held at Casteau (near Mons) and Leopold there agreed to an overall command of the Allied troops under General Gamelin. On 16 May he was ordered to abandon the strongly held Antwerp–Namur line and fall back behind the Scheldt to hastily improvised defensive positions. There, between 18 and 20 May he resolutely held the infuriated German forces at bay. On this latter date he was visited by his chief Ministers (Spaak, Lieutenant-General Henri Denis, Pierlot, and Arthur Vanderpoorten) and begged to give up the unequal struggle. He refused. General Weygand, who had now succeeded Gamelin, held a council of war at Ypres on 21 May, at which Leopold undertook to cover the left flank of a pincer operation designed to cement the Arras–Albert axis. This involved a still further withdrawal by

Leopold. The pincer operation failed disastrously. On 25 May, exactly one week after Brussels had been occupied by the Germans, Leopold's Ministers again begged him to resign himself to the inevitable, as they proposed doing; they were leaving to set up a government in France; and he had before him the example of King Haakon of Norway, Queen Wilhelmina of Holland, and the Grand Duchess Charlotte of Luxembourg, all of whom were now in exile. His reply was that he could not, at this critical hour, desert his troops.

The situation grew more and more confused and army commanders at times lost contact with one another. It was a débâcle that turned into a grim charade of *sauve qui peut*, and recriminations were bound to follow. Lord Gort, commander of the British Expeditionary Force, decided (apparently without being able to inform Leopold) to make the historic withdrawal to Dunkirk, and in the eventuality it was the heroic last stand of the Belgians on the river Lys that contributed in no small way to the success of Dunkirk. Informed by his Chief of Staff on 27 May that the army could not hold out any longer, Leopold immediately sent messages to the French and English that he must surrender. Seven hours later, at midnight, he asked for an armistice. Unconditional surrender was demanded. He had no choice. And hostilities ceased at 4 a.m. on the morning of 28 May.

Before constituting himself a prisoner and retiring with his family and entourage to the Château de Laeken, Leopold wrote both to the Pope and to the President of the United States to explain his position and then addressed a last message to his troops:

'History will record that our army has more than done its duty. Our honour is safe. These fierce combats and these sleepless nights cannot have been in vain. I ask you not to be discouraged but to bear yourselves with dignity . . . I am not abandoning you in this hour of misfortune which overwhelms us and I insist on watching over your future and that of your families. Tomorrow we must set to work with firm resolution to see our country rise again from its ruins.'

In eighteen days of bitter fighting Belgium had lost 308 officers and 5,790 other ranks. More than 500 soldiers were reported missing, and a further 2,000 prisoners-of-war died in captivity.

Though it should not have done so, the suddenness of the Belgian collapse surprised everybody, and it was some little time before it was realised that the only person who had kept his head was Leopold. He had not delivered Belgium over to the Germans. He had merely surrendered with his armies who were with him in Flanders. Other troops, who were stationed mainly in the Congo, were quite free to continue the struggle. His government, now in France, was equally free to carry on, particularly since all gold reserves had been prudently taken abroad as well as the printing presses, plates for paper money, and other important securities. Bewildered, lost, and angry the Belgian government in France could only lick its wounds and reflect on the sorry situation. Equally lost, Paul Reynaud was openly accusing Leopold of treason and the reception given all Belgians in exile in France was far from cordial. Even in England the conclusion was hastily reached that there had been, if not treason, at least betrayal in that Leopold had not warned of his intention to surrender, and it needed the stout defence of Leopold by Admiral Sir Roger Keyes, M.P.,[1] and a High Court action which Sir Roger brought against *Daily Mirror* newspapers, to prove to the whole world that Leopold had indeed sent messages of his intention and had given the Allies almost twenty-four hours' warning, fighting on to the last. That the messages had not got through was not his fault.

How wounding all this must have been to Leopold can easily be imagined. He had tried to play his role to the full. He had repeatedly warned his Ministers of their earlier follies. He had been blunt. He had been honest and courageous. He had been the *preux chevalier* his father would have wanted him to be. He had lived up to the legend of 'gallant little Belgium' of the First World War and had loyally co-operated with the Allies in every detail of strategy. And now, within hours of his surrender, self-indulgent politicians of the past were seemingly issuing a proclamation that he no longer reigned. On 31 May the Belgian Parliament caught up with the government-in-exile at Limoges and the entire Cabinet (with the solitary exception of Antoine Delfosse, the Minister for Communications) were again repudiating Leopold's actions and pledging themselves to

---

[1] Keyes had led a British flotilla (the cruiser *Vindictive*, two submarines, and three blockships) in the famous raid on Zeebrugge on St George's Day 1918. The harbour was blocked and the port's career as a German naval base was ended. In 1940 he was appointed Special Liaison Officer to King Leopold.

continue the fight alongside the Allies. On 2 June Leopold felt it necessary to ask for an envoy to be sent to Switzerland to whom his position could be explained and the situation clarified. He had *not* treated with the enemy. He had merely laid down his arms and informed the French and British of his intention so to do. He was now a prisoner-of-war like any of his soldiers.

On 10 June Mussolini cynically declared war on France. On 14 June Paris fell and Hitler arrived, flushed with triumph. The Belgian government-in-exile were driven to reappraise the situation, and on 18 June, having withdrawn to Bordeaux, they sent messages to the Argentine minister in Switzerland and to the Papal Nuncio there to explore the possibilities of treating with Germany. They also made arrangements for the government of the Belgian Congo and Ruanda-Urundi for the duration of hostilities. On 22 June the French capitulated. Four days later Pierlot contacted Leopold, indicated his willingness to resign, stressed the necessity for treating with the Germans over the fate of both soldiers and civilians, and suggested the time had come 'to negotiate with the Germans the conditions of an armistice or a convention concerning Belgium'. Once again Leopold was the one not to waver and to keep a realistic grip on the situation. He refused either to make an armistice or to reconstitute a government. He was participating in no political manoeuvring, nor was he receiving any politicians. He was a prisoner-of-war, along with his forces, in forcibly occupied Belgium.

The Belgian government, on the other hand, was at a complete loss as to what to do. One man only, Marcel-Henri Jaspar, objected to the government's approaches to Germany and came to London to make a radio broadcast on 23 June with the object of rallying all Belgians everywhere to continue the war. On 24 June the Belgian government repudiated Jaspar. From the beginning of July it re-established itself at Vichy alongside the government of unoccupied France, and its mind was finally made up for it by the Germans themselves who on 20 July announced that no members of the Belgian government-in-exile would in any case be allowed to return to Belgium. On 21 July Pierlot at long last accepted Leopold's various statements on his true position and the position of Belgium, and in a note dated 6 December Spaak affirmed that a state of war still existed between Belgium and Germany 'for an independent Belgium, for a liberated King'. On 10 May 1941 Spaak broadcast from London an official statement of the events of the eighteen-day war, and in July the official detailed account of what had happened was published by Evans Brothers on behalf of the Belgian Ministry of Foreign Affairs.[1]

So ended that sorry story of confusion and vacillation. The repercussions were going to make themselves evident much later, after the liberation of Belgium, when Leopold was not lightly to be forgiven for having kept his head at the real moment of crisis while others were losing theirs. Thus it can be claimed that the post-war constitutional conflict really burgeoned during these bitter months when the King, in opposition to the unanimous advice of his Ministers, decided to share the fate of his armies and not go into exile along with his government. In doing so, Leopold believed sincerely that he should give precedence to his rank as Commander-in-Chief of the armed forces rather than to his political function as Head of State. Over the five years down to the outbreak of war, as we have seen, he had taken a more personal concept of the way in which his kingly prerogatives should be exercised than had his father. Yet his political intervention had always been scrupulously restricted to cabinet level and all his actions had sprung from his real and legitimate desire to ensure the correct functioning of democratic institutions, being at all times covered by those Ministers who were politically responsible. This time, however, he was acting contrary to the prescriptions of the constitution, and against his Ministers.

Meanwhile, inside Belgium itself, efforts had to be made to return to some sort of normality under German jurisdiction. The very first problem was to cope with the vast numbers of refugees in France and Leopold was quick to call upon the Red Cross to give all the help it could. Between the end of June and 10 October they were returning at the rate of between 10 and 15,000 a day. Actual figures are impossible to ascertain, but it is known that no fewer than 306 special trains brought back a total of 327,000 and that there were at one time, in the south of France, approximately 45,000 Belgian registered motor-cars. Communications, transport, and industry slowly crept back to something approaching normal. The Germans fixed prices and salaries, exacted an indemnity for their 'occupational expenses', and not unnaturally commandeered all stocks of food and 'live' meat. Rationing became increasingly severe and the hard winter of 1940 caused such misery that Leopold, through his sister

[1] *Belgique: La Relation Officielle des événements 1939–1940.*

Princess Marie-José (who had married Prince Umberto of Italy), sought an interview with Hitler at Berchtesgaden. Coldly correct and speaking French throughout the interview, he made no concessions of any kind himself but came away with the promise of an immediate amelioration in food supplies and the return of 50,000 prisoners-of-war.

In June 1941 Princess Josephine-Charlotte was confirmed, and there is in existence a moving photograph of the royal family taken to commemorate the event in the gardens of the Palace of Laeken. Loneliness and bewilderment are manifest. Soon after the tragic death of Queen Astrid the motherless children came to be cared for by Mlle Mary Lilian Baels, daughter of Henri Baels, a former Cabinet Minister and Governor of West Flanders. As the years passed real bonds of affection undoubtedly developed. The outcome was that on 11 September 1941 Cardinal van Roey, the Primate of Belgium, solemnised a marriage between Leopold III and Mlle Baels and later issued a proclamation to that effect which he ordered to be read out in all churches on 7 December. Leopold stipulated that his wife renounced the title and rank of Queen, and that she would bear the title of Princesse de Réthy. No child born of the marriage would have a right of succession to the throne. Immediately, of course, a vilification campaign began. He had married a commoner. He had had to go to Austria to consult a dentist there. He had spent a honeymoon in Austria. He had fallen for German blandishments and made full and selfish use of all the facilities they were prepared to grant him to break the monotony of his so-called imprisonment at Laeken. It is important to stress that the marriage was used as still another weapon to secure Leopold's later abdication, and that subtle propaganda methods were used to work on a bewildered people suffering the harsh realities of occupation to reject the Princesse de Réthy, to scorn Leopold for self-indulgence in the midst of his people's troubles, and to remain faithful to the beloved memory of the great Queen and mother that Astrid had undoubtedly been.

All Leopold could do, of course, was to bear all this with dignified silence and scrupulously continue his promises to remain a prisoner-of-war and to bring all the aid he could, as Commander-in-Chief of the armies, to his suffering people. Princesse de Réthy created her own special secretariat to give war aid as widely as possible and Leopold in turn charged his officers to look particularly to the needs of children deprived of their parents. This in effect meant that they

were freed of their allegiance to him and so were able, in large
numbers, to begin mobilisation of the vast Secret Army that,
in liaison with London, was slowly building up its strength and
resources to strike its own blow for the liberation of Belgium in
common accord with the Allies once the invasion of France began
in 1944. Leopold's last direct intervention came in the winter of 1942
when the Germans began massive deportations into munitions
factories in Germany. By letter to Hitler he protested strongly. Hitler
refused to give way, but he did allow special exemptions for women,
young girls, war orphans, and children whose fathers were already
prisoners-of-war. It is estimated that by his insistence at this time
Leopold saved some 500,000 Belgians from deportation. On 7 June
1944, the day after the Normandy landings, Leopold was arrested
by the SS and removed to Germany. Princesse de Réthy and the
children were made to follow two days later. On 7 March 1945 the
royal family was moved from Germany to Strobl in Austria and it
was there that they were freed by the American Seventh Army on
7 May 1945, the day that Germany finally capitulated.

The Germans, of course, had begun the occupation by wooing
the Belgians and in particular by praising the gallant stand of the
Belgian armies. It is more than probable that Hitler envisaged at
this time the complete annexation of Belgium to the Reich and its
division into two loosely federated states of Flemings and Walloons.
In proportion as the essential temper of the Belgian people asserted
itself, however, and as state functionaries set an example by stubbornly refusing to comply with German demands, so were the
Germans compelled to take increasingly stringent measures. Within
two years more than 3,000 burgomasters, aldermen, and magistrates
had been replaced by collaborating Rexists or Flemish Nationalists.
The University of Brussels closed its doors in 1941. In November
1943 the Rector of the University of Louvain was arrested and
imprisoned for refusing to hand over to the German authorities
class lists of undergraduates, who were wanted for forced labour.
Professors at Ghent and Liège were arrested for similar offences.
The Gestapo moved in and showed no mercy. And as German
tyranny grew so did the Belgians come either to recruit themselves
into the Secret Army or to form amongst themselves various types
of resistance groups which were put into contact with the Belgian
authorities and British Intelligence in London, whose task became

that of co-ordinating all the various efforts towards the final show-down.[1]

At one time there were no fewer than 200 clandestine newspapers in circulation. Elaborate cell systems developed to hide shot-down Allied air force personnel and eventually to pass them along cunningly contrived escape routes back to safety in England, once again to become combatant. Similar escape routes were also devised by hundreds of able-bodied Belgians whose one wish was to get to England and join either the Belgian forces there or recruit themselves into one or other of the special services to be returned clandestinely to Belgium for liaison work with resistance workers. So were trained personnel secured for membership of the Secret Army and so were saboteurs and propagandists co-ordinated in their efforts to cause the maximum of disruption and dismay at the most opportune moments to suit the Allied cause. Nor did intellectuals scorn to use the only weapons they had to hand. One outstanding example was a lavishly mounted production of Schiller's *William Tell*, put on with the glowing approval of the Germans who forgot the message Schiller was preaching and who, in great discomfiture, were later forced to ban performances because of the patriotic fervour they were causing. Another is the play *Le Jeu des Quatre Fils Aymon* which the distinguished playwright Herman Closson wrote especially for an itinerant Rover Scout theatrical group, and which was performed in theatres and market places throughout Belgium before being finally banned in 1941. Such gadfly approaches were infuriating to the slow-witted, bovine German official. And acts of sabotage, passive resistance, and industrial go-slow reached such alarming proportions for the Germans that, once they had grasped that appeals made to Belgians by Rexist and Flemish Nationalist collaborators had no effect other than the often audacious assassination of such collaborators, they had to be ruthless.

Final statistics available have made the Belgian reflect soberly but proudly on those dark years of occupation. The eighteen days' war cost the country some 20,000 dead, soldiers and civilians. Necessary Allied bombardments between 1 January and 31 August 1944 caused the death of 6,500 civilians of all ages. A further 2,622 were

---

[1] It was a great privilege and an exhilarating experience to be working with these magnificent resisters from all conditions of life, who daily gave proof that the spirit of Counts Egmont and Horne (and of Thyl Ulenspiegel) still manifested itself in a fierce national pride.

killed in the final stages of fighting for the liberation of Belgium. The Ardennes counter-offensive launched by von Rundstedt on 16 December 1944 caused the death of a further 1,205 civilians. An overall count suggests that between 1943 and 1945 some 20,000 civilians were killed, and that the grand total for the war must be around 40,000. To these must be added 12,000 political prisoners who died in German concentration camps along with 26,800 deported Jews.[1] Materially speaking the country as a whole lost some 35 milliard francs, or 8 per cent of its total worth in 1939—a percentage figure, incidentally, exactly the same as that after the First World War.

[1] Of a total of 28,000 Jews deported only 1,200 returned. It must be remembered, however, that the vast majority of these were not properly speaking Belgians, but Jews who had sought asylum in Belgium between 1933 and 1939. Few Jews of Belgian nationality (i.e. those already established in the country before 1933) were deported. They were made, nonetheless, to suffer humiliating indignities and deprivation and went in constant fear of deportation at the slightest whim of the German officials.

Chapter 9

Government-in-Exile

WE LEFT MEMBERS OF THE BELGIAN GOVERNMENT-IN-EXILE huddled together at Vichy and in a state of considerable anxiety and indecision. Marcel-Henri Jaspar's broadcast from London had had to be disclaimed since tentative and indirect approaches to the Germans were at that time being made. The blunt German declaration of 20 July 1940 that in no circumstances would members of the exiled government be allowed to return to Belgium left them with little alternative but to pursue the war, somehow. And when on 1 August the Bank of France refused to honour cheques drawn by the Belgian government and Pétain was ordered by Germany to end all diplomatic relations with countries under Nazi occupation, France itself remained no longer a possible refuge. On 20 August the government resigned on the grounds that it no longer had state funds at its disposal and correctly informed Leopold of this. Members now separated. Albert de Vleeschauwer, to whom the administration of the Belgian Congo had been entrusted, arrived in London as early as July. Camille Gutt, Minister of Finance, joined him there in August. Pierlot and Spaak, whose first intention seems to have been to go to the United States, were detained in Spain for some weeks and arrived only in October. On the 22nd of that month a new government was formally constituted with Pierlot as Prime Minister, Spaak as Minister for Foreign Affairs, Information, and Labour, Gutt as Minister of Finance, Economic Affairs, and National Defence, and Albert de Vleeschauwer as Minister of Colonies and Administration of Justice. The new government at once declared itself, and was accepted, as a full partner in the Allied camp and undertook to be bound by all international agreements entered into by the Allies.

In this connection the government's first urgent duty was to regularise its current foreign policy. Belgium was not officially at war with Italy, though the Italians had broken off diplomatic relations at the time they declared war on France and had since shown insolent and brutal indifference to Belgium's plight. This situation was cleared up on 29 November 1940 by what was tantamount to an official declaration of war, and the government soon had the satisfaction of seeing its colonial troops playing a major role in the effective drubbing and routing of the Italians in Abyssinia. Immediate steps were also taken to sever diplomatic relations with Romania, Bulgaria, Hungary, and Finland, despite considerable material interests Belgium had in those countries, while on the other hand she was quick to recognise the provisional Czech government under Dr Benes and to establish friendly relations with the *Comité National Français* headed by General de Gaulle. In December 1941 war was officially declared on Japan, and on 1 January 1942 Belgium became a signatory to the Washington Declaration which formed a wartime coalition against the Axis and became the first important step towards the evolution of the United Nations.

Impressed by the fact that their English allies were now conscripting men to the armed forces up to the age of forty-one, the Belgians felt that they could do no less, and by a decree of 3 December 1940 they conscripted all eligible Belgians in all countries (including the U.S.A. and Canada) and made clear that any attempt to evade conscription would be punishable on the cessation of hostilities and the return to normal.[1] These conscripted Belgians usually fought in special units alongside the British, and the main army training centre was at Leamington Spa in Warwickshire. A Belgian section of the Royal Navy was created, and, since Belgium had disbanded her navy before the outbreak of war, a number of British warships were handed over to Belgian command and in turn became the nucleus of Belgium's post-war fleet. The Belgian air force had been completely destroyed during the eighteen-day war. Belgian air force personnel were, therefore, integrated into the Royal Air Force. In addition the Belgian merchant navy was able to put thirty-four ships at the disposal of the British merchant fleet, and more than 200 Belgian trawlers had managed to find refuge in English ports during the débâcle of May 1940.

Firm backing also came from the Belgian Congo. At first be-

[1] The Belgian age-limits for conscription were seventeen to thirty-five years of age. All such able-bodied Belgians were encouraged to leave occupied Belgium as best they could and rally to the cause in England. Draft dodgers from outside occupied Belgium were prosecuted after the war, and much publicity was then given to the prosecution of Walter Baels, brother of the Princesse de Réthy.

wildered by the unprecedented turn events had taken, the Congolese quickly rallied themselves and the Governor-General, Pierre Rijckmans, voiced the feelings of all in an important speech made on 21 July 1940: 'The Government has only one aim: to win the war, to liberate Belgium and restore to her a Congo intact, capable of contributing to the rebuilding of the country. To win the war means, of course, helping Great Britain to win it.'

Similar feelings of anger and demonstrations of eagerness to fight were made by the natives, one of whose spokesmen summed up tersely the whole situation by declaring that 'if that is the way Hitler treats the white people, what can we expect if he is victorious?' A territorial army was quickly mobilised, but although their numbers were great they lacked arms. De Vleeschauwer left for the Congo to help co-ordinate all effort in aid of the Allied cause, and on 21 January 1941 two agreements, one economic and one financial, put the immense wealth of the Congo at the disposal of the Allies. In brief, it was determined that once the Congo's own essential requirements had been met the surplus was to be handled, as required, by the government-in-exile. The whole of the Congo's gold production and foreign exchange was also ceded to the Bank of England against payment in sterling.

The effort made was phenomenal by any standards. In the first year alone the Congo contributed £7 million. A public subscription launched at Leopoldville by the Governor-General for the purchase of planes to be put at the disposal of Belgians fighting with the R.A.F. realised £250,000. And when Pierlot visited the Congo in company with de Vleeschauwer in 1942 he was able to reveal with pride that the contribution for the fiscal period from 1940 to 1943 would be no less than £28½ million. Meanwhile General Paul Ermens, who was in command of the Belgian colonial forces, had raised and equipped three brigades of 10,000 men. These, as we have already briefly mentioned, fought alongside the British in the Abyssinian campaign, were warmly congratulated by General Wavell, and one detachment led by General Gilliard had the supreme satisfaction of accepting the capitulation of the Italians at Gallo-Sidaeo on 3 July 1941 and taking prisoner 15,000 Italian troops (of whom some 9,000 were native irregulars), together with vast quantities of war materials.

Turning to what might be called 'home' affairs the government-in-exile had first of all to cope with some 23,000 Belgian civilians who had arrived in England mainly in June and July 1940, and also to handle the vexed question of its own gold reserves. These, amounting to some $260 million in value, had been deposited in Paris before the invasion of Belgium. After the total collapse of the Allies the Belgian government then in France requested that these reserves (at that time in Bordeaux) be transferred to London. The French transferred them instead to Dakar, and later, on German instructions, had them returned to France for delivery to Germany. The Belgian ambassador to the U.S.A., Georges Theunis, was now instructed to obtain from the Americans a writ of attachment against French reserves held by the Federal Bank of New York to recover the loss. The matter was speedily settled. The New York courts authorised an attachment on 5 February 1941 and the next day the Belgians had their own gold once again at their free disposal. The French, of course, challenged the ruling, but after much argument the American courts reiterated their competence in the matter and declared it closed on 8 August 1941.

To cope with the Belgian civilian population a cabinet decree of 28 November 1940 created a Ministry of Labour and State Insurance to ensure that the Belgian colony offered a full contribution to the British industrial war effort, and also to look after the social and material well-being of those Belgian citizens undertaking such work. It was essential to carry out an occupational census, and this was achieved with the collaboration of the British government to cover all males between the ages of sixteen and sixty-five and women between the ages of sixteen and fifty. Special training courses lasting six months were set up and an Anglo-Belgian Labour Exchange undertook the placement of all successful trainees. Rough estimates would indicate that fully 90 per cent of both men and women attending these courses were absorbed into the war effort. In addition, and in collaboration with the Diamond Corporation and the Diamond Trading Company, a diamond-cutting industry was set up (drawing on industrial diamonds from the Congo, which produces 80 per cent of the total world output) and Belgian diamond-cutters so employed sold vast quantities to the U.S.A., thus ensuring for Great Britain a steady flow of foreign exchange stock.

Camille Gutt, as Minister of Finance, also made several important fiscal decisions. The exchange rate for the Congolese franc was fixed at 176 to one pound sterling. In October 1940 holders of $3\frac{1}{2}$ per cent Belgian bonds which had fallen due on 29 May were informed that it had been decided to pay these in full, capital and accumulated interest, up to 29 November and that reimbursement would be in English currency at the rate of 123 Belgian francs to the pound. Holders of such bonds in occupied territories, however, would have payment deferred until the liberation of their country. A regular service of foreign loans was restarted, and so impressed was the rest of the free world by the financial stability of the Belgian government-in-exile and the measures it was taking to safeguard that stability, that the price of stocks held by the Belgian state and quoted on the London Stock Exchange rose steadily throughout the whole period of exile.

Thus the Belgian exiled government was able not only to bear all its own expenses but also to make a serious contribution in all fields to the Allied cause. Camille Gutt made in addition an out-and-out gift of £100,000 to the Spitfire Fund. The planes in which the officers, pilots, and other Belgian ranks flew with the R.A.F. were all paid for from Belgian funds. Ships handed over to the Belgian navy were maintained by the Belgians. And all army equipment used by Belgians was again paid for in full. The all-out war effort of the Allies was supported without stint or reservation, and it was a triumphant Colonel Piron who led his crack brigade of 3,000 troops, all trained in England, from the Allied landings in Normandy on D-Day, through Normandy towards Le Havre, and thence to take part in the liberation of Brussels itself on 4 September 1944 amid the delirious joy of the almost unbelieving *Bruxellois*.

Probably the most important decision taken by Camille Gutt, however, and certainly one of the best kept secrets of the war, was to print on British government presses an entirely new issue of Belgian paper money which would accompany the government-in-exile on its return to liberated Belgium and so effectively kill at one blow the inflationary situation created by the Germans. The idea briefly was to call in all paper money on a given date (9 October 1944) and only to issue in exchange new notes to the value of 2,000 Belgian francs per person. Any surplus amount would be credited to the owner, but 'blocked' for the time being, the onus eventually being placed upon the owner to prove that he had come by this money legitimately and not through any kind of transaction with the Germans or through illegal black market activities. Bank accounts and securities were similarly 'blocked'. In the event, about 40 per cent of the sums 'blocked' were soon released, it being obvious that the money had been legitimately acquired. The remaining 60 per cent were indefinitely 'blocked' and converted into a forced loan (*assainissement monétaire*) carrying an interest of 3½ per cent.[1] It was a stroke of genius, necessary though draconian, and immediately put the Belgian franc in good standing on all international money markets.

Meanwhile, the government-in-exile was well aware towards the end of 1943 that its return to Belgium was now a matter of months and not years. Pierlot felt it important that Leopold should be alerted as soon as possible to the position the government would take up on its return and a special emissary, François de Kinder (a brother-in-law of Pierlot), was sent to advise the King accordingly. It was requested that on the liberation of Belgium Leopold should immediately proclaim Belgium's determination, according to the Washington Declaration, to continue the war against both Germany and Japan until final victory; that he should announce Belgium's full participation in the necessary economic and political restructuring of the shattered world; and that he should make it clear that all collaborators would immediately be prosecuted. The messenger left on 3 November 1943. The King's actual wording in his reply was unfortunately never known as de Kinder was caught and shot by the Germans on his way back. It had to be assumed (and probably correctly) that Leopold refused to be drawn and still saw it as in the best immediate interests of his country that he should strictly maintain his position as a prisoner-of-war.

Brussels was liberated on 3 September 1944. The last important agreement entered into by the government-in-exile took place two days later when, by the London Convention, representatives of the respective exiled governments of Belgium, Holland, and Luxembourg signed an economic treaty to replace in effect the treaty made between Belgium and Luxembourg on 25 July 1921. So was Benelux born. Under this Convention, implemented on 1 January 1948, import duties on trade between the Benelux countries were formally abolished and a common customs tariff on imports from countries

---

[1] By January 1945, 179 milliards of francs had been affected. By that date also 73 milliards had been declared 'free', 42 milliards were temporarily 'blocked', 64 milliards indefinitely 'blocked'. It was calculated that out of 100 milliards in circulation roughly 12 or 13 milliards would be declared irredeemably 'black' and confiscated by the state. When the whole operation was finally wound up the confiscation figure was only 4,412 million. A fine tribute to the patriotism of the Belgian people as a whole.

outside Benelux was instituted, though quota restrictions were to remain temporarily in force.

On 8 September 1944 the government-in-exile returned to Belgium.

Chapter 10

The Royal Question

OF THE MANY PROBLEMS with which Pierlot and his government (and indeed successive governments) had to contend as Belgium struggled back to normality, that of the future of Leopold, involving the whole future of the Belgian monarchy, was the most important, the most fraught with both hidden and overt dangers, and the most explosive. Increasingly it became obvious that the constitutional position needed careful reappraisal; that it was anachronistic in terms of a modern democratic society; and that, ironically, it had required a man of Leopold's character and temper, by his own actions – however altruistic and directed towards the best interests of his country as he imagined these to be – to bring all this to the boiling. It must also be reiterated that, if Leopold now became in some measure a victim of his own character, he was equally at the centre of a series of vindictive political intrigues and was constitutionally in no position to defend himself as any ordinary citizen might have done.

It is to be remembered that monarchy in Belgium was born of the Belgian revolution of 1830 and was at the outset far from welcomed by those powers which had vanquished Napoleon. Belgian acceptance of a truly national dynasty coincided with the growth of national sentiments throughout the country, and the new monarch, Leopold I, was regarded by the Belgians as their first true national King. He was to make the Crown the bedrock of the country's unity and the symbol of all the liberties finally secured after so many centuries of struggle. The choice of a monarchy was again inevitable in that the people of Belgium had always lived under a monarchy. All they had known of a republic was through the French revolutionary armies, and this form of rule had left very bad memories in men's minds, irrespective of their political or philosophical beliefs.

Yet although the Belgians who drew up the constitution of 7 February 1831 were unanimously agreed on the monarchy as being the best form of government, they were nevertheless firmly resolved to found a monarchy that should be totally different from that which they had just got rid of. They were self-made men, a type of bourgeoisie unlike any other bourgeois classes to be found in power elsewhere in Europe. They owed nothing to anybody and everything to their own individual effort – and to the relatively excellent schooling the King of the Netherlands had thoughtfully provided in his desire to put Belgium on a sound economic footing. They started with no historical traditions of government behind them. They were a 'new' people, and their rise to importance and power was due to the economic revolution which, since the end of the eighteenth century, had substituted for a mercantilism functioning under state control one in which individualism and free competition were given full scope. They were also reared on the writings of those eighteenth-century philosophers who had inspired the French Revolution, and the political philosophy thus handed to them bore for them the stamp of truth. They wanted a parliamentary system of government in which the executive authority would be wielded collectively by the Head of State *and* his Ministers, who would be chosen from among members of two Houses of Parliament and who would without question be responsible to both Houses – as opposed to the Dutch system in which the executive authority was vested solely in the Head of State who governed with the help of Ministers he had personally chosen *without* reference to Parliament.

'Gentlemen,' said the Vicomte (Charles-Hippolyte) Vilain XIIII,[1] 'I shall declare myself in favour of a constitutional monarchy, but one which is founded on the most liberal, the most popular, and the most republican principles'. The result was that the constitution became a compromise arrangement between the Liberal left wing and the Catholic right, and it was conceived and drafted in such a way that wide variations in the exercise of authority were not only possible, but permissible. Again, the question of peace and war was uppermost in all minds, and speed was essential if Belgium were to be allowed to exist as a separate nation. So it was that, as first King of the Belgians, Leopold I was brought immediately, by unavoidable

[1] Member of an old aristocratic family settled in Flanders. His forebear Vicomte Jean-Jacques-Philippe has been President of the States of Flanders under Austrian rule. The descendant had formed part of the deputation to London to invite Leopold to take the Belgian throne and played a vital role in drafting the new constitution.

necessity, to play a part in interpreting the constitution and so setting a pattern for his successors to follow.

In a country which had only just won its independence and in which everything had yet to be organised he had personally to take charge of negotiations with other powers. He had to be in effect his own war Minister. He had to keep fully abreast of all that was happening and to intervene regularly in public affairs. In short, the pressing needs of the times demanded that he both reign and govern, as they gradually shaped his own personal conception of the role of the sovereign which he read into the constitution. It was, so he believed, the sovereign's duty actively to participate in the discussions of his Ministers and exert a guiding influence over their actions. He must favour neither one party nor another. He must be strictly impartial in all his undertakings. He must scrupulously obey the constitution, not only in the spirit but in the letter. He must place his country first and foremost and must refuse to accept a Minister's resignation if this, in his opinion, was at the time not in the best interests of Belgium. He must not act as a rubber stamp to ministerial decisions, but take his time and ponder the advisability (or otherwise) of giving his royal assent.

Obviously, he took as much advantage as possible of the liberal institutions set up by the constitution and he widened the Crown's sphere of influence as far as it was possible for him to do so. When he died (10 December 1865), deeply and unanimously regretted by his people, he bequeathed to Leopold II a powerful monarchy enjoying a considerable degree of political influence. Leopold II was not slow to exploit his inheritance. Following in his father's footsteps he presided over cabinet meetings, and even towards the end of his life, though he appeared more rarely in public, he maintained direct contacts with his principal Ministers. He received members of Parliament in audience and maintained relations with various political groupings, keeping them advised of his own ideas and opinions. He also ran the Congo as his own personal venture and made an unwilling country the heir to one of the richest colonies on the continent of Africa. He was in no doubt that the Crown had the right to express its opinions and he considered that the sovereign should enjoy a real measure of freedom of action within the executive.

Leopold II had repeatedly flouted the letter and spirit of the constitution, and his heir and successor, Albert I, mounted the throne in particularly difficult circumstances. Not only had the monarchy

lost its popularity, but a social quarrel was for the first time dis-
rupting the country. Though Belgium was proportionately as rich
as France or the German empire, and though the overall income
of its inhabitants exceeded that of the Netherlands or of Italy, the
working classes were reduced to the most abject poverty and were
beginning to be articulate about their grievances. For the first time
also the claims of the Flemish-speaking regions were beginning to
have considerable effect on the country's political development. From
the outset, Albert made it a rule to follow all political developments
by means of regular discussions with the Prime Minister and members of the Cabinet. He did not preside over cabinet meetings, however, but preferred to remain discreetly active in the wings.

The First World War willy-nilly changed all this. Indisputably
he assumed personal command of the armed forces, acquitted himself brilliantly and courageously, and was equally indisputably in
charge of all cabinet meetings called to prosecute hostilities and
bring the war to a successful conclusion. When peace came he prudently and cautiously retreated to his former role, was careful never
to interfere in political quarrels, and – living more and more on his
'legend' – conformed more and more to the ideal pattern of a constitutional monarch that the growing Socialist Party advocated.
His role was to be no different from that of the King of England.
It was under Albert that the Belgian monarchy recaptured the popularity it had known under Leopold I and that the seeds were sown
for the dissension that was to engulf Leopold III.

As we have briefly pointed out, Leopold III was determined conscientiously and to the best of his ability to put his country first and
foremost, come what may. He was equally determined to show that
he was the worthy son of a noble and well-beloved father. Yet the
very props he needed to sustain him in playing his role at the most
difficult period, not only in the history of Belgium but also in the
history of the whole of western Europe, were one by one denied him.
His father had been passive, whereas he had to be active and take a
more personal concept of the way in which his prerogatives should
be exercised. His father had denied him all precedent for this. And
at a time when he was beginning to make an impact the tragic death
of Queen Astrid removed for him a most important stabilising
element in his life, isolated him as no other monarch had been
isolated, and gave birth to another 'legend' which again did not
centre on him. The harsher realities of the international scene now

demanded even more resolute action on his part. He was going to be called upon to be the champion of 'gallant little Belgium' all over again. He must be prepared. He must not fail. Yet fail he did, though valiantly and certainly through no fault of his own. To the end, however, he kept a sense of proportion in all matters and put the interests of his people first, even though this did ultimately mean violating the constitution by refusing to take the advice of his Ministers and go into exile along with his government. As a prisoner at Laeken he had ample time to brood on his misfortunes, on the fickleness and slipperiness of politicians, on the ingratitude and incomprehension with which he was now having to contend. He was hurt and humiliated, and his resolve hardened, leading him to be less adaptable and diplomatic at the crucial moment when these qualities were most needed.

Within twenty-four hours of his return to Belgium Pierlot was presented with a memorandum written by Leopold on 25 January 1944 and which seemed to ignore completely the earlier communication that should have come to him via de Kinder. The memorandum proved to be a closely argued justification of Leopold's own conduct throughout the period of Belgian occupation, demanded an apology from the government for the attitude they had taken, and finally reiterated the necessity for continuing with the policy of independence-neutrality. This was a challenge that Pierlot could not accept, particularly since he had already pledged Belgium's support to the United Nations and said Belgium would prosecute the war to the end against both Germany and Japan. On 19 September 1944 Pierlot obtained an overwhelming vote of confidence from Parliament for his policies. In that he was still held a prisoner by the Germans, Leopold was declared 'incapable of reigning' and his younger brother, Prince Charles, was elected Regent almost unanimously, forty-five members preferring to abstain and only two votes being positively registered against him.

Once again the situation can only be described as unfortunate, if inevitable. Prince Charles, as the second son of King Albert, had escaped all the publicity, and it would indeed seem that his parents had urgently connived at this. Nor had the two brothers at any time in their lives been very close to one another. The war years forced Prince Charles to cease to be a nonentity. To escape the attentions of the Germans he had to go into hiding. When the final push came he judged it prudent to identify himself with the resistance and go into the *maquis*. There he proved to be a first-class officer and leader of men. He rejoiced in having at long last an important task to fulfil and he acquitted it bravely and with distinction, becoming increasingly popular among all the resistance movements. It was impossible for the average Belgian not to make invidious distinctions between the patriotism of Charles who was risking his life for his country along with fellow countrymen from all walks of life and the leisured ease and comfort in which King Leopold was supposed to be playing his part as a prisoner-of-war. To be fair to Prince Charles he recognised the falsity of his position and the delicate nature of the role he was called upon to play as Prince-Regent. He was at first reluctant to accept office. Having accepted, however, he gave of his best.

In February 1945 the socialist leader Achille Van Acker formed a new government to replace that of Pierlot, which, drawing its cabinet members from all four parties, had only six Catholic Ministers out of a total of eighteen. Parliament was now well to the left, drawing its strength mainly from the Walloon provinces, and therefore anti-Leopold. Nevertheless, when the liberation of Leopold was announced on 7 May, the presidents of both Houses sent telegrams of congratulation. No reply was received. On 9 May an official delegation headed by the Prince-Regent and Van Acker left for Austria. Three days of talks led to nothing other than a formal request from Leopold to his brother to carry on for the time being as he (Leopold) was at the moment too sick to contemplate an immediate return to Belgium.

More discussions followed with Van Acker on 5 June. A further meeting on 14-15 June led to Leopold submitting for Van Acker's approval the texts both of a radio broadcast he proposed making to the nation and of the speech he would make from the throne. When Van Acker returned to Brussels with this information, however, the government threatened to resign, claiming that it could not be held responsible for what might happen should Leopold return. The whole situation now became incredibly confused. On 11 July Leopold, still persisting in an attempt to find some solution to the impasse, proposed that a commission of three Ministers be appointed to examine his record and at whose disposal he would place all his private dossiers. He had meetings with the Cabinet between 8 and 14 July, and was then threatened with a full parliamentary debate unless he abdicated. He had interviews with the Queen-Mother and

Prince Charles on 13–14 July, and then addressed a well-argued letter to the government through his brother. He desired Prince Charles to make it plain that he did not wish to impose himself; as always he put his country first; but he was given to understand that a large section of the population wanted him back. How then could he honourably abdicate? He would wait until tempers had calmed when, at the next regular elections, the will of the people could be made known. Three days later, on 17 July, Van Acker opened the Royal Question to a full parliamentary debate, during which an attempt was made to destroy Leopold politically by proving that he had believed in a German victory and had acted from 28 May 1940 as if the war were over. Nothing was settled – how could it be when the consciences of some politicians were far from easy on this score?– and the entire group of Catholic Ministers resigned from the government as a protest. On 30 September 1945 Leopold moved with his entire family from Austria to settle at Pregny in Switzerland and issued a touching proclamation to the Belgian people, reminding them that he was the only one still in exile, but he was always ready to do the people's will: 'the Belgian monarchy is founded on the common will of all Belgians'.

With the dissolution of Parliament in January 1946 and new elections called for in February, Leopold reminded the government of his earlier suggestion that the elections should be used to decide whether the electorate wanted him back or not. He was coldly rebuffed and told that the principle of monarchy was not in question. Constitutionally, the monarchy was functioning perfectly. It was Leopold who was the stumbling-block. Between February 1946 and March 1947 government succeeded government. The Royal Question was obviously being shelved in favour of matters of more immediate national concern, and Leopold therefore decided to appoint his own commission to examine his behaviour over the war period. It was called on 14 July 1946 and consisted of nine men, all with an impeccable war record, seven of whom were lawyers and all of whom represented all shades of political opinion, the linguistic regions of Flanders and Wallonia, and the universities of Louvain and Brussels. Their report was published on 25 March 1947 and in its scrupulosity refused to consider whether or not Leopold had acted unconstitutionally in staying with the armed forces instead of following his government into exile. Leopold was judged politically. The government's accusations of *attentisme* were repudiated. Leopold had acted at all times in the best interests of his people. Not unnaturally, such a cold and legally phrased document failed to make converts to the King's cause.

In March 1947 a new socialist–Catholic coalition government headed by Spaak, which managed to last until the elections of June 1949, agreed that the time had come to drop the Royal Question. At once Pierlot was up in arms and published a series of twelve articles in *Le Soir* defending his *own* behaviour. Not to be outdone, a fiery Walloon, Victor Larock, raked up all the dirt he could in a series of fifteen articles published in *Le Peuple* and claimed that Leopold had visited Austria more than once as the honoured guest of the Germans. It was now clear that those who wished to assuage their own misgivings and feelings of guilt were going to make Leopold the scapegoat. It was becoming equally clear that the Royal Question was dividing the country in a most dangerous way: Catholics were backing Leopold as against socialists and Liberals; Flemings were backing him against Walloons; Flemings were almost to a man Catholic.

Spaak manoeuvred adroitly. On 18 January 1948 he informed Leopold that on 27 March the vote would be granted to women for the first time and that the electoral lists would then be completely revised in preparation for a general election to be held in June 1949. Leopold should prepare himself against this and make clear to the new electorate what his position was. On 22 June 1948 Leopold wrote to the Prince-Regent and revived the idea of a popular consultation. The Lower House, dominated by the Social Christians, was in favour, but the Senate rejected the suggestion on 28 October and the Liberals now countered with their own suggestion that the government should establish its own commission to decide Leopold's future, and on which Leopold would be represented by two of his own nominees. This Leopold rejected. On the eve of the 1949 elections he summoned the Prince-Regent and Spaak to a meeting in Berne and made it finally clear that he had had enough. The elections were upon the country. A decision, for better or for worse, must now be taken.

With no single political party having an overall majority it took between June and August 1949 for a coalition government to be formed. The Liberals now supported the Catholic proposition for a national consultation as to Leopold's return, though they warned the nation of the danger of such a consultation bringing in its train bitter Flemish–Walloon controversies. On balance, however, the risk was worth taking if the constitutional crisis was once and for all solved. The Liberals advised, however, that they could not accept a simple majority in such an appeal to the people. Leopold refused to be bound by figures, remembered his constitutional rights, and acidly retorted that he would decide as to whether any majority he might have was sufficient for his return. Spaak insisted on a 66 per cent majority in favour as a minimum. Leopold said 55 per cent and it was left at that.

On 12 March 1950 the electorate went to the polls to answer the simple question: 'Are you in favour of King Leopold III resuming the exercise of his constitutional powers?' National overall figures showed that 57.68 per cent said 'Yes' and 43.32 per cent said 'No'. Broken down on a regional basis, however, the figures revealed only too clearly Liberal apprehensions and how far already the constitutional crisis had eroded the unity of the nation. The Flemish provinces alone had polled 72 per cent in favour of Leopold, whereas the Walloon provinces had polled 58 per cent against him and the Brussels agglomeration 52 per cent against. The lowest favourable percentage for Leopold in the Flemish provinces was recorded in Antwerp (68 per cent) and the highest in the province of Limburg (83 per cent), predominantly agricultural and noted for being the most conservative and Catholic province in the whole country.

The next day the Prime Minister, Gaston Eyskens, left for Geneva to acquaint Leopold with the results and to ask (somewhat naïvely in the circumstances) what Leopold intended to do about them. Leopold properly retorted that it was up to Parliament to assume its own political responsibilities in the matter. Rumblings of discontent were now heard from various Walloon separatist movements and animosity between the Flemish and Walloon communities broke out. The Liberals withdrew their support of Eyskens' government and he had to resign on 19 March, unable to solve the dilemma. On 22 March Spaak appealed to Leopold to consider the greater good of the country and to put an end to an impossible situation by abdicating in favour of his son and heir, Prince Baudouin. The Prince-Regent charged Paul van Zeeland, a Catholic, with the task of forming a new government. The Liberals made it clear that they would not support Leopold's unconditional return. Van Zeeland left to consult Leopold and secured from him a compromise arrangement that he would temporarily delegate his powers and duties to his son.

There was again stalemate. All the Prince-Regent could do was to dissolve Parliament and call for new elections.

These were fought, of course, solely on the Royal Question, and to the relief of many the Social Christians were returned with an overall majority. Jean Duvieusart, as Prime Minister, had constituted his Cabinet by 8 June. On 27 June he announced the imminent return of Leopold. At once discord broke out. The trade unions let it be known that they would not recognise Leopold. There were demonstrations against Leopold on 6 July and a mass rally on 8 July in Brussels to pay homage to Prince Charles. Further demonstrations took place in Antwerp on 10 July and between 10 and 12 July the whole of the Black Country went on strike as a protest. Nonetheless, Duvieusart persisted. On 20 July the united chambers voted to end the regency, socialists, Liberals, and communists refusing to register their vote. And in the early hours of the morning of 22 July Leopold, accompanied by Princes Baudouin and Albert, slipped quietly into his Palace of Laeken.

As was only to be expected, loyalist demonstrations and counter-demonstrations followed the news as it leaked. By 28 July there were half a million on strike in the Walloon provinces alone and two days later the strike had become so general that the port of Antwerp could not operate. An unfortunate incident at Grâce Berleur, near Liège, led to the killing of three socialist demonstrators by the police. And on 31 July a huge socialist rally of some 100,000 members planned a concerted march on Brussels. Meanwhile Leopold had received a delegation from a non-political organisation, the National Confederation of Political Prisoners-of-war and their Descendants. By 8 p.m. on the night of 31 July he had to acknowledge that the dice were too heavily loaded against him and that the only way out was abdication. An abdication message to the press was read out at 6.45 a.m. on the morning of 1 August by the Minister of Public Instruction. On 3 August this was submitted to Parliament. On 11 August 1950 the position was finally clarified when Leopold created Baudouin Prince Royal and instructed him to act for him in a temporary capacity. He hoped that national unity and amity would now centre on the heir to the throne in such a way that he himself could finally bow out. On 16 July 1951 Leopold III judged that the moment had arrived. At a moving ceremony held in the Royal Palace at Brussels Leopold III became the ex-King and Baudouin I began his reign by looking his father straight in the eyes and

exclaiming: 'My dear father, I am deeply touched by the nobility of
your utterance. I promise you to do all in my power to show myself
worthy to be your son.'

'An irascible people' is what Lord Palmerston, in a moment of
irritation, once called the Belgians. They almost certainly felt that
about Leopold and he had no illusions about them. They are obstinate yet loyal. Having decided on the course of action to be taken
they pursue it to the end. They are, however, ready to compromise
once the wisdom of compromise action has been made evident. And
such a compromise solution both the Belgian people and Leopold
almost tacitly agreed upon when Baudouin became Prince Royal for
a trial period before the final and irrevocable abdication. Good sense
on both sides eventually prevailed as tempers calmed. The Belgians
are also both practical and traditionalist. As the Royal Question
meandered along it became evident that it was the ambiguous nature
of the constitution which allowed for too wide a freedom in interpretation of the sovereign's prerogatives that was most at fault. This
must be rectified. Consequently a commission composed of top-
ranking magistrates and politicians of all trends of opinion was set
up by the government early in 1949 and instructed to make 'a moti-
vated recommendation on the application of constitutional principles
regarding the King's prerogatives and the relationship between the
great constitutional authorities'. The commission reported on 20 July
1949 and the conclusions it reached secured the approval of the three
traditional parties.

The report is more remarkable for what it does not say than for
the positive recommendations it puts forward. In the first place it is
accepted without question that Belgium is and must remain a monarchy. Secondly, the inviolability of the King's person is reaffirmed –
even though Leopold III played on this by reminding his people that
he could not be deposed, and that if and when he abdicated he
would decide the time and (in the event of a national referendum)
the percentage of votes in favour of abdication that he would accept.
Thirdly, it is stressed that the part played by the King in the government of his country can never be a purely passive one: it is his duty
to express his personal opinions and wishes to his Ministers who are
his only advisers; acts performed by the executive proceed from the
intentions of the government *and* from those of the King; the King's
share in decisions countersigned by a Minister must never be
revealed; and should Ministers be unable to secure the King's ap-

proval, no other resource is open to them other than that of tender-
ing their resignations. The King still appoints and dismisses his
Ministers. He can still refuse to accept a resignation and instruct a
Minister to try again and again to form a government. He still decides when the situation has become so impossible that Parliament
must be dissolved and new elections held.

On the other hand, the root causes of the quarrel with Leopold III
were squarely faced. It is obvious, argues the commission, that
Article 68 of the constitution (stating that the King commands the
armed forces on land and sea, declares war, makes treaties of peace,
alliance, and commerce) is totally unsuited to the complexities of
modern existence and modern warfare. If the King takes *personal*
command of his forces, then he can no longer be available to
discharge his supreme duties as Chief of State. Henceforward his
priorities must lie in that direction. As to treaty making, this again
must become a concern of special parliamentary procedure, particularly since nowadays any opposition on the part of the King to a
government backed by a parliamentary majority has obviously become impossible: the government derives its authority solely from
the confidence of Parliament. Finally it is emphasised that, while
his Ministers must be directly responsible for all the King's acts
and opinions, the government's agreement must precede any royal
initiative. If the King acts on his own or against the advice of his
Ministers, the Crown is no longer shielded and has made any application of the principle of ministerial responsibility impossible. This
golden rule of a parliamentary monarchy must always be scrupulously observed. And by the same token all the King's acts are
binding on the entire government – though minor acts require only
the agreement of the Minister concerned. It is up to the Prime
Minister, in consultation with the King, to decide which is a major
or minor act and whether the agreement of the entire government
is necessary or not.

To sum up, the Belgians have not seriously altered the 1831 constitution. They find it works to their satisfaction once ambiguities
have been cleared away. They want a King in active pursuance of
his stipulated duties. They have been well served (as they are honest
enough to acknowledge) by their present royal house. And, men of
spirit themselves, they feel they need a man of spirit as Head of State.

Chapter 11

Post-War Reconstruction

THE 'LONDON GOVERNMENT' OF PIERLOT, as it came to be called, sought a mandate on its return to Belgium to carry out three urgent and important tasks: firstly, to put the economic position of the country on a healthy footing; secondly, to punish all who could be shown to have actively collaborated with the enemy; and thirdly, to prosecute the war along with the Allies. As a gesture to the undoubted stout resistance communist groups had put up during the German occupation, Pierlot introduced three of their number into his government – but they were to resign in protest on 16 November 1944 when measures were taken to disarm all former resistance groups. Of the Gutt plan to achieve immediate financial stability in liberated Belgium we have already spoken,[1] and it is only necessary to note here that its full and immediate beneficial effect was blunted by the von Rundstedt offensive in the Ardennes in December 1944. Prosecution of collaborators was too relentlessly pursued in that resistance groups were allowed too much licence to denounce, and it is certain that vindictiveness crept in and that attempts were made through loopholes possible in the denunciation system to settle not a few private scores. In the event, 83.5 per cent of the cases brought before the courts were either thrown out or held as non-proven, and a total of no more than .64 per cent of the whole population paid the penalty of collaboration.[2] As to the successful prosecution of the war, there is little to say other than that the Belgian armed forces who had so joyously taken part in the operations of the Second Front moved as tried veterans into Germany and their numbers were swollen by eager young Belgians who, now the opportunity had at last arrived, were only too anxious to prove their mettle.

Despite all the strenuous efforts the Pierlot government were

---

[1] See above, Chapter 9.
[2] But not Degrelle, who succeeded in escaping to Spain.

making, however, it soon became obvious that they were out of touch with the realities of the situation. Too much hope was pinned on the Gutt plan, yet this was only one of four elements which in the long run did make for a more rapid post-war recovery than elsewhere in Europe. The other important factors were that Belgium had not turned into a battleground over which the Allies had to fight their way inch by inch; that the port of Antwerp had been captured intact from the Germans, thanks to the admirable foresight of the Belgian resistance forces who had elaborated a scheme to prevent its sabotage; and that the Belgian government had accumulated large dollar credits from the wartime supply of copper, uranium, and other minerals from the Congo to the Allies. Pierlot tended to assume that the devastation he found was mainly due to German plundering. He was unable at once to cope with the fact that the entire network of railway communications was disrupted, and that a total of 905 locomotives and some 65,000 waggons had just vanished. Nor could he immediately tackle the problem of coal output, vital to the entire industrial effort, which in October 1944 had sunk to an abysmally low figure of 688,000 tons and which in the first six months of 1945 only reached 1,100,000 tons—barely 45 per cent of the normal pre-war output. Steel production in consequence reached only 5 per cent of its normal figure. Matters were still further complicated by inadequate food supplies, for how could coal and steel workers attempt anything like a normal day's work after years of privation under the German occupation and *now* still underfed? Disillusionment was widespread and had in it, of course, an important psychological element.

The crunch came in November 1944 when the Allied High Command requested that all resistance forces be disarmed. A communist-inspired hunger-march of loyal resisters descended on Brussels on 25 November and besieged Parliament. For an hour or so a ding-dong struggle raged between them and the gendarmes who had in self-defence to open fire. Some people were wounded, though fortunately not seriously. But Pierlot was now completely discredited. The two most important and concrete moves of his ministry were first to begin negotiations with the trade unions for pegging the wages of all workers to the rising cost of living and secondly, on 28 December 1944, to institute a social security scheme to protect workers against loss of income through accident, industrial illnesses, sickness, incapacity, old age, premature decease, and unemployment.

Pierlot bowed out gracefully on 12 February 1945 and the socialist leader Van Acker was able to form a ministry which deliberately excluded all the 'men of London', with the solitary exception of Spaak who retained his control of Foreign Affairs. The Cabinet included six Catholics, five socialists, four Liberals, two communists, and a technical expert. Van Acker proved to be a popular and dynamic personality who put the final seal of success to the social measures instigated by Pierlot and tackled the coal situation resolutely. He also had to take first soundings on the Royal Question, and when his six Catholic Ministers walked out on him in protest during the debate he opened on Leopold on 17 July 1945, he forthwith replaced them with a mixed bag of technical experts, noted members of resistance movements, and members of a small and ephemeral Democratic Union Party, which then had hopes of forming a new political party that would group Catholics and Liberals together. In other words, Van Acker was out to show that he was going to have a government which, as far as humanly possible, genuinely represented all the people.

But the time for a general election to sound the wishes of the whole of Belgium had now come. This was held in February 1946, and the returns, as was to be expected, considerably modified the composition of Parliament. The Social Christians, replacing the former Catholic Party, took 92 seats in the Lower House and 83 in the Senate. The socialists had respectively 69 and 55 seats; the Liberals, 17 and 12; the communists, 23 and 17; the Democratic Union, one seat in the Lower House. Attempts by the Social Christians to form a government failed because the socialists would not accept their attitude on the Royal Question. Spaak then formed a makeshift socialist government on 13 March which lasted exactly eighteen days. And then Van Acker bounced back into power, announcing a triple attack on coal supplies, on rising prices, and on securing an increase in exports. His coalition government of socialists, Liberals, and communists collapsed some four months later when support was withdrawn in the Senate over an accusation that the Minister of Justice, Adolphe Van Glabbeke, had intervened to protect a firm prosecuted for economic collaboration with the Germans. Another socialist, Camille Huysmans, took over more or less the same team, but his government fell when, on 11 March 1947, the communist members withdrew their support on the pretext of an increase of 24 francs in the price of a ton of coal.

It was only now that the country was prepared to face up to the logical consequences of the election results which had made the Social Christians the dominant party with the socialists a strong second. On 20 March 1947 Paul-Henri Spaak was able to form a coalition government of the two groups and to keep it in office for almost two years and five months. His Cabinet consisted of nine Social Christians, eight socialists, and two independents, and there is no doubt that his growing international prestige considerably strengthened his authority at home. He handled the Royal Question with firmness and decision. He coped with an unemployment problem that by 1947 had risen to some 220,000. He was able to announce by 1948 that the battle for coal had been won in that the production index (100 in 1936–8) had now reached 111. On 27 March 1948 women were for the first time given the vote and new electoral lists were speedily prepared against a forthcoming general election. He brought the National Bank under complete state control. By the law of 20 September 1948 he created a Central Economic Council and also Works Councils (long urged by the Central Federation of Trade Unions) to bring employers and employees together to deliberate on and concur in further developments in their own particular industrial fields. And, for good measure, he was already in 1948 working on an idea, first suggested by the Social Christian Duvieusart, which was to culminate in the World Exhibition held in Brussels in 1958.

But it is in the international field that Spaak made his name and in which he has for so many years remained a dominant figure. There his far-sightedness and wisdom have put Belgium at all the important conference tables and increased her prestige and standing among all modern Western nations. She is listened to with respect. For centuries, down to the last war, she has inevitably and traditionally been the cockpit of Europe for all internecine struggles among the Western nations. Not unnaturally, therefore, she has been quick to give her full support to present attempts at bringing about a lasting peace in Europe based on a sound European economic policy. She has also realised that since she was once the pivotal point for all wars she can now become the pivotal point for peace. Shrewdly she has manoeuvred this and today the Belgian capital, Brussels, bids fair to become at least an economic capital for the whole of western Europe. In the year 1968 the headquarters of the Common Market, of Euratom, and of the Coal and Steel Community were all grouped together in one massive star-shaped building at the far end of the Rue de la Loi. Already the term 'Eurocrats' is being attached to functionaries who work there. And President de Gaulle was not unhelpful in declaring that SHAPE and NATO must leave France. Immediately the Belgians offered asylum. Since 1967 the forces of SHAPE have been stationed on the site of the former Belgian military and air force training area at Casteau, near Mons, and on 16 October 1967 the Belgian Prime Minister (Vanden Boeynants) formally handed over the newly constructed head-quarters of the Atlantic Alliance to the Secretary-General of NATO, Manlio Brosio. These are situated at a point along the road between Brussels and the city's international airport at Zaventem. True, as the Belgian press with wry humour pointed out, neither Mons nor Brussels can vie with Paris as places of entertainment, but the basic aim of SHAPE and NATO is *not* to cater for the leisure of their personnel.[1]

All this steady progression towards making Belgium a European international centre stems from the initiative of one man, Paul-Henri Spaak, in his socialist youth a firebrand advocating insurrectionist strike action in a vain attempt to shake his party out of the torpidity into which it was plunged in the early 1930s. He has always put his country first, and imaginatively has always been one step ahead of others in doing so. It was this that led him to see the importance for Belgium of the policy of independence-neutrality at the time it was advocated. And he has since seen that the obverse side of the coin, so to speak, is to have Belgium the powerhouse of a United States of Europe.

Immediately after the war, from April to June 1945, he repre-sented Belgium at San Francisco and played an active part in the drafting of the United Nations Charter and in securing the sig-natures of forty-seven nations thereto, thus creating the United Nations Organisation to which Belgium has given her full support ever since – though with increasing misgivings that it is being ren-dered impotent through misuse of the veto. He brought equally enthusiastic support to the drafting of the Charter of the Rights of Man and to the creation and development of the specialist organi-sations, UNRRA and UNESCO, which have resulted from the creation of UNO. He grasped the significance of the Marshall Plan,

[1] Jean Dusart in *La Lanterne* (10 April 1967).

and the importance of its timing, and quickly made Belgium one of the sixteen countries adhering to it and so to some extent financially benefiting over the tricky economic period between 1948 and 1952.[1]

It was, of course, the dread of Soviet propaganda and the near belligerency of the Russians at this time that had prompted inspiration for the Marshall Plan. Poverty-stricken Europe must be given every assistance to become economically solvent again and so healthy enough to resist any communist blandishments. On the other hand, Marshall Aid, valuable and indispensable though it was, made it quite clear to the whole of western Europe that henceforward the two great world powers were going to be the Soviet Union and the United States. About this, something positive must be done in Europe itself. Thus Spaak became a passionate advocate for a five-power pact, well within the framework of the Charter of UNO, whereby Great Britain, France, and the Benelux countries signed an agreement for mutual aid in military, economic, and social matters, to extend for a period of fifty years. Significantly the pact was signed in Brussels on 17 March 1948 and came henceforward to be known as the Brussels Treaty. It was a regional defensive alliance, just in case, and also the first positive step to be taken towards achieving some semblance of European unity.

Hardly had the Brussels Treaty been signed than a conference of some 800 participants was called at The Hague in May 1948 to discuss the possibilities of creating a genuine European movement. From these deliberations resulted the Council of Europe, with its permanent secretariat to be established at Strasbourg and its aims and objectives clearly defined by the Treaty of London of 5 May 1949. Ten nations signed the original treaty, of which the Benelux countries were ardent supporters, and their aim was given as that of seeking 'to achieve a greater unity between Members for the purpose of safeguarding and realising the ideals and principles which are their common heritage and facilitating their economic and social progress'. The number of participating nations has gradually

---

[1] The Marshall Plan got its name from a lecture given by General George Marshall, the U.S. Secretary of State, to the alumni of Harvard on 5 June 1947. Urgent financial aid was given to France and Italy at the end of 1947, though President Truman did not sign the plan until 3 June 1948. Aid was to last for five years, and recipients must agree to economic co-operation among themselves. The Marshall Plan was superseded by a plan for military aid on the outbreak of the Korean War (1950–53), but by that time some 15 milliard dollars had been distributed.

increased to eighteen. The work of the Council is conducted by a committee of Ministers – in effect periodic meetings of the Foreign Ministers of the various member countries – and by a Consultative Assembly composed of parliamentary representatives of the member states, chosen somewhat arbitrarily on a proportional basis according to the estimated importance of a particular country. Thus, Belgium has six representatives and France eighteen. One of the first important moves of the Council of Europe was to create a College of Europe for research and study into European affairs, and this (significantly) was founded in Bruges on 19 May 1950. The latest important development has been the creation, on 1 January 1962, of a Council for Cultural Co-operation to draw up proposals for the cultural policy of the Council of Europe. Naturally, education has been shown to be a chief concern and the aim of the Council for Cultural Co-operation in this direction is given as being 'to help to create conditions in which the right educational opportunities are available to young Europeans whatever their background or level of academic accomplishment, and to facilitate their adjustment to changing political and social conditions'.

On 16 April 1948 in Paris, Belgium signed the Convention for Economic Co-operation which established the Organisation for European Economic Co-operation (OEEC) and which has since become the Organisation for Economic Co-operation and Development (OECD). The initiative to start such an organisation was taken by joint action of the British and French governments in July 1947, and it constituted the first realistic step towards economic integration of the whole of western Europe. A further logical step forward from this was the creation on 19 September 1950 of the European Payments Union, which was called upon to administer the financial arrangements resultant on the application of the Marshall Plan. More important still, however, for Belgium was the ratification of the so-called Schuman Plan by the Treaty of Paris, signed on 18 April 1951, which established the European Coal and Steel Community, comprising Belgium, France, Italy, West Germany, Holland, and Luxembourg – but excluding Great Britain and the Scandinavian countries.

Meanwhile the *coup d'état* in Prague which in 1948 brought Czechoslovakia firmly into the Russian camp, the Russian blockade of Berlin, the victorious offensive of Mao Tse-Tung in China – all these events made it quite clear to the greater powers of the free world that some positive counter-defensive measures were needed. And so at Washington on 4 April 1949 NATO came into existence with the Benelux countries eagerly subscribing and, as the Korean War got under way, France becoming the natural headquarters as thousands of American troops returned to Europe . . . again, just in case. The direct consequences of this defensive alliance for Belgium have been threefold: firstly, NATO eclipsed the earlier Brussels Treaty and led to the signing, on 23 October 1954, of the Paris agreements, which extended the Treaty of Brussels to include Germany and Italy, allowed Germany to become a member of NATO, and instituted the Western European Union; secondly, on 21 January 1951, Belgium felt obliged, in order fully to meet her military commitments to NATO, to extend the period of compulsory military service to two years; and lastly, as we have already noted, she has now become the host country not only of NATO but also of SHAPE.

So, triumphantly, did Spaak lead Belgium into the council chambers of all the greater powers and speak up eloquently and persuasively for her to play a role fully commensurate with her strategic and economic importance to her allies. And he carried the rest of Benelux with him. Unfortunately, however, the very future of Benelux was threatened at home, and the economic and political situation in Belgium itself, tying in so closely with the Royal Question, made Spaak's position increasingly precarious and had him constantly looking over his shoulder. It was only at the beginning of 1947 that Holland was sufficiently recovered from the ravages of war to seek an implementation of the terms of the London Convention, and it was not until January 1948 that she was ready formally to abolish import duties on trade with the Belgian–Luxembourg Economic Union, established on 25 July 1921, and to agree to a common customs tariff on imports from third countries. Quota restrictions still had to remain temporarily in force and the intended completion of the customs union and its extension into an economic union had to be delayed. Within months of the signing of this agreement Belgium was building up for herself enormous credit balances in Holland (by 1950, 7½ million Belgian francs and a further 300 million advanced from the International Monetary Fund). On the other hand, Holland was dumping on Belgium agricultural produce at anything between a half or a third of the price Belgian farmers had to ask, and the same situation threatened to spread to industry as the Dutch industrial effort intensified.[1] Not unnaturally there was much discontent felt throughout Belgium at this situation, and the discontent was aggravated by increasing unemployment, the general world economic depression, and Great Britain's drastic devaluation of the pound sterling by almost a third on 18 September 1949. All the smaller countries, Finland, and the British Dominions (excluding Canada) had to follow suit, and even France and Germany devalued by 22 per cent and 25 per cent respectively. Belgium devalued by 12.35 per cent and at the same time was able to negotiate with Holland on 15 October 1949 a pre-union agreement which began the systematic co-ordination of monetary and commercial policies *vis-à-vis* third countries and the liberalisation of most remaining internal trade barriers.

The main cause of the domestic troubles which the Spaak government had to face (apart from the Royal Question) was the fact that the nation as a whole had still not come to terms with the new political alignment of the immediate post-war years. The Catholic Party, though basically still the party of the peasantry and the leisured middle classes, was becoming increasingly dominated by its left-wing Christian Socialists – in other words its working-class element. Hence the change of name of the party to Social Christians. Hence also a new element of divisiveness within the party on almost any matter of principle – a divisiveness which, as we shall later see, was to topple a strongly-based Social Christian government on the linguistic question in 1968. The Socialist Party, now the most homogeneous group, had put the communist bogy behind it and its moderate intellectual leaders were guiding its working-class members along lines of social development and reform not dissimilar from those advocated by the present Conservative Party in Britain. The Liberal Party, now the most conservative of all the parties, disputed its following of middle-class supporters with the Social Christians and was striving hard to seek a new image for itself – this leading in 1961 to the abandonment of the title of Liberal Party (proudly held since 1846) in favour of the supposedly more modern and appealing title of Party of Liberty and Progress (PLP). To confound matters, however, all this was bedevilled not only by the Royal

[1] The seriousness of the situation from the Belgian point of view can be judged from the fact that the average hourly wage of the Belgian worker was in 1951 B. francs 24.70. The Dutch worker was paid only 16.30 francs. If social security costs are added to this Belgian figure, then the Belgian working man was earning almost twice as much as his Dutch counterpart.

Question (with socialists mainly anti-Leopold and Liberals divided), but also by a profound disquiet as to their economic future felt by the middle classes and farming communities of all parties, and by a menacing intransigence over linguistic and scholastic questions from the Flemings and the Walloons.

Spaak's tenuous retention of office had been threatened in May 1948 over the question of state subsidies to free (Catholic) technical education. The final break came a year later over growing unemployment and the manner in which state allocations in terms of social benefits were being made to the unemployed. The Prince-Regent dissolved Parliament on 18 May 1949. At the general elections held on 26 June, and at which women for the first time registered their vote, the Social Christians gained an overall majority in the Senate (92 seats), but could only command 105 places in the Chamber of Deputies (a gain of 13); the socialists had 66 seats in the chamber (a loss of 3) and 53 seats in the Senate; the Liberals had 29 seats in the Lower House (a gain of 12) and 24 in the Senate; the communists had 12 seats in the Lower House (a loss of 11) and 6 seats in the Senate.

It was impossible for the Social Christians to form a government without the support of either the socialists or the Liberals. Moreover, the situation was further complicated by the fact that, following on the 1947 census, the number of deputies had been increased by ten – eight of the new seats going to the Flemish provinces and two to the bilingual Brussels agglomeration. This meant in effect that there were now 104 Flemish deputies as against 76 from the Walloon provinces and 32 from the Brussels agglomeration, and their alignment on the Royal Question was threatening to cut right across party loyalties. Negotiations dragged on throughout the summer until, with reluctant Liberal support, Gaston Eyskens was able, on 11 August 1949, to constitute a Cabinet consisting of nine Social Christian and eight Liberal Ministers, and to tackle the problem of drafting a bill for a referendum on the King's return. The bill was immediately adopted by the Senate, but was only approved by the Lower House in February 1950 after a stormy passage resulting in 117 being in favour and 92 against. We have already discussed in some detail the results of the referendum held on 12 March. Discontent in the Walloon provinces led to strikes as Eyskens left to consult with Leopold in Geneva, and since the Liberals now withdrew their support of the Social Christians, Eyskens had to resign on 18 March. Six weeks of uncertainty and mounting tension and strikes followed. Parliament was finally dissolved on 30 April and the new elections held on 4 June exacted the appropriate penalty from the Liberals for their ambivalence, and further discredited the communists. The Social Christians took 108 seats in the Lower Chamber (a gain of 3); the socialists held 77 seats (a gain of 11); the Liberals could muster only 20 deputies (a loss of 9); and the communists lost 5 seats, thus reducing their representation to seven.

Four days later the new Prime Minister, Jean Duvieusart, was able to form his Cabinet, and, secure in his overall majority, to make immediate plans on 20 July for the return of Leopold and the ending of the regency. The sorry sequence we have already discussed. Four days after Prince Baudouin took the oath as Prince Royal, Duvieusart himself resigned to be succeeded by Joseph Pholien, formerly Minister of Justice. Paul van Zeeland took over Foreign Affairs and immediately associated Belgium with United Nations policy over the Korean War, which had started on 25 June. On 10 January 1951 Belgium signed decrees empowering the Minister for Defence to send Belgian units to serve under Eisenhower in the North Atlantic army. Belgium also promised to contribute 10 per cent of Western Union defences, and to meet her obligations raised the period of compulsory military service to two years on 7 March 1951.

In home affairs the Social Christians began by reducing state subsidies to the coal mines and to the railways, concentrating on highway development and the provision of new housing, and managed to pay off a large proportion of the national debt to Canada and the United States. From 1950, indeed, the economic situation of Belgium became increasingly stronger and budgets were being balanced, even though wages and prices were beginning to chase one another to an extent which alarmed the economists. A particularly vigorous period of economic activity from the second half of 1950 onwards was, of course, sparked off by the Korean War. A slight period of economic recession in 1953 was quickly overcome, so that the nationalisation of the Suez Canal on 28 June 1956 provoked no real crisis. Indeed, it may be said that from 1957 onwards there has been full employment in Belgium – a situation stimulated to a great extent by preparations made for the Brussels World Fair of 1958.

True, there were symptoms of a new recession early in 1958, but the effective institution of the Common Market on 1 January of that year undoubtedly had a great deal to do with warding off an impending slump. The improvement in the situation continued throughout 1959 and 1960, and in 1961 it attained the proportions of a genuine boom that reached its peak in 1963, despite the disturbances in the Congo during January 1959 and July 1960, and also despite internal political troubles during the first quarter of 1961. Since 1963 there has been an unprecedented level of economic prosperity, accompanied, of course, by the well-known trend towards inflation, on which the authorities are keeping a cautious and vigilant eye.

Chapter 12

Baudouin I (1951–   )

PROBABLY THE MOST ASTONISHING THING that the modern commentator on Belgian affairs has to bear in mind is that already King Baudouin I has reigned longer than did his father, Leopold III, though happily in far more favourable circumstances. Leopold III, starting from a position of strength and with enormous goodwill about him, was powerless to stop the steady process of disintegration and consequent campaign of calumny that brought the royal household to an ebb of popularity unknown and undreamt of since the heyday of Leopold II. Baudouin, the most reluctant monarch ever to succeed to a throne, had to have the courage to clear up the sorry mess about him and make a constitutional monarchy in Belgium work all over again. That he has triumphantly succeeded is due to his disinterested devotion to his country, to the efforts he made to overcome his shyness, loneliness, and inexperience, to his transparent honesty and integrity of purpose – and to the careful schooling for his important task that his father had already given him and to whom he was always able to turn both in the days of the regency and the early days of his reign. Not unnaturally, Baudouin at first considered himself an usurper and had little use for those politicians who, in his view, had hounded his father from office. Yet he was always punctiliously correct and treated with the silent contempt they deserved those who, in a frenzy of frustration and unabated hatred of Leopold, now claimed that Baudouin was but a puppet king since his father still stayed on at the Palace of Laeken.

The Early Years

Duvieusart had most properly tendered his resignation once Baudouin had become Prince Royal, and the resignation had been accepted. Joseph Pholien in turn tendered his resignation as Leopold finally abdicated, but this time the resignation was not accepted and Pholien soldiered on until 9 January 1952, when he was defeated over his fiscal policy which included a rent freeze, a tax on exports, and a 50 centimes per hour increase all round in the wages of manual workers. Jean Van Houtte replaced him, but the overall majority of the Social Christians was reduced to nine in the Senate and to eight in the Lower House. This trend towards unpopularity was further emphasised later in the year at the *communal* elections, held on 12 October 1952, when the party was eclipsed, particularly in the large towns, with substantial gains to the socialists and (less so) to the Liberals. Nevertheless, Van Houtte was able to remain in office until March 1954, when Parliament was dissolved primarily in order to bring about constitutional changes in procedure necessitated by Belgium's various commitments to her Western allies.

In 1952 and 1953 Baudouin carried out the centuries-old tradition of making his 'joyous entries' to the principal towns of Belgium to show himself to his subjects. And on 9 April 1953, amid tremendous enthusiasm, Princess Josephine-Charlotte married in Luxembourg Prince Jean, heir apparent to the Grand Duchy. Slowly the royal image was reasserting itself on more modern, more youthful, and more sophisticated lines, and the people liked what they saw. When the 1954 elections confirmed the fall in popularity of the Social Christians first noted at the *communal* elections, leaving them in a minority position, Baudouin was called upon to carry out his first piece of persuasive manoeuvring to help constitute still another coalition government. He acted most competently. The veteran socialist leader, Achille Van Acker, was able to form, on 23 April 1954, a bipartite government consisting of nine socialists and seven Liberal cabinet Ministers, and to remain in power a full four years until 23 June 1958, during which time the delicate negotiations for setting up the European Economic Community (ratified by the Treaty of Rome, on 25 March 1957) were carried through and complemented by a further treaty creating the European Atomic Energy Community (Euratom) to establish a common market in the nuclear industry. In all of this, of course, Paul-Henri Spaak was again a prime mover and an indefatigable champion of Belgium's interests and the role she would have to play.

With the rugged, robust, and down-to-earth Van Acker, Baudouin was quickly on friendly terms. They liked and respected one another, and from this liking Baudouin drew strength and confidence further to assert himself to the exercise of his royal prerogatives. He decided, with full ministerial approval, that the time had come for him to make a tour of the Belgian Congo, to show himself to his peoples there, and to get first-hand information on present problems and discontents. He left on 15 May 1955 and, after a tumultuous reception two days later at Leopoldville, covered some 10,000 kilometres. At Leopoldville he made it quite clear that he was on a fact-finding tour to be properly informed in his efforts to seek a solution to the Congo question, and on his return to Belgium on 13 June was in no doubt as to his popularity and the success of his mission. In a carefully prepared speech delivered on 1 July he stressed that the vital question, as he saw it, was the establishment of better and more harmonious relationships between the whites and Congolese; he underlined the hardship and real deprivation that many Congolese families suffered through almost enforced migration from the country to the towns to cope with rapidly expanding industrial development; and he announced the creation of a special King's Purse (*Fonds du Roi*) to alleviate this suffering and to help bring about decent living and family conditions for these displaced persons. The speech received respectful and world-wide comment.

Baudouin was no less resolute in now turning his attention to the economic and social problems that faced Belgium itself and, in this instance ably helped and guided by his father, received on 30 May 1956 a delegation of industrialists to whom he was equally forthright. Belgium, he argued, had always been in the vanguard of social progress and must remain so. How, he asked, was Belgium to face up to present-day consequences of this policy which already afforded its workers higher salaries and a shorter working-week than other industrial competitors? There must be a more determined effort and a co-ordination of policies at the managerial level to increase production to a maximum of efficiency – and this, in his opinion, could only come about on a basis of sound human relationships and mutual trust which must involve everyone, from the shop-floor upwards, in proper consultation. To this theme he was again to return when, at the official opening of the prodigiously successful World Exhibition in Brussels on 17 April 1958, he stated that 'technical know-how will not of itself create a civilised world. For technology to bring progress in its train it must be paralleled by corresponding changes in moral attitudes and by a firm will to work together in a common constructive effort.'

Economic Policy and Planning

In point of fact Belgium was already in process of realising the full implications of the role she had so assiduously sought as a leading commercial power in the creation of the New Europe and was having to adjust her economy accordingly. She must henceforward reckon with the fact that she had deliberately courted the choice of Brussels as the headquarters of the various European organisations set up under the Treaty of Rome, and her policy must now be essentially directed towards the balanced expansion of her economy, to continual adjustment to her position in the European Economic Community, and, consequently, towards diversification of her production. Brussels would rapidly become the commercial brain of Europe, the hub of great European industrial concentrations, the nerve centre which could issue instructions and send out authorised representatives to co-ordinate the progress of the international enterprises established within the Common Market. And the entire country must be geared to meet the agreed-on gradual reductions of internal customs tariffs inside the Common Market (roughly 10 per cent year by year so that by 1970 at the latest all should have disappeared) by a correspondingly greater economic and industrial effort.[1]

There must be an economic rejuvenation, parallel in intensity and importance to that of the 1870–1920 boom which had attracted foreign investment from all over the world and which had sent out highly skilled Belgians in control of industrial enterprises in places as far apart as Egypt, Russia, China, or Argentina. Fortunately the situation was favourable. To attract foreign investment there must be an abundance of highly skilled manpower and, thanks to the most efficiently organised education services (of which we shall speak fully in a later chapter), this was readily forthcoming. Nonetheless, nothing must be left to chance and an immediate important move educationally was the Schools' Pact of 1958, made law on 29 May 1959, which sought to end once and for all the struggle between Church and state for control of education and to emphasise the need for a more harmonious and imaginative policy for Belgium to play her part, along with the greater powers, in strengthening the

---

[1] This was in principle achieved by 1 July 1968 – eighteen months sooner than envisaged.

position and influence of the Western world. Monetary and price stability was also a prerequisite, and once again Belgium was most favourably placed in comparison with many other countries, statistics (using the basis of 1958=100) revealing that the wholesale price index is only lower in Federal Germany and in the United States. As for consumer prices, the Belgian index figure to date is the lowest in the Common Market with the sole exception of Luxembourg, and lower than the United Kingdom.

This happy state of affairs, resulting in an increase in the investment section of the gross national product from about 17 per cent in 1955 to over 22 per cent in 1966 and to a corresponding attraction of foreign capital (2.5 billion francs in 1959; 3.4 billion in 1960; 6.8 billion in 1962; 18 billion in 1965), was considerably strengthened by the passing of the so-called Economic Recovery Laws of 1959. The law of 24 May 1959 was aimed specifically at the smaller industries and provided for wider access to professional and trade credits for the skilled trades, light industry, and small and medium-sized businesses to modernise, re-tool, re-convert, and extend. The law of 17 July 1959 deals with general expansion and enables industrialists to obtain long-term credits for the creation, extension, conversion, and modernisation of all industries and skilled trades *so long as they are in keeping with the interests of the economy in general.* The law of 18 July 1959 has instituted special measures designed to combat economic and social problems in certain regions designated as 'developing regions'. These 'developing regions' are notable for such problems as structural unemployment, population migration, and daily or weekly commuting of manpower (so wasteful of time), and most favourable interest rates are granted on loans made to industrialists who elect to settle in these areas.[1] Finally, two Royal Decrees of 20 March 1961 and a third of 24 March 1961 have provided for state intervention in the remuneration of workers affected by the reconversion of their industries, for the reclassification of unemployed workers who change their place of residence, and for state aid in the selection, professional training, or reclassi-

---

[1] The successful implementation of this law has (ironically) exacerbated antagonisms between Flemings and Walloons, and if (as seems today possible) Belgium eventually becomes a loosely-knit two-state federation of Flemings and Walloons, then history must record the part played by the law in attracting foreign capital to establish 'clean' industries in formerly underprivileged Flemish areas at the expense of the outmoded industrial economy of Wallonia.

fication of personnel recruited with a view to the creation, extension, or reconversion of industrial enterprises.

To supplement the Economic Recovery Laws the government set up in 1959 a Bureau of Economic Planning, with the chief task of elaborating a medium-term economic and social development programme. This programme must itself fit in with the general framework of expansion planned for the national economy and deal in particular with production, the working population and employment, exports and investments, and income and the utilisation thereof. There then followed in 1962 the creation of the National Investment Corporation, entitled to issue state-guaranteed debentures and also to extend its support to private enterprises in the form of temporary capital participation, the holding thus acquired, however, being restricted to a maximum of 80 per cent of the capital invested. Its main task is seen as coming to the help of companies wishing to increase their production capacity, to rationalise or modernise their plant or equipment, to improve or reorganise their financial position, to operate a merger. It equally gives full financial encouragement to companies belonging to the same economic sector who desire to standardise their technical or commercial departments. Up to January 1968 the National Investment Corporation had participated with investments reaching almost 1,200 million francs.

Nevertheless, and despite the fact that over the last eight years' working of the Economic Recovery Laws direct or indirect foreign investment has totalled some 58,000 million francs and provided almost 44,000 new jobs, there is no room for self-complacency. Scarcely had Vanden Boeynants become Prime Minister on 19 March 1966, at the head of a Social Christian–Liberal coalition government, than a new law had to be passed (14 July 1966), complementary to the July 1959 laws, to cover special assistance for the speeding-up of reconversion projects, the economic development of the coalmining areas, and to help other regions at grips with urgent crucial problems. And later in the year, during the course of an important address delivered to the *Société d'Etudes et d'Expansion* on 20 October 1966, Vanden Boeynants spelled out the message as clearly as possible:

'Contrary to initial hopes, the application of the laws of 17 and 18 July 1959 has not produced any fundamental change in the industrial structure of the country. In fact, a large proportion of investments within the framework of the above laws was made in the steel sector – 41 per cent, followed by the metallurgical industry – 25 per cent, and only 10 per cent in the chemical industry. The credits granted have, to a large extent, been used to finance increases in capacity rather than bring about qualitative changes. I do not wish to say that this was a mistake, but that the preparation of our economy for a Europe of 1970 depends now, above all, on qualitative and structural changes.'

He stressed that special attention must be given to the problem of an orderly reduction in the output of coal mines which were costing the state more than 7 billion francs annually in subsidies and therefore placing too heavy a burden, in view of foreign competition, on the steel and electricity sectors in particular. He urged his audience to accept the fact that the time for individualism in industry and the traditional Belgian concept of the family-based small firm was long past:

'Companies of a certain size are better able to adapt themselves to the technical and economic conditions of modern production, to the possibilities offered by the Common Market for mass production, and to the severely competitive criteria of a worldwide market... The very nature of their size is a source of strength [and] in the enlarged perspective of the Europe of 1970 there is less reason than before to fear that concentration will lead to monopoly or impair the free-play of competition.'

He concluded by forecasting the implementation of yet another law, passed on 31 March 1967, aimed at correcting regional deficiencies in the expansion of the economy and at stopping the decline of industrial sectors without the prospect of the creation of new activities to replace them. And wisely, if only because of traditional distrust of too much state interference at provincial and local levels, this latest economic law challenges local enterprise to make the fullest use of what is termed a Regional Economic Expansion and Reconversion Fund, and prove that it can make a serious effort at reconversion and economic expansion that are both in its own and in the nation's interests. Obviously, of course, an attempt will be made to restrict the advantages provided to those regions which need them most. But the onus will be on the regions to rethink their economic policies and stake their claims accordingly. The local industrialist, businessman, and financier is still very much in the picture.

Benelux

It would seem that amid all this careful economic planning to safeguard Belgium's future interests within the framework of the Common Market, the role to be played by Benelux, and indeed its importance, has to some extent been eclipsed. This is only partly true, though it must be remembered that when the idea of Benelux was first mooted no one could have foreseen even the possibility of achieving a European Economic Community in our time. Thus, Benelux came to be seen as a necessary first step towards the goal, and without Benelux the Common Market could never have existed as at present constituted in the same way as Benelux could not have existed without the earlier Belgian-Luxembourg Union of 6 March 1922. This important step not only created a customs union free from internal tariff barriers, but also established parity of esteem between the Belgian and Luxembourg francs, created a common gold and foreign exchange reserve in the National Bank of Belgium, provided for the joint negotiation of trade agreements, established a large degree of integration in the administration of customs, formed a common pool for the receipt of customs and excise duties to be divided between the two countries on the basis of their populations, and introduced unified trade statistics. The two countries signed a second convention on 23 May 1935 to establish a common system of import and export licensing, and the Belgian-Luxembourg Economic Union then came properly into being. A new Belgian-Luxembourg convention was signed on 29 January 1963 and came into force on 1 August 1965. Its chief aim was to codify and clarify earlier agreements and to abolish previous administering bodies in favour of complete parity of control between the two countries.

It was on the basis of the pre-war success of the Belgian-Luxembourg Economic Union that Benelux was dreamed up in exile. It began with a simple monetary agreement implemented on 21 October 1943 and led to the Benelux Customs Convention of 5 September 1944. This we have already briefly noted.[1] We have also noted the difficulties that beset Benelux in the immediate post-war years,[2] leading to a pre-union agreement of 15 October 1949, and there can be no doubt that these difficulties, vexatious though they were at the time, were of inestimable service in that their solution helped clear the ground for a smoother and swifter inauguration of the Common

[1] See above, p. 128.   [2] See above, pp. 149–50.

Market. While negotiations for establishing the Common Market were afoot, little further beyond implementation of the 1949 pre-union agreement took place on the Benelux front, but once the Common Market had become a reality the Benelux countries were at last able to sign the Benelux Economic Union on 3 February 1958 and agree that it should come into effect as from 1 November 1960, though a delay of five years was allowed before certain articles in the treaty were to be fully implemented. When the Benelux Committee of Ministers again met in October 1965 it was found that decisions that would have to be taken within the framework of the Common Market would effectively remove the need to implement most of the outstanding treaty articles. So the matter rests, it being very unlikely that the scope of the Benelux Economic Union can now be broadened much further. What it can do and what it is doing with all the powers of persuasion at its command is to urge strongly the acceptance of Great Britain into the Common Market with the least possible delay.

Gaston Eyskens (1958–61)

At the 1958 elections Van Acker's Socialist–Liberal coalition government had to give way to the Social Christians, whose influence had been on the increase and who, in effect, have remained in power ever since. Eyskens first tried to govern with a slender majority but soon (within four months) had to come to terms with the Liberals and so managed to retain office for almost three years. The situation was tricky because of Gaston Eyskens' somewhat inept earlier involvement in the Royal Question, but Baudouin had by now much more self-assurance and Eyskens was wise enough to encourage the King to make the fullest possible use of his royal prerogatives on the basis of his already proven ability. Baudouin was allowed, for example, considerable latitude and independence of action over the Congo question. He successfully opposed the removal of the Governor-General, Henri Cornélis, whose policies his Ministers no longer favoured. And on 13 January 1959 it was Baudouin, not Eyskens, who addressed the Belgian people on the nature and importance of the Fourth of January uprisings in Leopoldville, telling them in no uncertain terms that they would very soon have to grant the Congolese their independence. Similarly, despite the pleas of his Ministers, who feared for his safety, he insisted on leaving for a further fact-finding tour of the Congo the following December.

In May 1959 Baudouin left for what turned out to be a triumphant state visit to the United States, during the course of which he made a moving appeal for world peace at a joint session of Congress. It was now for the first time, thanks to the wide coverage given his tour through the medium of television, that the Belgian people came to see Baudouin as he really was—relaxed, gay, capable of real enjoyment and real understanding if only he were allowed to be himself. It was another Baudouin they saw, and a Baudouin they liked and wanted to welcome back. Yet once again the royal image was to be set back a little. In April 1959 Albert, Prince of Liège, had announced his engagement to the Italian Princess Paola Ruffo di Calabria. The Belgians were looking forward with tremendous enthusiasm to the junketing that would accompany the first real piece of pomp and royal ceremony since the war—only to learn that Pope John XXIII had agreed to marry the couple in the Vatican, Baudouin having arranged this as a purely family matter without troubling to consult his Ministers. There was an outcry. Let Baudouin and the rest of the royal family be themselves as much as they pleased, provided they did not forget they were the *Belgian* royal family and what their Belgian duties were. In this instance their duty was to provide an excuse for a junketing, and, moreover, not to exacerbate anti-clerical feelings. Pope John tactfully withdrew his offer, Baudouin announced full ceremonial plans for the wedding to be held in Brussels, and on 2 July the marriage was solemnised in due form to everyone's ultimate satisfaction.

Baudouin's December visit to the Congo led to the Round Table Conference called in Brussels for January 1960, and on 21 February he made a special speech to the assembled delegates, urging careful phasing of the move to independence. When independence finally came on 30 June 1960, Baudouin considered it his duty to be in Leopoldville and to make a suitable and sincere congratulatory speech in the presence of the recently elected Prime Minister, Patrice Lumumba. The insults and invective which the politically intoxicated Lumumba churlishly conjured up in his reply were taken by Baudouin with considerable dignity and restraint. The Belgians had every reason to be proud of their young king, and prouder still they were when he became engaged on 16 September 1960 to the Spanish Doña Fabiola de Mora y Aragón and married her in Brussels on 15 December. Queen Fabiola has since won the affections of the Belgians in much the same way as did Queen Astrid. The royal couple have become the kind of symbol the Belgians always hanker after – in this case one of soundly based domestic felicity which releases energy for disinterested devotion on the part of both to every facet of Belgian life. The fact, distressing for Queen Fabiola, that she has proved unable to bear children has probably endeared her in even more subtle ways to her people, and has at the same time focused attention on the heir-apparent, Prince Albert of Liège, and his family. Baudouin and Albert, as brothers always very close and liking and doing the same things, have in their own separate ways placed the royal family firmly in the modern idiom and more surely in touch with the realities of the present age. Once again the Belgian people are being well served.

The main preoccupations of Gaston Eyskens' ministries were those of stabilising the economy in view of a general world recession and of coping with the consequences of the granting of independence to the Congo. The Economic Recovery Laws we have already discussed. Towards the end of 1959 Belgium had more than 7 million tons of surplus coal and it became imperative to close down unprofitable mines and to reduce the working days to four per week. This naturally led to a series of strikes in the Borinage and throughout Hainaut, and there were also demonstrations in Ghent at the enforced closure of a number of textile factories. To ensure a balanced budget for 1960 drastic economies had to be effected. One immediate result was the reduction in September of the period of compulsory military service to twelve months.

An inevitable sequel to the granting of independence to the Congo was the so-called Austerity Programme, whereby on 7 November 1960 Eyskens published a bill for economic expansion, social progress, and financial rehabilitation. He proposed to reduce expenditure by 11,000 million francs and to increase taxation to the tune of some 4,000 million. Subsidies to unproductive coal mines, particularly in the Mons region, were to be cut, but in return a five-year plan for industrial expansion was announced, calculated to create some 20,000 new jobs annually. Public works were also to be extended over a period of fifteen years at the cost of 148,000 million francs. The bill was reluctantly accepted by both Houses on 18 December, but two days later the Socialist Trade Union, predominantly Walloon in membership, ordered a general strike on the grounds that increased taxation and reduction in social benefits would force the workers to bear the brunt of the programme. The

Catholic Trade Union, on the other hand (some 800,000 strong and mainly Flemish, whereas the Walloon membership was only around 700,000), refused to strike, declaring that the various provisions of the bill *in toto* held many future advantages for the workers. Baudouin had to cut short his honeymoon and return to Belgium on 29 December. The strike, virtually total throughout Wallonia, prolonged itself into January 1961. Some serious rioting occurred, particularly in Brussels and Liège. It was thought prudent to recall some troops from the NATO forces in Germany. One man was killed in Brussels, another died of wounds in Liège, and many were injured. Mounting pressure from the Catholic Trade Union, combined with dismay on the part of the Walloon socialists, led to the latter eventually seeking a compromise solution whereby the changes in social security provisions should be submitted to a tripartite Commission for Labour and Employment. This was agreed. The strikes ended. The bill became law on 13 January 1961 and was given the sanction of the Senate the following month.

From the point of view of present-day difficulties, however, the most important aspect of the strike was that it highlighted for the first time the divisive nature of Walloon and Flemish aspirations. A delegation of Walloon socialist deputies petitioned Baudouin to intervene on the grounds that the government was deliberately disadvantaging the industrial south by establishing newer and more productive industrial plant in the Flemish provinces. They asked for structural reforms, both economic and political, that could only lead to federalism. Following this lead, the ardent Socialist Trade Union leader, André Renard, created his Walloon Popular Front movement, designed to bring about Walloon separatism as the sole basis on which the declining Walloon industrial output could match the menace of growing Flemish aspirations. Not unnaturally, the Flemings riposted in kind, conscious of their numerical superiority and determined, now that they saw themselves for the first time since 1830 not the underdogs, to hold on to and extend all the advantages that were accruing to them. With the death of André Renard in 1962 most of the fire went out of the Walloon Popular Front movement, but the damage was done.

This became clear when the Liberals withdrew their support of the government over differences on the application of the Austerity Law and so forced a new election. Baudouin dissolved Parliament on 20 February 1961, but was firm enough to make two stipulations:

that the coalition government should remain in office until after the elections and that the law should not become operative until after the new Parliament had assembled. The elections were held on 26 March, and for the first time since the war right-wing conservatives, standing as independents, and members of the extremist Flemish People's Union won seats at the expense of the Social Christians. The constitution of the two chambers now became as follows:

	Deputies	Senate
Social Christians	96	47
Socialists	84	45
Liberals	20	11
Communists	5	1
Flemish Nationalists	5	2
Independents	2	

A Social Christian and socialist coalition was the only possibility and this was headed by Théo Lefèvre, with Spaak as vice-premier and also in charge of Foreign Affairs. The Liberal Party, discontented with its present image and poor following throughout Belgium, now decided to change its name to that of Party of Liberty and Progress (PLP), hoping thereby to attract discontented Social Christians to its banner.

Théo Lefèvre (1961-5)

Of course, this was nothing more than a marriage of convenience between the two major parties, but it worked and the government was able to pass complicated legislation on the linguistic problems, deal with various intricate social security problems (which provoked a doctors' revolt in 1964), and yet manage to remain in office for a full span of four years and three months. Lefèvre began by promising that the controversial issues of the Austerity Law would be closely re-examined and then went on to announce a programme of state planning for industry, fiscal reform, the establishment of a coal directorate, the definition of linguistic frontiers, and a solution to the problems of bilingual Brussels. We will deal fully with the linguistic problems in a later chapter, though it is necessary to note here that by July 1963 matters had reached such an impasse that the government sought to resign and had to be prevented by Baudouin from so doing.

Meanwhile, full employment was maintained, industrial expansion continued, and several new and important industrial plants were opened by British, American, German, and Japanese companies. With only 0.3 per cent of the total world population Belgium was now accounting for 3.5 per cent of world trade. On 1 July 1962 the African mandate territories of Ruanda-Urundi became independent and diplomatic relations were at last resumed with the Congo, many Belgians then returning either to take up their old jobs again or to act in specialist (especially teaching) or advisory capacities as required. In March 1964 Spaak paid an official visit to Leopoldville to discuss problems of giving technical and financial aid to the Congolese, to effect the proper transfer of formerly held Belgian military bases, and to obtain guarantees for the safety of Belgian citizens within the Congo. In August of the same year he was able to resume diplomatic relations with the United Arab Republic, obtain compensation for the sacking of the Belgian Embassy in Cairo in February 1961, and secure the return of all Belgian property that had then been sequestrated.[1]

The social security programme of the government ran into difficulties with the medical profession when it became known in the summer of 1963 that a health service, not dissimilar from that in Great Britain, was envisaged. The doctors threatened strike action and the government promised emendations. Mistrustful, the doctors for the first time felt the need for a union of their own and speedily created the *Chambres Syndicales des Médicins*, recruiting to its fold some 10,000 of the 12,000 registered practitioners. The Leburton Law, as it came to be called (after the name of the socialist Minister for Welfare, Edmond Leburton), came into force on 1 January 1964 and called for compulsory registration and fixed medical fees, as opposed to the free and voluntary National Health system as then in force. The doctors objected strongly to fixed fees for all patients, though they did accept state-regulated and state-paid fees for medical treatment of pensioners, widows with low incomes, orphans, and permanent invalids. A general medical strike was called for 1 April 1964. The government retaliated by calling up all doctors under the age of forty-five for military service.[2] The doctors took their revenge by reporting for duty minus their own personal items of medical

---

[1] For details, see below, p. 223.

[2] *All* able-bodied doctors in Belgium are liable for military service until they reach the age of forty-five.

equipment (stethoscopes and the like) which the government was legally bound to supply and was in no position to do in such quantities. Much confusion followed which everyone enjoyed at the government's expense, for the doctors, of course, had taken great care to have emergency cadres laid on during the strike to cope with the requirements of the really and dangerously ill.

To solve the deadlock the rectors of the four universities offered their mediation. Agreement was finally reached on 25 June – again a typical Belgian compromise – whereby 60 per cent of the doctors agreed to a new standardised fee arrangement (the other 40 per cent being free to opt out), the government undertaking in discussions with trade unions and employers that health insurance subscriptions would not in the immediate future be increased to meet the deficit the changes would entail. This became law on 1 July 1964. The system is financed by equal dues paid by workers and employers and by a substantial contribution from the state. The insurance system pays 75 per cent of the agreed fees charged by the general practitioner and 100 per cent of the agreed fees charged by a specialist in certain circumstances. The following table should make the position clear:

Care	Agreed Fees	Reimbursements Widows Orphans Pensioners Disabled, etc.	All others
Visit to general practitioner	63 frcs.	63 frcs.	48 frcs.
Practitioner's visit to home of patient	79 frcs.	79 frcs.	59 frcs.
Visit to specialist	126 frcs.	126 frcs.	95–126 frcs.

By a Royal Decree of 31 December 1965 the state contribution towards the purchase of prescribed medicines became 10 per cent only of the cost. Thus the patient pays 90 per cent, though his contribution may not exceed 50 francs for patent medicines (22 francs for widows, orphans, etc.) nor 20 francs for prescriptions made up by a dispensing chemist. All in all, an ingenious compromise device which respects individual freedom and dignity (so dear to the Belgian) and which seems to be working smoothly.

By October 1964, at the time of the *communal* elections, a crushing defeat was registered for both the government parties, with corresponding big gains by Liberals (whose new image was asserting itself) and smaller gains for the communist and national groups. Plainly the Lefèvre administration was losing the confidence of the people, chiefly over its handling of the linguistic problems and the health service fiasco, but also because it was running into some financial problems and was obviously going to have difficulties in balancing the budget. In 1964 the relatively modest growth in industrial output was not matching up to higher wages and a consequent rise in consumer and wholesale prices.

Pierre Harmel (1965–6)

A general election was called for 23 May 1965 and the results of the polling bore out the trend noticed the previous October. The Social Christians lost heavily to the Flemish party in Flanders, to the French-speaking independents in the Brussels agglomeration, and to the PLP everywhere. The Social Christians retained only 77 seats and the socialists only 64. The PLP increased its representation to 48. The Flemish Nationalists took 12 seats (an important gain of 7), the communists 6, and the independents 5. The PLP were now a force to be reckoned with and it was not until 27 July that Pierre Harmel was able to form a further coalition government of Social Christians and socialists. Harmel's first task was to wipe out the 1965 budgetary deficit he had inherited and to stimulate industrial output. He also announced a programme of making Belgium more regional in character, of conceding cultural autonomy, of establishing commissions to find ways of improving relations between the Flemish, Walloon, and Brussels regions, and a new impetus to the promotion of scientific research. He stressed that Belgium's future at the heart of a modern Europe demanded remodelling and replanning along these lines, and that an important element must be a new policy of social and human progress which gave its immediate attention

'to encourage every boy and girl to continue their education or training right up to the uttermost limits of their aptitudes. This obliges us to deal with the problem of the university, higher education, and technical training from the broadest possible standpoint and with a complete absence of any prejudice.'

Given the strength of the PLP in the new Chamber of Deputies

Harmel had at first tried to form a tripartite government and had failed. The fact that he had failed meant that his ministry must be of short-lived duration. He was sniped at from the Flemish provinces on the grounds that his Cabinet contained fourteen French-speaking Ministers as opposed to thirteen Flemings. Surely the numbers were disproportionate and could only jeopardise Flemish interests. What again about all this talk of regional responsibility if there was not to be regional representation in the Cabinet?[1] He was praised, however, for giving his Cabinet a new pyramid structure, flanking himself with five co-ordinating Ministers who, in turn, were assisted by a series of Ministers and Secretaries of State. And he was given credit for making Mme Marguerite de Riemaecker Minister for Family and Housing and so introducing the first woman in Belgian history into cabinet proceedings.

Paul Vanden Boeynants (1966–8)

In January 1966 the doctors demanded a 25 per cent increase on their agreed fees in view of the extra paper-work involved in operating the Health Service. The government would only offer 5 per cent. A threatened strike was only averted on Baudouin's personal intervention on 6 February. A month later Harmel had to admit that he could no longer carry Parliament with him and the shrewd and dynamic Vanden Boeynants managed to achieve a Social Christian–Liberal (PLP) coalition and keep everybody happy by carefully balancing his Cabinet on a basis of regional/linguistic differences. He assumed office on 19 March 1966 and his Cabinet, consisting of twelve Social Christians and seven Liberals, was linguistically split to contain twelve Flemish-speaking members, six French-speaking, and five from the bilingual Brussels agglomeration.[2] Spaak was dropped as Foreign Minister in favour of Pierre Harmel. He had in any case become more and more absorbed in international work on a non-political basis and he finally resigned from the Socialist Party in July 1966 to devote himself more wholeheartedly to this. Vanden Boeynants promised to make every effort to effect reconciliation between the language groups, to work hard for a widening of the concept of the European Economic Community (in this sense he has

[1] *De Nieuwe Gids* (29 July 1965).
[2] Arithmetic differences are accounted for by the presence of Secretaries of State.

proved a strong protagonist for Great Britain), to keep public spending within reasonable limits but at the same time to encourage industrial output both nationally and regionally,[1] and to give every possible support to NATO.

In July 1967 the Council of Ministers of the European Economic Community agreed on merging the separate commissions of the Common Market, Euratom, and the Coal and Steel Community into one, and this came into practical effect when they were all decanted into one massive new building in the Rue de la Loi in February 1968. On 31 October 1967 Vanden Boeynants, in an address to the Council of Ministers, urged the necessity for integrated European technological co-operation to face up to the American challenge; he made the point again with equal firmness on an official visit to London on 14–15 November 1967 specifically for talks on the subject of Great Britain's entry to the Common Market. And within two days of the devaluation of the British pound sterling on 19 November 1967 the Belgian National Bank was granting Great Britain a loan of 2,500 million francs over and above her contribution through the International Monetary Fund (in which Belgium participates to the extent of one per cent of her national budget).

Much thought was given to repeated demands from the Congo for technical aid of various kinds, for since the savage Congolese rebellion of 24 November 1964 (when Belgians and other whites had been held as hostages or killed, and a dramatic rescue operation had had to be mounted by Belgian parachute troops), Belgium was chary of needlessly risking the lives of her nationals with no means of protecting them, or of incurring again the possible displeasure of the United Nations if she sought to afford help and protection should they be in danger. In the event, she did agree in October 1967 to facilitate the recruitment of personnel for the Congolese universities and secondary schools, and she signed an agreement with Ruanda relative to financial and technical aid she was prepared to provide for 1968. The report of a special mission of two representatives of the Christian and Socialist Trade Unions to the Congo in November was optimistic enough for some 200 technical personnel to be released for service there, though it was stressed that the Belgian government was at present only authorising a limited and selective resumption of such assistance.

[1] We have already discussed the measures taken in this direction. See above, pp. 159–60.

Official estimates released on 6 October 1967 revealed that the economic situation of Belgium remained steadily progressive, though constant vigilance was necessary. Investments throughout the whole of Belgium since the beginning of the year, either for projects under way or projects definitely decided upon, amounted to over 42 milliard Belgian francs and were making 24,603 new jobs available. Most new jobs were being created in Hainaut, whereas Antwerp (as was only to be expected because of its unrivalled port facilities) enjoyed the largest influx of capital. The Belgian Minister for Economic Affairs, Jacques Van Offelen, gave further evidence of the watch that was being kept on the economy of the country when, receiving a special envoy from President Johnson on 4 January 1968, he stated that:

'American investments are important for us because they represent some nine-tenths of the total of foreign equipment installations in our country. These investments concern primarily the areas of the country which are experiencing economic difficulties... The Belgian position is to obtain the largest possible quota of the export of American capital for Belgium so as to ensure the carrying through of projects already started as well as those under negotiation, and in addition those which will come up at a future date.'

On 27 January 1968 the Belgian government called for a 4 per cent increase in the gross national product annually between 1968 and 1970. And the Minister for State Insurance, Placide De Paepe, announced that his department would be spending in 1968, in direct and indirect payments on social allowances, 163,000 million francs – a record for the country.

In his capacity as Foreign Minister Pierre Harmel recommended the readaptation of NATO to secure improved co-operation and greater sophistication in the use and deployment of its resources, and to show that Belgium at least would play her part to the full announced on 21 November 1967 a plan for the structural reorganisation of the Belgian armed forces between 1968 and 1972. Further to implement this a Belgo–German agreement was signed on 14 December 1967 for the purchase by Belgium of 334 Leopard tanks of German manufacture, the contract calling for delivery to start in February 1968 and to spread over a period finishing early in 1970. In return Germany undertook to place orders on the Belgian market, spread over three years, and amounting to 4,535 million Belgian francs – only 5 million francs short of the Belgian order for tanks.

The Fall of Vanden Boeynants

Meanwhile, the political situation on the linguistic front had been steadily worsening and a rueful Vanden Boeynants had to admit publicly that 'as soon as the language problem is raised all groups entrench themselves in fixed positions which make dialogue impossible'. The crisis erupted over the University of Louvain, when a caucus of eight Flemish Social Christian members of the Cabinet resigned in protest at the government's refusal to commit itself to a transfer of the French-language faculties to French-speaking territory. On 7 February 1968 Vanden Boeynants had no other alternative but to tender his resignation to the King, and the situation was so explosive that Baudouin could do none other than accept it. It was a sorry and tragic moment, full of portents for the future, for it was the first time in Belgium's history that a government had fallen over the language issue. A group of Social Christians attempted to save the situation and explored every avenue to constitute another acceptable government. It was fruitless. It seemed that the Flemish surge towards autonomy was irresistible. Accordingly the group's spokesman, Paul-Willem Segers, had to advise the King to dissolve Parliament and call for a general election.

Amid considerable gloom and in some confusion of mind the Belgians went to the polls on 31 March, conscious that the polling was bound to be a veiled referendum as to whether Belgium should remain a unified state. Their confusion arose from the fact that they found the main political parties now hopelessly split and presenting them with a bewildering list of candidates from which to choose. The Flemish and the French-speaking wings of the Social Christians were fighting the election separately. Vanden Boeynants was determined to seek a vote of confidence on his undoubtedly successful term as Prime Minister and therefore would have nothing to do with either wing of the Social Christians. Instead he stood with a list of his own in Brussels. The socialists generally held together on the basis of a complicated compromise on economic decentralisation, though this did not stop their Flemish wing breaking free in Brussels and thus presenting the electorate there with two socialist lists. The Flemish Nationalists were bound to win votes in Flanders from both the Social Christians and the socialists on the basis of an electoral campaign which emphasised the granting of equal social opportunities for all Flemings and championed federalism, with Brussels to be administered as a state district. Traditionally right-wing, they were now noticeably attracting to their banner some outstanding but politically radical youngsters.

The results of the elections were better than was feared. The Social Christians retained 69 seats (a loss of 8), the socialists 59 seats (a loss of 5), and the Liberals 47 seats (a loss of one). On the other hand, the Flemish Nationalists and the left-wing Walloon Federalists almost doubled their representation by taking 20 seats (a gain of 8) and 12 seats (a gain of 7) respectively. The communists lost one seat to retain five. On 1 April the King began consultations with Vanden Boeynants on the formation of a new government, for in principle the outgoing coalition government could have carried on with a majority of ten and Vanden Boeynants himself had scored a huge personal triumph in Brussels, candidates on his list carrying off nine of the twelve contested seats. In practice, however, Vanden Boeynants had first of all to mediate between his Flemish and French-speaking wings and restore some semblance of unity. He failed. Every alternative was tried, including a proposal for a three-party 'national' government which the socialists rejected. The nub of the problem was that if constitutional changes were to be introduced to bring about any form of federalism and so do away with Belgium as a unitary state, then such changes must be carried through Parliament by a two-thirds majority. And on this very question of federalism the Flemish and French-speaking wings of the Social Christians proved to be as suspicious of one another as were the Flemish Nationalists and the Walloon Federalists.

The weeks slipped by and on 7 May King Baudouin again urged Vanden Boeynants to try to give him a government. Again Vanden Boeynants failed. It was not until 17 June, after nearly five days of delicate negotiations, that the former Catholic leader, Gaston Eyskens, was able to announce a coalition with the socialists and to proclaim the sixty-fourth – and largest – Cabinet since Belgium was founded in 1830. It is divided painstakingly between fourteen Flemish and fourteen Walloon Ministers with Eyskens himself, as a moderate Fleming, acting as link between the two groups. To satisfy growing pressure for more Flemish and Walloon autonomy he has now set up separate Ministries of Education, of Culture, of Regional

Economic Development, and has also created new Ministries for Relations between the two national groups, the one headed by a Fleming, the other by a Walloon. Needless to say, the government still does not command the two-thirds majority necessary for implementing constitutional reforms.

Chapter 13

The Language Dilemma

THE COLLAPSE OF VANDEN BOEYNANTS' GOVERNMENT over the language issue has now made it quite plain that the traditional concept of a strongly centralised unitary state, governed from Brussels, is fast disappearing; probably to be replaced by a form of federalism which lines up the Walloons and the Flemings, not so much in mutual distrust and antagonism as in some form of concerted (if not joint) action to reject the idea of a mighty, centralised, and Frenchified Brussels which, though housing only 10 per cent of Belgium's total population, claims to be in control of their separate destinies.[1] For all practical purposes, however, we have to remember that the present language conflicts in Belgium date from the founding of the kingdom of Belgium in 1830, and to understand fully how the present impasse has been reached we must glance at the historical background to the linguistic relations between the Flemings and the Walloons.

The linguistic frontier in Belgium dates from at least the third century when the Salian Franks began to filter within the confines of the Roman empire. This movement was accelerated in the fifth century when the Romans, threatened by invasion from the Goths, began to withdraw their legions from the north and thus facilitated the crossing of the Rhine by the Franks who quickly settled on territory as far south as a line roughly running from Maestricht across what is now Belgium, passing to the south of Brussels and Lille, and reaching the North Sea near Boulogne. Because this district was sparsely populated the invaders became firmly rooted

---

[1] It is an interesting phenomenon and, while I would not wish to press the comparison at all closely, I find it equally interesting that this attitude coincides with the waves of national individualism now evident not only in Brittany, Wales, and Scotland, but also in Russian satellite communist countries; exactly as the nineteenth-century awakening of the Flemings to a new pride in their language, literature, and culture coincided with similar linguistic-cultural revivals throughout nineteenth-century Europe.

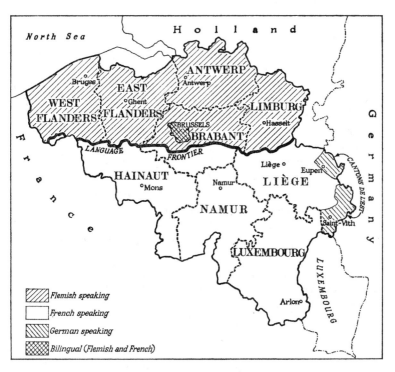

THE LANGUAGES OF BELGIUM

and were able to establish there both their own customs and their native Germanic tongue. Why the invading Franks never moved south of this east to west line across Belgium remains a mystery.[1] Other Franks, of course, and particularly under such leaders as Clovis, did pour into what was then called Gaul, but here they were slowly absorbed by a people of superior numbers and superior civilisation, and soon came to adopt the religion, customs, and language of the Gauls. Thus, French came to be spoken from the Mediterranean as far north as the Maestricht–Boulogne line, and above that line dense Frankish colonisation made the low Germanic tongue of the Franks supreme.

When Charlemagne's empire was partitioned in 843 at the Treaty of Verdun, no attempt was made to have political boundaries follow linguistic frontiers. After all, the official written language was Latin and the common people had no need to understand what was going on. Between the eleventh and fourteenth centuries the French language gained considerable prestige throughout the greater part of Europe and the songs of the *trouvères* were certainly known and appreciated in the provinces of Brabant, Liège, and Flanders, where French influence was most strong in that the Count of Flanders owed his allegiance to the Kings of France. Nevertheless, throughout the Middle Ages the Flemish tongue sturdily maintained itself and French, though undeniably spoken by most members of the Flemish bourgeoisie, never became in any sense predominant. Nor did the rival languages become standards around which opposing political and religious factions might rally.

Indeed, in the Burgundian and Habsburg periods each new prince upon his accession took his oath in Flemish and the Emperor Charles V not only had part of his education in the Netherlands but also spoke fluent Flemish. The first marked change came during the Spanish period under Philip II, when for the first time French came to be regularly employed for correspondence between the provincial states and all acts pertaining to the whole territory were drafted in French. Even then, however, it was still an accepted principle that those who governed at a local level should use the language of their subjects. The revolt of the Netherlands against Spanish oppression led to the secession of the Northern Provinces, formally recognised by

[1] One theory is that a line of Roman fortifications along the road from Cologne to Boulogne held the Franks from colonising south of the present linguistic boundary.

the Treaty of Westphalia in 1648, to become a strong and independent Holland. The Southern Provinces (today known as Belgium and comprising the two linguistic groups of Flemings and French-speaking Walloons) were linked first to Spain, then to Austria, and finally came under French domination between 1792 and 1815. The great favour which the French language and culture enjoyed throughout the eighteenth century both at Frederick the Great's court in Berlin and also in Vienna meant, however, that even under Austrian rule (1714–92) French became the predominant language in these Southern Provinces, and again under Austrian rule the Flemish bourgeoisie were already taking great pride in sending their children to be educated either in France or in a Walloon city, and disdaining their own language and culture.

The creation of the United Netherlands in 1815 might have seemed at the time politically desirable, but no real arguments could then be put forward from a nationalist point of view to justify the move. For two centuries the Northern Provinces and the Southern Provinces had existed separately, and after the revolt in the sixteenth century they had been divided by religion. The Northern Provinces were largely Protestant; the Southern Provinces were almost entirely Catholic, the Dutch-speaking Flemings most fervently so. Again, after the political separation the Southern Provinces had followed Spain in her decay as an economic power and their foreign trade had been practically wiped out when the Dutch closed the Scheldt and thus deprived the port of Antwerp of access to the open sea. Attempts made at developing the port of Ostend had been frustrated by joint action on the part of the Dutch, French, and English. The Southern Provinces, therefore, had no love for their Dutch neighbours, no real feelings of affinity, and it is significant that when the Dutch rose in revolt against the Napoleonic régime the southerners remained quiescent. Thus, once the union between Holland and Belgium had been effected at the behest of the major European powers, the Dutch were all too ready to regard Belgium as conquered territory and the Belgians to consider the Dutch as foreigners and usurpers.

Nevertheless, and despite the ill-feeling which the historical past had engendered between the Dutch and the Belgians, this enforced union did arouse a new interest in Netherlandish culture and literature among the Flemings, and gave impetus to a nascent Flemish movement. King William of Holland, as ruler of the United

Netherlands, naturally did his best to further the movement and so as an indirect consequence not only paved the way to Belgian independence, but at the same time added an extra dimension to the language problem: it was now inextricably caught up with educational issues which in their turn were later to impinge on and further complicate the religious and political attitudes. King William created new state secondary schools which adopted the Dutch language in all Flemish-speaking provinces, even to the point of using Dutch to teach Latin. Courses in the Dutch language were also provided in secondary schools throughout the Walloon provinces. Courses in Dutch language and literature were automatically offered in the three new universities he created for Belgium. The elementary-school system was revised on the Dutch pattern. And a new teacher-training college which King William opened at Lier in 1817 gave all its instruction in Dutch and became an important centre of Netherlandish sentiment.

Yet all William's attempts at fostering a new pride among the Flemings in their own language served only to intensify the differences between the Flemish-Belgian way of life and that of the Dutch; to alienate the French-speaking Flemish bourgeoisie; to make the Catholic clergy in Belgium increasingly suspicious of Dutch intentions; and to assume that encouragement of the Flemings to assert their linguistic rights was a clumsy Protestant move to infiltrate into that part of Belgium where the hold of Catholicism was traditionally strongest and most fervent. It was remembered, as never before, that throughout history the Southern Provinces had always held themselves apart and fought their own battles for their own individual conception of freedom. And the last two hundred years had intensified this feeling of national separateness and proved most convincingly that the accident of a common language (if only the language itself were involved) could safely be ignored in drawing political boundaries.

Thus, when the 1830 revolution came it sought not only to dissolve the political union with the Dutch but also to lessen the cultural and linguistic affinities with Holland. The leaders of the revolution were all members of the bourgeoisie and, as such, Flemings and French alike, were admirers of the French language and culture, and despisers of all things Netherlandish. French became the official language of the new kingdom. All new laws and regulations were written and published in French, though arrangements were made for translations of all official pronouncements to be issued in those provinces where the Flemish or German languages were in common daily use.[1]

The Flemings reacted patiently and realistically. They had to admit that Flemish was at a grave disadvantage in that it was predominantly a popular tongue and as such lacked stability: there were almost as many dialects and variations in popular speech as there were *communes*. What was lacking was discipline in the use of the language and some measure of conformity. But this could only come slowly through education and through the writings of Flemish men of letters, among whom the novelist Henri Conscience (1812–83) set an example for later authors to follow, and among whom also Frans Willems (1793–1846), the philologist, secured official recognition in 1844 for a new standardised form of Flemish on which he had been working for some five years. Leopold I also helped by appointing Conscience as Flemish tutor to his own children. By 1849 it had become politically possible to arrange regular philological conferences with the Dutch and to elaborate with them a project for a dictionary which would further stabilise orthography, grammar, and syntax. And recommendations from these conferences were finally adopted in 1864 (with some opposition from certain Flemish regional writers who deplored the passing of the colourful dialect forms) to make Flemish as a written language and as spoken in the schools and by intellectuals indistinguishable from the Dutch tongue.[2]

This Royal Decree of 21 November 1864 meant that parity of esteem between the Flemish and French tongues could no longer be indefinitely delayed. In 1873 the use of Flemish was made obligatory in all Flemish judicial proceedings and the same ruling was applied to all public administration throughout the Flemish provinces in 1878. The School Law of 1850 had made it obligatory for Flemish to be taught in all state secondary schools throughout the Flemish provinces as the second language, though difficulties of implementation immediately arose through a shortage of really competent

---

[1] An 1846 census revealed that 2,471,248 Belgians spoke Flemish as against 1,827,141 whose 'natural' tongue was French.

[2] The story of the rise and development of an indigenous Flemish literature (and also of how the great names in Belgian literature of French expression came to be of pure Flemish stock) is fascinating but too complicated to be discussed here. Interested readers should consult my *Modern Belgian Literature (1830–1960)*, London, 1966.

teachers, and it was not until 1864 that it became practically possible to continue the teaching of Flemish at an advanced level in the topmost forms of the secondary school, and not until 1874 that native Flemish speakers were leaving the universities in sufficient numbers to be recruited into the schools to teach the language thoroughly and efficiently. The first linguistic School Law was passed on 15 June 1883. It stipulated that all courses in the lower forms of secondary schools in Flemish areas must be given in Flemish, though French should be taught to promising pupils to enable them to continue their education at various advanced levels without feeling disadvantaged, and French courses must always be available for pupils who could not profit from instruction in Flemish. Secondary teacher-training courses in Flemish were started at the University of Ghent in 1884 and subsequently at the elementary teacher-training college in Bruges (later transferred to Ghent). On 6 July 1886 the Flemish Royal Academy of Letters came into existence. And a law of 15 April 1898 finally allowed Flemish to take its place beside French as an official language.

All these later measures and subsequent reforms in favour of the Flemish-speaking provinces were in effect due to the defeat of the Liberals by the Catholics in the 1884 elections – a defeat which kept the Catholics in power until after the First World War. The Catholics were only too aware that they owed their electoral triumph to the support of the Flemish provinces and they looked to their Flemish Catholic electorate as the main defence against the steady encroachment of radicalism and French free-thinking tendencies. And so it was that for the first time the linguistic question became intimately involved with religious belief which in turn was now much concerned with the political issues of the day. Radicalism flourished in the heavily industrialised Walloon provinces. The predominantly agricultural Flemish provinces remained cautiously conservative in approach and became more self-assured and positive as the reactionary hold of the French-speaking Flemish bourgeoisie weakened before a strong, youthful, and vigorous Flemish literary movement that had by now firmly established itself.

The one thing the Flemish intellectuals now lacked was a university and it became unthinkable that the State University of Ghent should continue to give instruction entirely in the French language, particularly now that satisfactory Flemish teacher-training courses were well established there. The struggle to secure complete *flamandisation* was a long, difficult, and bitter one and was not helped by the First World War hero and spiritual leader, Cardinal Mercier, who declared unequivocally that the language in higher education should be an international language and that for the Flemings it must be French. Attempts to provide separate French and Flemish sections failed in 1911 because of strong opposition from militant Flemings who demanded all or nothing. The situation was further bedevilled during the First World War when with their curious lack of *savoir-faire* and total misunderstanding of the true temper of the Belgian people the German occupying forces attempted to woo the Flemings and opened in 1916 a completely Flemish university in Ghent. Unfortunately, as usually happens in such circumstances, a number of naïve hotheads and extremists for the Flemish cause were attracted by the bait and became collaborators. Recriminations and trials followed the cessation of hostilities and the 'German' university was closed, though in his speech from the throne on 22 November 1918 King Albert was careful to promise the Flemings greater equality of status and a speedy solution to the university problem. Much compromise and patient and skilful negotiation resulted in a complicated bilingual arrangement on 31 July 1923, which satisfied nobody, and it was not until 5 April 1930 that Ghent received its purely Flemish charter.

The death of Cardinal Mercier in 1926, the noticeable decline in prestige of the French nation and the French way of life in the period between the two wars, the world-wide recognition now being accorded distinguished Flemish men of letters, and the determined efforts of various socialist Ministers who came to power after 1918 — all these factors now combined in the between-the-wars period to strengthen the Flemish cause. Political leaders were now emerging who had outgrown the inferiority complex of their predecessors; there were brilliant young doctors, lawyers, priests, and writers who wrote and spoke Flemish for all purposes of both their private and public lives; and there had emerged (unfortunately) an extremist movement, the Flemish National Front (VNV), whose aspirations for separatism stemmed from the anguished fumblings of groups of Flemish soldiers and padres who had manned the Yser front towards the end of the war. By 1933 the VNV, under its dynamic leader Staf de Clercq, claimed some 60,000 members and was actively campaigning for an autonomous if not a completely independent Flemish state. The movement came to parallel Degrelle's Rexist movement, was fired with similar nazified mystical ideals, likewise fished in the politically troubled waters of the late 1930s, and of course collaborated actively with the German occupying forces during the Second World War.

A law passed on 31 July 1921 obliged Ministers to communicate with provincial authorities in the language of the region. Separate Flemish sections were created in all *athénées* (academic grammar schools) in Flemish provinces and some key *écoles moyennes* (middle schools which took pupils only up to the age of fifteen) were completely turned over to instruction in Flemish over a three-year period on a year-by-year intake. On 10 September 1926 the socialist leader Camille Huysmans made teaching in Flemish compulsory in all *écoles moyennes* throughout the Flemish-speaking provinces, reserving a few classes in history, geography, science, and commerce only still to be given in French, and a year later, on 13 September 1927, he introduced a very complicated formula for Flemish *athénées* which in effect allowed all subjects to be taught partly in French and partly in Flemish with a marked bias in favour of the latter tongue.

In 1929 a huge Catholic and Flemish-inspired congress met at Dendermonde and passed several important resolutions which were finally embodied in the linguistic laws passed in the summer of 1932. In all government Ministries there were to be separate French and Flemish services. A Flemish Military Academy was established and the army itself was made bilingual in the sense that parallel French and Flemish units were created. All instruction at both the primary and secondary levels must henceforward be given in the language of the region, the other language (French or Flemish) becoming the first modern language to be studied. The Brussels agglomeration, where well over half the population now spoke French, was charged with ensuring that Flemish-speaking schools were provided for Flemish children living in predominantly French-speaking areas (and vice versa, of course) on the understanding that the language of the region was also taught as the first modern language after the first three years of schooling (i.e. from the age of nine).[1] Meanwhile

---

[1] These laws were harsher than might at first appear, in the sense that for the first time in the history of Belgium they deprived the parent of the right to have his children instructed in his own mother-tongue should he happen to be a Fleming, say, working in French-speaking Wallonia. By the same token, parents fortunate enough to be living in the Brussels agglomeration

the two 'free' universities of Louvain and Brussels matched the changeover of the State University of Ghent to becoming purely Flemish by offering parallel courses in French and Flemish, and so in effect becoming bilingual and giving a tidy pattern for the country of one French-speaking state university (Liège), one Flemish-speaking state university (Ghent), and the 'free' universities to deal with all comers. A further law of July 1935 made it obligatory for any defendant in a court case to be heard and tried in his mother-tongue, no matter where the offence was committed, and all was tidied up by a commission of 1937 which not only conceded full cultural autonomy to the Flemings but also gave French and Flemish equal official standing in their respective provinces in much the same way as holds in the various cantons of Switzerland.

Thus, on the outbreak of war there were no substantial grievances left in the minds of most Flemings and it was hoped that a certain harmony might now prevail, and so smother the aspirations of those diehard Flemings who still hankered after a separate Fleming state. The Flemings, it was felt, would be realistic and face the fact that the Dutch tongue they speak has a very limited and restricted use in the modern world and can never compete with universal languages such as French or English, praiseworthy and important though its literary output may be. In turn surely the Walloons must allow the Flemings their justifiable pride in their not undistinguished past and their literature and culture.

Unfortunately matters have not worked out that way at all for a variety of good reasons, unforeseen at the time of the passing of the 1932 laws. These laws had also required that a language census be taken every ten years. The first (and only) census took place in 1947 amid almost universal chaos and bitter acrimony resulting from disputes as to which villages along the language frontier should be considered bilingual or French- or Flemish-speaking. The results of the census, however, were shattering for the Walloons in that they revealed 51.3 per cent of the population speaking Dutch, 32.94 per cent speaking French, 15.7 per cent French and Flemish in the Brussels agglomeration, and one per cent speaking German. There was every indication that this trend would continue. The Walloons were further disheartened by the fact that not only was their own

escaped this restriction on their personal liberty. In other words the *Bruxel-lois* was privileged. So were sown the first seeds of growing distrust of bureau-cratic control of the rest of Belgium from Brussels.

industrial apparatus outmoded, their coal-fields exhausting themselves, their communications inadequate to cope with any modernisation attempted, but also that the Brussels bureaucrats seemed to be deliberately favouring the Flemings by setting up new technological projects in the Campine area and attracting foreign investment to that end. They equally strongly argued that it was nonsense in the modern post-war age still to compel them to teach Flemish as the second modern language when they should be becoming proficient in German, English, Russian, Spanish. The Flemings, of course, for the first time since the creation of the kingdom of Belgium in a position of unassailable strength, blandly refuted these charges, but did not make the situation less difficult by truthfully pointing out that the swing of modern industrial plant to Flemish territory was inevitable given the rapid technological advances made since the war.

Successive governments coped as best they could with the mounting discontent from Wallonia and the smooth (and understandable) intransigence of the Flemings. The coalmining industry of Wallonia was given government financial support and commissions were set up to consider the tricky nature of the linguistic boundaries as evinced by the 1947 census. A bill was passed in February 1962 to stabilise the boundaries by transferring Mouscron-Commines from West Flanders to Hainaut and the Voer region from Liège to Limburg. The Primate of Belgium, Cardinal Léon-Joseph Suenens, also mediated by declaring that henceforward the archbishopric of Mechlin should be renamed the archbishopric of Mechlin (Malines)-Brussels and that Antwerp should form a new and separate diocese. The bishops in conclave, as governors of the 'free' Catholic University of Louvain, reaffirmed that bilingual courses should continue even though Louvain itself was undisputably within Flemish territory. And on 8 November 1962 a new language law was passed which declared Brussels bilingual, insisted that all schools in the now clearly defined Flemish areas must teach in Flemish, and that in Brussels there must be a sufficient supply of Flemish-teaching schools, the decision as to whether a child attended a French or a Flemish school there being dependent on the language spoken by the father.

The following year another attempt was made to adjust the frontiers of the nine provinces, giving the French provinces a further 86,439 inhabitants, the Flemings 20,377, and the Brussels agglomeration 2,886, with the intention of increasing the number of its *communes* from nineteen to twenty-five. Predominantly Flemish-speaking *communes* in Brussels would be administered in Flemish, though a French-speaking minority could demand to have its documents presented to it in French. It was this decision which created such a storm of protest that Lefèvre threatened to resign and had to be prevented by Baudouin from so doing.[1] A compromise was found in July to guarantee the full rights of French-speaking minorities in any of the disputed Flemish *communes*. A further law passed in July 1963 reinforced the schools' decision of November 1962 by abolishing such schools as were still giving parallel classes in French and Flemish. All the teaching personnel in a given school must now speak the same language. And by the same token a dual Ministry of Education was instituted with each French-speaking administrator having his Flemish opposite number.

All these various conciliatory measures, ingenious though they were, satisfied no one and, indeed, the decision to make Brussels bilingual in this curious way incensed its one million inhabitants, emphasised the linguistic divisiveness, and confirmed the Flemish and Walloon provinces alike in their growing belief that Brussels had for too long had too much say in what should and should not be done with the remaining 8 million inhabitants outside the agglomeration. Brussels was tartly reminded that the Belgian flag flew only over Brussels. The Flemings had their lion and the Walloons their cockerel. Brussels was Brussels, so be it. But Flanders was Flanders and Wallonia was Wallonia. Extremists in Wallonia now urged complete political and economic autonomy for the Walloon provinces, while the Flemings sought separatism only on linguistic, administrative, judicial, and cultural grounds. Non-extremists, while against any form of federalism, saw the only possible solution to lie in some form of decentralisation.

By 1966, though a lot of the fire had gone out of the Walloon movement towards independence through the death four years earlier of its leader, André Renard, the Flemings were beginning to feel both frustrated at Harmel's attempts to 'freeze' the language situation and impatient with the bishops, who appeared to them

[1] The one international and important airport Belgium possesses is on Flemish territory in the Brussels agglomeration. So intransigent is the attitude that all administration is carried out in Flemish, much to the bewilderment of the traveller and the fury of the French-speaking *Bruxellois*.

still too wedded to Cardinal Mercier's belief that French must be the language of higher education throughout Belgium and were showing extreme reluctance to declare unequivocally that the University of Louvain was and must be Flemish. Student clashes occurred in Louvain late in 1965 and assumed more serious proportions in March 1966 to coincide with Flemish extremist rioting in Antwerp. It is to be remembered that the University of Louvain, its foundation dating from 1425, had carried out all its teaching in the French tongue for the last three centuries and that it was as late as 1912 that Cardinal Mercier had grudgingly allowed Dutch-language courses to be started there. The university had become bilingual only as the State University of Ghent had received its Flemish charter. The bishops now decreed that as from the beginning of the academic session of 1966–7 the Flemish department of the university should have autonomous status, but that there was no question of the university not remaining united in its present form in Louvain. They failed, however, to spell out clearly how exactly this autonomous status was to be achieved or how the problem of growth of the Flemish faculties was to be dealt with.

It was this 'growth' problem which finally led to the débâcle of 1968. The French faculties were by now bursting at the seams and it was imperative for them to implement their own expansion programme without delay. They proposed expansion into the area lying between Louvain and Brussels. At once Flemish professors and students were up in arms. The French-language community, consisting of some 10,500 students and 800 professors, which had dominated the university for so long, was now proposing to 'Frenchify' the region between Brussels and Louvain (a distance of 15 miles) and extend thereby the domination of the French language, already an accomplished fact in Brussels, over a good part of Flemish Brabant. All French-speaking faculties must migrate at once into Wallonia. That was the only solution. Serious street-fighting broke out in Louvain in January 1968 and was followed up by demonstrations throughout the whole of Flanders. The bishops were appealed to and had by now ruefully to confess that they themselves no longer spoke with one mind: the Flemish bishops were taking the side of their own national community, aware that their prestige would dwindle to nothing if they supported the central government.

In February 1968 Vanden Boeynants was challenged to declare

that the French-speaking faculties would be moved with a minimum of delay to French-speaking territory. He refused to commit himself to a step which was bound to shatter the revered traditions of one of the oldest and most distinguished of European universities. The eight Flemish Social Christian members of his Cabinet resigned *en bloc* and their spokesman summed up the position as they saw it, speaking in impeccable French, at a press conference:

'We will not have peace in this country as long as the French-speaking community refuses to adapt itself to the reality of Belgium as it is today; as long as French-speaking citizens demand language facilities wherever they settle in Flanders (the Flemings who form 60 per cent of the population would not dream of demanding Dutch-language schools in Wallonia); and as long as bilingualism continues to mean that Flemings have to speak French. The French-speaking community in Louvain is an island with demands on its Flemish surroundings. It is nonsense to speak of a split of Louvain University. It has never been united.'

Never?

It is sad to think that the kind of linguistic apartheid which is already enforced in both primary and secondary schools should be extended to one of Europe's ancient universities – to the largest Roman Catholic university in the world.[1] Vanden Boeynants genuinely tried to form a 'national' government and thereby spread bilingualism, in the hope that this would eventually soften what it is difficult not to dub 'tribal' antagonisms. The root cause of all the trouble is that the balance of power is still shifting from the Walloons to the Flemings, although the Walloons still retain a tradition of cultural superiority and will not readily let the Flemings forget this. When one talks with both staff and students at Louvain it quickly becomes apparent that the fundamental complaint against the Walloons has been not so much their presence in Louvain as their tendency to dominate – their irritating air of effortless superiority. That inferiority complex still lingers with the Fleming and makes him nowadays even more frustrated and discontented when he reflects that the 5 million Flemings in the country today control twice as many parliamentary seats as the 3 million Walloons, and he is still (apparently to him) getting nowhere. In the long run, of course, the Flemings must have their way, but let good sense

[1] The French-speaking faculties of Louvain are now (1969) at Ottignies.

prevail. Most thinking people would not now feel inclined seriously to challenge a recent statement by the Flemish National leader, Frans van der Elst, that:

'The basic issues in this country are now finally brought into the open. The very structure of Belgium is at stake and no lasting solution will be possible on the basis of the unitary state we have had so far.'

Chapter 14

Education in Belgium

THE REALITY OF THE DIFFERENCES which divide the Belgians in language, religion, politics, and social standing finds its fullest expression in education and, as we have recently seen in discussing the unfortunate collapse of Vanden Boeynants' government, political and educational issues, religious and linguistic differences, economic and social problems, are so closely intertwined as to produce situations of the greatest interest and from which important lessons can be drawn. Education has been a major political issue throughout Belgium since the breakaway from Dutch rule. 'Dutch' William's capable, but despotic and unintelligent, attempt to impose on the Belgians his own more advanced system of schooling was one of the main causes of the Belgian revolt. In the years immediately following the creation of the new kingdom of Belgium the Liberal and Catholic parties were soon involved in repeated clashes on educational issues. The Catholic Church maintained that, since a religious society must in every respect be superior to the lay body, then it alone had the right to educate. The Liberals naturally opposed such an attitude, maintained that there must be a state system of education, and constantly reminded the Catholics that Article 17 of the constitution states quite explicitly that 'education is free; any attempt to curtail this freedom is prohibited and offences in this direction are punishable by law. Public instruction given at the expense of the state is also governed by law.'

Between 1830 and 1847, while the new kingdom was establishing itself, a kind of uneasy truce existed. On 4 August 1834 the 'free' Catholic University of Louvain was reopened, but three months later, on 20 November 1834, the Liberals triumphantly countered the move by opening the 'free' University of Brussels and seized the opportunity to stress that *their* university was open to all comers irrespective of religious beliefs or observances. The following year saw the opening of the two state universities at Ghent and Liège.

In 1842 the first School Law on primary education was enacted, making it obligatory on each *commune* to support at least one primary school, though local authorities were permitted to adopt 'private' (i.e. Catholic) schools and make them serve the purpose if they so thought fit.

The years 1847 to 1884 witnessed the gradual hardening of positions, the beginnings of Catholic intransigence towards teachers in state schools and parents who sent their children to these schools, retaliatory measures on the part of the Liberals, and (to confound the situation) the birth of the Belgian Socialist Party. The Liberals had been in undisputed control of the nation's affairs since 1857. The new Socialist Party engineered the downfall of the Liberal government in 1884 and the defection of left-wing Liberals to the socialists to bring about this defeat gave the country thirty years of Catholic control (1884–1914). The days of the enlightened Liberal bourgeoisie were over and never again would a Liberal government take office.

Meanwhile a law regulating secondary education was passed in 1850 and in effect substituted for the collaboration between Church and state which the 1842 School Law had brought about both separation and competition. Almost the whole of secondary education up to this time had been in the hands of the Catholic Church. The Prime Minister, Charles Rogier, now created a whole series of *athénées* (academic grammar schools taking pupils from the age of twelve to the age of eighteen) and *écoles moyennes* (lower-grade secondary schools which catered for pupils between the ages of twelve and fifteen only), strategically placed throughout the country, all under direct governmental control. Various clergy could be invited to give and supervise religious instruction in the schools, but all teachers and inspectors were to be nominated by the government and the government would likewise draw up the general programme of studies.

In 1879 the then Liberal Minister, Van Humbeek, revised the earlier 1842 law on primary education by insisting that it was the government's duty to decide on how many schools a *commune* should be called upon to maintain, and how many classes and teachers there should be in any one school. Teachers, it was stressed, were state functionaries and *communal* authorities had no longer absolute rights of suspension or dismissal. Teachers must be paid a fixed minimum salary and the *communes* must be responsible for keeping all school buildings in proper order. All poor and necessitous children were to be educated free at *communal* expense in official state schools. By the same token private (Catholic) schools lost all their subsidies and the *communes* were henceforward forbidden to adopt Catholic schools rather than build and maintain their own. All ecclesiastical inspection had to stop. Religion was deemed more properly the concern of parents, but a room was to be at the disposal of a priest who might give religious instruction before or after school hours according to parental wishes. Finally, all teachers in government-subsidised and state schools must be trained in state-controlled teacher-training colleges, and no diplomas issued by 'free' training colleges would in future be recognised in government-sponsored schools.

A second School Law on secondary education was passed in 1881, and while it aimed to modernise the curriculum and bring the work in the *école moyenne* in balance with work in the lowest forms of the *athénée* (and so facilitate the passage of promising bright pupils to the *athénée*), its principal objective was to create many more state-controlled secondary schools of both types. Girls' secondary education had also now become of prime interest to the Liberals and the hold of the Catholic convent girls' schools was equally challenged, and the challenge equally bitterly resented.

These two school laws brought the struggle between state and Church for control of the education of the child to a sorry climax of invective, calumny, and abuse. Both sides were driven to exaggerate and distort the true facts when they found that some advantage was to be gained by so doing. Uncompromising attitudes were adopted by the Church on the one hand and by the Masonic Lodges, by now the bastions of Liberal thought, on the other. And all ultimately turned on the irreconcilable elements in the philosophy each propounded.[1] As the Catholics came to power they immediately sought to redress the balance by passing a third School Law on primary education in 1884, amending it in 1895, and by restricting, in 1897, the permitted number of *athénées* and *écoles moyennes*, taking away from the latter the prestige they had begun to enjoy as being in some measure preparatory for advanced work in the *athénée*.

The 1884 and 1895 amendments to the 1879 Liberal School Law

[1] Readers interested in further details should consult my *Power and Politics in Belgian Education* (London, 1963), pp. 68–121.

on primary education have remained fundamental, all subsequent pieces of legislation being mainly concerned with necessary elaboration of basic and fixed principles. Among these the autonomy of the *communes*, which the Liberals had so flouted with their steam-roller tactics, was paramount. Each *commune* would itself now determine the number of schools it needed, would be responsible for its own budget for education, would appoint its own teachers, and would be free to choose them from either the state training colleges or Catholic institutions. It could 'adopt' a school which was recognised as efficient by all general standards and such a school would be entitled to the same subsidies as any other. In 1895 religious instruction became compulsory in all schools and training colleges, though a written parental declaration of opting out was admissible, such children (or students) then being obliged to follow courses of moral instruction during the periods set aside for religion, it being conceded that there existed three cults: Catholic, Protestant, and Jewish.

The turn of the century was marked by vigorous campaigning on the part of the professional (state) teachers' organisation for compulsory education and by a real effort on the part of the more moderate Catholics in office to end the bitter feuds on the schools' question. On 19 May 1914 the *Loi Poullet* was passed to make education immediately compulsory throughout the country up to the age of twelve and to arrange for extension to the age of fourteen, by progressive stages, for no later than 1921. In the event, the First World War postponed implementation until 1922. A further and final law intended to modernise the whole approach to education was passed on 13 May 1936 (the Bovesse Plan[1]), but this again had to go into cold storage until the ravages of the Second World War had been healed.

It must not be supposed, however, that in this present post-war period, and despite the Schools' Pact of 20 November 1958 (of which we shall speak later), the struggle between Catholics and non-Catholics for the education of the child is ended. The Belgian being what he is, this would be asking the impossible. Men's minds today are just as sharply divided and as uncompromising from an ideological point of view as they were fifty years ago. And the situation is now further bedevilled by the language question. At the moment of writing, statistics show that between 55 and 60 per cent of chil-

[1] Named after François Bovesse, Minister of Justice in van Zeeland's Cabinet.

dren are in attendance at Catholic schools. The state-school system caters for a definite minority of pupils. Equally, between 55 and 60 per cent of the total school population is Flemish. In the University of Louvain itself, French-speaking and Flemish students are almost equally divided in numbers – some 11,000 of each – but there is evidence that the French-speaking faculties are recruiting faster than the Flemings, and it is inevitable that foreign students registering to study in Louvain should opt for the French-speaking faculties.

No wonder, then, that education is still very much a major political issue throughout Belgium. Every teacher, parent, student, and pupil is acutely politically conscious in a way that is scarcely true of any other country. Each is aware of the part educational issues have played and will continue to play in his life and determined (individualistic Belgian that he is) to fight for his rights as he sees them and to secure, in historic phrase, *un redressement de ses griefs*. Let either a Catholic or a socialist government gain an overwhelming majority in Parliament to the extent that the Liberals cannot act as a decisive mediating influence, and the storm-clouds will burst again. Sanity and realism in educational issues (except for the unfortunate Louvain business) would now, however, seem to prevail. It is accepted that roughly half the population believes in the Church's right to interest itself directly in the education of the young and will seek every constitutional and lawful opportunity for increasing the efficiency and influence of the Church. It is equally accepted that the other half believes profoundly in the advantages accruing from state-controlled education in all its forms and will again seek every lawful means for reducing any monopolistic tendencies on the part of the Church. Today there are in evidence few of the bitter enmities between families and sections of the population such as existed in the first part of the century. Many sound Catholics send their children to both the state primary and the state secondary school. The state universities of Ghent and Liège are open to all comers. So is the 'free' University of Brussels, and it usually has its small sprinkling of Catholic students who are regarded as not perhaps quite orthodox in their attitude by ardent fellow-Catholics. Only the University of Louvain insists that all students and all members of the teaching staff shall be practising members of the Catholic Church.[1]

In such circumstances the role of any government is a very

[1] Foreign students, of course, are exempt from this requirement.

awkward one. All it can hope to do is to reconcile conflicting interests. It must never interfere unless the welfare of the whole nation is in jeopardy. It must never dictate but must dispense its benefits impartially and justly. Consequently, it cannot prescribe any particular system of education, but may only demand that each individual receive an education of which it has determined the broad principles and over which principles it does have control. Thus there can never be any educational planning on an overall national scale as recently in France or Sweden. So it is that all recent reforms have not aimed at altering the structure of education so much as legalising unmistakable trends in a given direction and at seeking a proper and just solution to problems created by present aspirations and socio-economic trends.

Since the implementation of the Bovesse Plan, education is now compulsory throughout Belgium for eight full school years starting from the age of six, and pupils may attend schools controlled either by the state, the Catholic Church, any one of the nine provinces, or by a township. The same pattern holds for all secondary and technical education, and intending teachers for any school have, in effect, to decide under which authority they prefer to serve. Kindergartens exist for children between the ages of three and six, and the most recently released figures show that over 96 per cent of children between the ages of five and six, and over 85 per cent between the ages of three and six, attend such schools. The schools are attached to a primary school and inspection is carried out by a primary-school inspector. Should more than thirty parents petition for the setting-up of a kindergarten within their *commune*, then there is a legal obligation upon the *commune* to provide these facilities.

The avowed aim of the Bovesse Plan was to bring harmony, cohesion, and simplicity into the entire school system; to ensure that every child would be able to obtain the education he required as well as full preparation for the career for which he was suited; to develop the already well-established systems of child and vocational guidance; to achieve parallel classes of study that would make for easy change from one type of education to another; to replace the workshop apprenticeship system by vocational education that did not neglect the cultural aspects. Consequently, no child now undergoes any examination hurdle of any kind to enroll in that form of post-primary education his parents seek for him. All school fees (partly abolished for children up to the age of fourteen in 1947)

have since 1959 been abolished in every type of educational institution except the universities. And this means that no matter where a
parent decides to send his child to be educated – to a state school, a
provincial school, a local township school, or to the privately controlled Catholic sector – the state foots the bill. It follows that there
is neither need nor desire in Belgium to follow the fashionable swing
to some form of comprehensive education, nor is there any pressing
urgency to raise the school-leaving age beyond fourteen: most pupils
now are staying voluntarily at school until at least sixteen.

On completion of his primary-school education at the age of
twelve a pupil passes either to a technical school, to the *école
moyenne*, or to an academic-type grammar school (*athénée* for boys,
lycée for girls, *collège* in the Catholic sector). Pupils who enter the
technical school directly at the age of twelve are generally the less
bright pupils academically, but they are required to follow alongside their technical/commercial programmes a common-core curriculum not dissimilar from that in the *école moyenne*. Pupils at the
école moyenne who at the age of fifteen have betrayed a definite
technical/commercial bent now join the technical school and will
work along with the brightest of the twelve-year intake to the
technical school for qualifications at either the technician's level
(eighteen plus) or the technologist's level (twenty-one plus). In
addition, pupils who have attended the *athénée*, etc., up to the age
of eighteen and are practical-minded rather than academic in their
leanings do not go on to the university but join the technical school
and qualify for the various higher-grade (technologist) diplomas.
The least able pupils from among those who entered the technical
school at the age of twelve complete their school course proper at
the age of fifteen, but are required to attend a further year to secure
a qualification as semi-skilled workers.

The *école moyenne* has had a chequered but not inglorious history since its establishment in 1850 to provide a three-year post-
primary education for pupils either not suited to or not desirous of
taking a full six-year academic course in the *athénée*. Inevitably it
became the poor relation of the latter and recruited mainly the
children of ambitious working-class parents or of the lower-middle
classes, providing a sound modern education which equipped them
either to hold subordinate (but not to be despised) positions in the
bourgeois hierarchy or to train to become teachers at the kindergarten, primary-, and middle-school levels. At the same time oppor-

tunity has always existed for a pupil to transfer at the age of fifteen to the *athénée* and so prolong his studies a further three years. In time, a number of *écoles moyennes* – mainly those remote from an *athénée* – came to be allowed to attach to themselves the three upper forms of the *athénée* and to function as such in fact, though not in name. This in turn meant that from 1924 onwards the work on the modern side of the *athénée* in the three lowest forms came to be identical with the work done in the *école moyenne*. A restructuring of the *école moyenne* in 1947 brought the curricula of the *école moyenne* and the *athénée* closer still, and on 12 March 1958 the lower cycle (twelve to fifteen) of technical/commercial education was brought into line to parallel as closely as possible the work in these classes in the *école moyenne*. The overall result has been to organise the *école moyenne*, in such a way that it also has its fully developed technical/commercial sections alongside academic ones, to become a school of general instruction, with inbuilt specialities, which postpones a pupil's obligation to make a final and (almost) irrevocable choice of his career until at least the age of fifteen.

It was hoped that the old-established *athénées* (*lycées* and *collèges*) would see fit to bring their lower cycle of instruction into line, but they have so far ignored the invitation to join in this experimentation. As a result a ministerial ruling of 5 October 1964 has decreed that every new secondary school opened since September 1963 and every new technical school opened since September 1964 must conform to this new pattern of a general education up to the age of fifteen. The fact is that the aim and main function of the *athénée* is still jealously preserved. It recruits mainly children from the bourgeois and professional classes. It seeks to train an intellectual élite and to provide a sound modern academic education for those who aim at professions or occupations demanding a certain measure of highly-trained intelligence. And it still can have its own primary school attached to it, particularly in the Catholic sector. Pupils entering the *athénée* are directed to either the modern or the classical side, mainly on the basis of an estimate of their potential formed during their last years in the primary school. Changes of subject emphasis are of course possible during the first three years, but from the age of fifteen onwards six specialist sections are available. Of all these, the Latin–Greek section is still the most popular, since it is the traditional form of preparation for university entrance. The Economics section is next in popularity, but it is to be remembered

that girls' schools have a predilection for this option. Next in order
come the Scientific A section (which devotes more time to mathe-
matics than Scientific B), the Latin–Maths section, the Latin–
Science section, and finally the Scientific B section (a creation of
1958 which places the emphasis on physics and chemistry).

Teachers are trained for work either with infants (women only) or
in the primary school, the *école moyenne*, or the *athénée*. Teachers
of infants usually enter training college at the age of fifteen and
follow a four-year course which must now include completion of the
upper cycle of secondary studies (fifteen to eighteen) in a less
specialised way than in the *athénée*. Primary teachers enter college
either at fifteen from the *école moyenne* or more rarely at eighteen
from the *athénée*. By the new School Law of 1958 the first and
second years of study in the training colleges are now assimilated to
the first- and second-year studies of the corresponding side of the
upper cycle of the *athénée*. The whole of the third and fourth years
of the training college are assimilated to the third (and final) year
of the corresponding side of the *athénée*. The importance of the
change is that a student in a training college can now not only earn
a primary-school teacher's certificate, but also a certificate of satisfactory completion of a full six-year course of academic education
which entitles him to prolong his studies, if he so desires, at a
university or at some other institution of higher education. Having
done this, he is not necessarily bound to return to teaching as a
career.

Teachers for the *école moyenne* are best classified as non-graduate
specialists, and they are sorted out during the first three years of
the ordinary primary teacher-training course and given two years'
intensive work in their chosen specialities after the completion of the
initial three-year course. Teachers in the *athénée* are all university
graduates and have followed a four-year course (into which professional training is sandwiched) in clearly defined areas of special
study. Technical/commercial teachers fall into two categories:
those who teach non-technical subjects on the basic common-core
curriculum; and technical/commercial specialists. The latter are
most often recruited after some time in industry, and then trained;
the former teach to the level for which they have been trained in the
ordinary training colleges.

Until 1965 successful completion of the full secondary-school
course in certain specified groupings of subjects automatically

entitled a student to attend the university of his choice. Since 1965 an additional entrance examination is required to sift out those students who can reasonably be expected to profit from a higher academic education of this kind. The examination is simple but searching. A candidate is required to write down in his own words a paraphrase of a passage that has been read to him and also to discuss and argue some problem presented to him within the field of his intended speciality. Apart from dentistry and medicine, which require respectively six and seven years of study to a first degree, all other subjects take four or five years and are divided into *candidature* (taken after two years) and the final first-degree examination.

All these various modern reforms, however, were not going to have their full impact and properly enable Belgium to play her chosen part in the vanguard of the New Europe and as an enthusiastic member of the Common Market, Euratom, and the European Coal and Steel Community unless some serious attempt were made to settle once and for all both the linguistic issues and the still vexed question of the peaceful coexistence of public and private education. It was generally accepted by all political parties that if a political federation of western Europe were to emerge from the Treaty of Rome, then Belgium could no longer afford the luxury of allowing petty internal divisions to sap her energies. To be able to live comfortably with their neighbours they must first learn to live comfortably amongst themselves.[1] To solve the problem of the relationship between Church and state the three main political parties (Social Christian, Socialist, and Liberal) announced on 20 November 1958 their 'gentleman's agreement' or *Pacte Scolaire*, the main provisions of which became law the following year on 29 May 1959.

The *Pacte* begins by recognising the need for a more harmonious and imaginative policy if Belgium is to play her full part in strengthening the position and influence of the Western world. The cultural and material development and growth of the whole country must be accelerated. It urges a raising of the compulsory school-leaving age, an equitable distribution of state grants for education among all kinds of schools recognised as efficient, and the abolition of all fees at all levels of instruction. It recognises the right of every authority (state, Church, province, or township) controlling its own system of schools to draft its own curricula in accordance with

---

[1] Of the attempts made to deal with the linguistic question we have already spoken in Chapter 13.

minimum requirements as laid down by the Ministry of Education. It leaves each authority absolutely free to decide its own teaching techniques. No political propaganda of any kind may take place in any school, and parents must be completely free to choose between the neutral state-school system and the Catholic schools. As heretofore, however, state schools will set aside two hours per week for either religious or moral instruction according to parental wishes.

It is made the prime responsibility of the state to ensure that throughout the country parents have sufficient schools of all kinds within reasonable travelling distance for their children. Should the Church, for example, decide not to provide a certain type of school for which there is a demand, then the state must open one of its own. On the other hand, should a number of parents feel disadvantaged because there is no school of their 'persuasion' (Catholic or state) within reasonable distance they may petition for such a school to be provided. Having agreed that there is a just complaint the Ministry may then either open a school, refund travelling expenses to an existing school, or 'recognise' a school whose staff ratio of qualified teachers has so far not allowed it to be considered efficient.

The abolition of all fees in all schools in both the public and private (i.e. Catholic) sectors has made it imperative to ensure that salaries, pension rights, and sickness benefits must again be the same in all similar types of school. The only differentiation allowed, indeed, concerns the provision of school buildings. Naturally the state is fully responsible for maintaining its own schools. Provinces and towns can get a 60 per cent subsidy for building projects. The Catholic schools (as previously) will get nothing, though this is more equitable than it sounds, for many teachers in Catholic schools are members of religious orders and do not personally touch their salaries, which are ploughed back into the funds of the order and thus used to provide extra amenities. School buildings and the extension of school buildings must now count among these amenities.

Much goodwill has been brought to bear on the problems involved, and the only two parliamentary votes cast against the bill which embodied the provisions of the *Pacte Scolaire* came from communist members. The Act is a sincere effort to end for ever the quarrel over the schools. And both main political parties have made serious ideological sacrifices. The Catholic Party has at last accepted the right of the state to create and maintain its own schools, and Liberals and left-wing members have in turn agreed to allow the Church parity of esteem (to the extent of having all recognised teachers in schools in the private sector state-salaried) with the state system. On the other hand, it should be noted that Protestants and Jews are excluded from the new legislative process, mainly on the grounds that for almost a hundred years they have been more than content with the educational provision made for them by the state. Their only alternative to attending state or Catholic schools is to open their own schools, for which they must be completely responsible. This they are hardly likely to wish to do.

It must be admitted that the Belgian educational system as it exists today is an extremely elaborate and complicated one, and made more complicated by the determination, in implementing necessary reforms, not to change the basic structure. Always loath to rush matters, the Belgians are in any case convinced that they have evolved the structural pattern in education best suited to their temperamental needs. They have moved cautiously since the last war and have arrived at their present position only after some twenty years of careful experimentation. Primary education has remained virtually unchanged since 1936. Facilities for kindergarten education have, on the other hand, been fully extended. And, because Belgium is at long last seen as moving from its previous traditional position as the chosen battlefield for repeated wars between rival powers in Europe to become a kind of powerhouse for a united Europe, a complete rethinking of the whole purpose of secondary and technical education has become imperative. More and more highly-skilled personnel at all levels of national and economic endeavour are needed. To cope with the demand all kinds of elaborations, permutations, and combinations are evolved to fit into the existing framework.

And what is this framework which remains so highly prized and therefore almost sacrosanct? That of a bourgeois-based society. The revolution of 1830 was a bourgeois revolution. The bourgeoisie has brought Belgium safely through crisis after crisis. It has remained virile and progressive because it has never hesitated to recruit to its ranks anybody from any walk of life possessed of industry, ability, and promise. It has ever scrupulously respected the right of the individual to safeguard his own liberty, property, customs, and traditions. It is no respecter of persons except on their own proven worth. It gears its educational system to give everyone an equal chance, not on a basis of *idem cuique* (the same for everybody) but on a basis of *suum cuique* (to each his own). To achieve this ideal the system has to be elaborate.[1]

[1] But out of the elaboration (to quote but one single topical example) Prince Philippe (the elder son of Prince Albert of Liège, himself the heir-apparent to the throne) is at the moment attending the Jesuit College of Saint-Michel, at state expense like everyone else and on exactly the same footing as many worthy and promising sons of local people.

Chapter 15

Towards an Independent Congo

THE GRANTING OF ITS CHARTER to the Belgian Congo on 18 October 1908 marked the beginning of some fifty years of enlightened rule, backed by a doctrine of paternalism towards the native Congolese, and brought a systematic and steady exploitation of the country's abundant mineral and hydro-electric resources as well as the application of modern and scientific techniques to the development of a large agricultural sector. Indeed, with the sole exception of the Union of South Africa, no other territory in what may be termed the black sub-continent has had such a high industrial and agricultural development as the Congo, and its importance (particularly as regards its mineral resources) became increasingly valuable from the end of the First World War.

Leopold II had bequeathed to his country a colony eighty times larger than Belgium and with a population of 11 million, then controlled by some 3,000 whites who with their successors sought assiduously over seventy-five years to weld the country (with its bewildering multiplicity of tribal loyalties and affiliations) into one politically unified whole. As for Leopold II, his own personal achievement (never having once set foot on his territories) must be unique in history. He had set out with the initial aim of conferring on the Congolese the benefits of European civilisation. He had occupied, explored, and pacified his colony and had obtained the blessing of the greater powers to do so. In the short span of twenty-three years he had established order out of chaos on the basis of a smoothly-running administrative machine. Slavery had completely disappeared. Missionary, capitalist, and civil servant were beginning to work in unison to further the introduction of Christianity, to promote the general welfare of the African, and to bring about necessary technical progress and efficiency for full economic development. He had built thousands of kilometres of railroads and highway and fleets of steamers were navigating all the available waterways. Already he was insisting that intending colonists must give evidence of their suitability, of a sound general educational level, and of civic competence. He performed the first important phase of opening up the Congo. It was now up to the Belgian government to build on the sound foundations he had laid.

In point of fact the administrative arrangements made for the Congo in terms of its charter and the development of educational services were such that no real changes were considered until after the First World War. On 7 August 1914 King Albert had proposed that the Congo basin be considered neutral territory, but a week later the Germans cut telephonic communications along the western bank of Lake Tanganyika and gave the 12,000-strong Belgian–Congolese army the opportunity it was itching for. In September 1914 a detachment helped the French wipe out a spearhead attack from the Cameroons and the following year a further detachment joined the French in their Cameroon campaign which put an end to all German resistance in this area. In November 1915 still another detachment answered an appeal from the British authorities and helped free Northern Rhodesia from a German invasion. The fourth and last operation to be mounted entailed the transformation of the Congolese army into a modern professional fighting force, demanded lengthy preparations and training, and resulted in the conquest of German East Africa, completed on 19 September 1916. Before the war ended, further assistance was rendered the British in East Africa where brilliant manoeuvring on the part of the Belgian Colonel Huyghé helped drive the last remnant of German forces for refuge to the neutral Portuguese colony of Mozambique on 9 October 1917. These African campaigns cost the lives of 257 Belgians, 2,500 Congolese soldiers, and 20,000 porters.

With the coming of peace, educational reforms within Belgium itself, the highly favourable opinions expressed by other European powers on Belgium's achievements in the Congo, the high compliment paid to Belgium by the League of Nations in 1924 whereby the former German colonial possessions of Ruanda-Urundi were placed under her trusteeship – all these things culminated in a renewal of effort to improve still further the general social administration both of the Congo and of her trustee territories. In Belgium courses in tropical medicine and in tropical agriculture and horticulture were by now well developed and eagerly attended. More and more specialists and able men and women were being attracted to service in the Congo. In the Congo itself, increasing numbers of Congolese were achieving posts of some responsibility. Congolese missionaries were by now everywhere actively at work. Hygiene and medicine were killing the tsetse fly and mastering the many diseases to which the native, through ignorance and superstition, was prone. The rate of African infant mortality was falling.

In 1920 the then Minister for the Colonies, Louis Franck, took a close look at administration at local government level. It is to be remembered that the first political relations established between Africans and Europeans were on a basis of treaties made with traditional chiefs, the native communities keeping their social structure and local institutions and characteristics. Once the Belgian Congo became a reality the government not unnaturally tried to base local government (as in Belgium) at the village level. The difficulty was that while a village might cover a vast area its population was small. It was found necessary from 1891 onwards to form groupings of villages into larger units, but even this meant that by the end of the First World War there were no fewer than some 6,000 such units. Franck advocated the grouping into *secteurs* of small tribal units too small to be administered by themselves, and the provision of modern government institutions. As the numbers of individual units were gradually reduced by this process (the number had shrunk to 2,496 in 1935 and to 432 twenty years later), so was the number of *secteurs* increased, rising from fifty-seven in 1935 to some 900 in 1960 for a rural population of 10½ million. It had been intended since 1891 that the small units themselves should be prepared for self-administration, but Franck's innovations speedily gave the *secteurs* their own budget, their own taxation, and an amount of self-government comparable with that in Belgium. The avowed aim was the establishment of an autonomous self-ruling system of local government as the foundation on which a central government for the whole Congo should eventually be built.

Changes were brought about in central government administration in 1926 by organising it at general, provincial, district, and territorial levels. General (central) administration was based on Leopoldville and was headed by a Governor-General assisted by a government council. There were at first four provinces (increased to six in 1934) and each had its own provincial governor and council. Each province was then divided into a number of districts administered by a district commissioner (with no district council), and each district subdivided into *territoires*, each ruled by a territorial administrator who (only since 1957) was assisted by a territorial council. It is important to note that, in pursuance of the doctrine of paternalism, while local government was virtually the monopoly of the Congolese, central government was reserved for Belgians.

This new reorganisation naturally called for thorough and enlightened training for future Belgian colonial administrators at all levels, and indeed veteran colonial administrators had been urging this for some years. The result was the creation in Antwerp of a Colonial University, financed by monies made available by the American Commission for Relief in Belgium. The first courses began in 1920. In 1923 the *Ecole Coloniale Supérieure*, as it had so far been called, became the *Université Coloniale*, and in 1949 it again changed its name to *Institut Universitaire des Territoires d'Outre-Mer*.[1] In 1926 money became available for the creation of a colonial commercial section to be attached to the *Université Coloniale* to specialise in the training of candidates, not as administrators, but for work in various colonial commercial undertakings. The aim of both courses was to give the students not only a general cultural background but also to equip them with highly specialised knowledge to serve usefully in conditions so different from their own. All the teaching staff were appointed by the Colonial Office, and they all had lengthy service of outstanding quality to their credit in the Congo as well as highly specialised knowledge of the subject they were called upon to teach. The professor of Swahili, for example, was a philologist of world-wide reputation who had spent years in the Congo studying the various Congolese languages and dialects.

The Minister for the Colonies now turned his attention to securing a more precise definition of the distribution of function in educational policy in the Congo. A commission he appointed in July 1922 finally enunciated certain principles which it felt should in future be closely followed. First, it stressed that the education of the Congolese must be conceived in terms of their environment; that a purely Belgian teaching certificate was not a sufficient qualification for work in the Congo and must be supplemented by familiarity

---

[1] The change of name is significant in that it marks the changing attitude of the post-1945 government to the doctrine of paternalism and colonial administration. A move was made in January 1946 to admit Congolese students to the Colonial University but, unfortunately, it came to nothing.

with the Congolese languages and customs; much more attention must be paid to local geography and history; the elements of hygiene, as well as agriculture and the arts and crafts of the native, must also have an important place on the programme. Secondly, it had to be recognised that the Congolese, in contact with the white man, lost much of his respect for his accustomed disciplines; character training and moral training must therefore be emphasised and there must never be a purely bookish and literary type of instruction to breed an aversion to manual work. Thirdly, all instruction must, as a general principle, be given in the tribal language: only those Congolese coming into repeated contact with the whites need learn a European language – French. There must be constant vigilance to avoid creating Europeanised Africans who would become social misfits in their own communities. Fourthly, the work of the various Christian missions received high praise and it was conceded that they were still the best equipped to carry on the good work of universal mass education throughout the Congo. Fifthly, it was emphasised that the work of civilising and instructing the Congolese must in the long run be left to the Congolese themselves, guided and helped by whites. The creation of numerous African training colleges for teachers became, therefore, an immediate and urgent necessity. Sixthly, it was felt still premature and unrealistic to insist on compulsory attendance at school except in the most important and urban centres which could maintain a highly efficient and well-articulated school system. For the rest, persuasion, blandishments, and bribes must be held out to entice the children to some form of elementary schooling. Lastly, the education of girls should seek to make them acceptable partners for their future husbands – roughly the same intellectual level, and so on – but predominantly good housewives and mothers with a proper respect for and understanding of modern medical standards of hygiene in the home.

It was on a basis of all these findings that the still present system of education in the Congo was finalised. It was accepted, as in Belgium, that education is 'free' in that anyone can open a school, given the usual moral and hygienic safeguards. To qualify for state subsidies, however, a school must be open to government inspection, must conform to the general programme of studies as laid down for the whole of the Congo, and must appoint properly trained teachers, using them only at the level for which their training fitted them.

Primary education starts with a two-year infant school which can also run special classes for older children to enable them to enter the primary school. There are then two levels of primary education. The first level lasts for two years and was given by Congolese teachers inspected by a European. In rural areas this school has been mixed, has accepted children of all ages, and academic instruction has been geared to meet all needs, while carefully watching for the boy or girl of promise. In the urban areas the children have been grouped within a narrow age range and better instruction has been possible. The second level of primary education has been either of three years' duration for the mass of pupils or four years for the most promising to enable them to move to some kind of post-primary education. These upper-level schools were in the past under the general supervision of Europeans.

Children from the three-year school might then move to an agricultural vocational school (two years), to gardening or horticultural courses (two years), to apprenticeship courses (two years), to a higher-grade agricultural school (three years), or to teacher-training for the lowest level of primary education. Girls could have training in domestic science (three years) or become assistant midwives (two years). Infinitely more choices were naturally available for children satisfactorily completing the four-year course. Girls could train to become children's nurses, home managers, housekeepers, etc. (four years). For boys there was a middle school (as in Belgium) of four years' study; a school for sanitary workers (four years); a middle-grade professional training school (four years); a higher-grade similar school (six years) for commercial and administrative training, for scientific instruction, and for the training of land surveyors. Finally there is the academic secondary school leading to the universities and similar in construction and length of courses to its purely Belgian counterpart. Needless to say, very few Congolese ever got so far. It was as late as 1956 that the first Congolese student graduated from the University of Louvain. It was in that year also that the Catholic University of Lovanium was opened at Leopoldville and two years later that the first state university was established in Elisabethville. At the time of the granting of independence to the Congo both universities were inter-racial, Lovanium having roughly two-thirds of its students black and Elisabethville only one quarter. In 1958–9 there was a grand total of 365 students at Lovanium and 219 at Elisabethville.

Nevertheless, statistics published in 1951 revealed that, in round figures, one and a quarter million Congolese children were in receipt of full-time instruction, though the Belgians themselves were quick to point out that much still remained to be done and that not many more than 25 per cent of the native population could be considered as fully educated. What they did *not* underline (and what in defence of Belgian administration in the Congo must now be done) was that in 1946 the percentage of school attendance stood as high as 56.1 in comparison with the incredibly low figure of 11.6 for the French African colonies; that in 1953 these figures were respectively 59.1 and 22.5; and that in 1958 they were at the high level of 77.5 as against the French figure of 34.8. In 1956 there were 7,000 self-employed Congolese living with their families in Leopoldville, and for the whole of the Congo the figure stood at 17,781. Of these 1,141 were professional people, 10,523 independent or semi-independent tradesmen, and 6,117 craftsmen. An impressive achievement by any count. And one which put the average annual income per head of population throughout the Congo higher than anywhere else in the various British, French, Portuguese, and Spanish African colonies.

On the other hand, it has to be admitted that the doctrine of paternalism led the Belgians to put all their effort into primary education and to neglect other branches. Louis Franck himself had seen as early as 1920 that if his reforms at local government level in the Congo were to produce the desired results, then a cadre of leaders capable of directing and advising at this level must be trained. The Vicar Apostolic also shared his view. Such a school was at once opened by missionaries for the training of the sons of African chiefs and it was soon followed by others. The whole scheme, however, was abandoned in 1929, though territorial and district officers protested, arguing that it had now become vital to prepare large numbers of civil servants to cope with the growing responsibilities of modern administration.[1] A golden opportunity was again missed, as we have seen, to send the most brilliant of the Congolese to the *Université Coloniale* in the immediate post-1945 period. Paternalism demanded that the Congolese should not leave his own country to come to western Europe without good reason: a Europeanised Congolese could so easily be a liability and not an

[1] Ironically it was the Catholic Church, which had supported the scheme, that felt it had to move the closure. These chiefs' sons were for the most part sons of polygamists and were likely to follow their fathers' example on return to their villages. Missionaries could hardly undertake the education of future polygamists,

asset. And French colonial policy which sought to turn the educated African into a Frenchman was viewed with considerable reserve.

Up to the Second World War, then, Belgium concentrated all her efforts on making the mass of the Congolese literate, on improving their living conditions and standards of medical care and hygiene, and on providing as many as could profit and would profit from the educational facilities available with sound, if subservient, positions in local government and in the many industrial and commercial enterprises she financed. The European who came to make a living and perhaps a fortune in the Congo was carefully scrutinised and hemmed about with restrictions to prevent exploitation of the African. He was also expected to take a deep pride and interest in all the affairs of the country which welcomed him and to give evidence of real patriotism. For these reasons, while it was always possible for him to send his children back to Europe to be educated, he was encouraged to keep them with him. To this end an adequate school service was set up and by 1960 it comprised no fewer than thirty-eight schools of different kinds – official or subsidised 'free' schools (mainly Catholic) – all adhering closely to the Belgian pro- grammes of study and including six *athénées*. There has never been any colour bar in the Congo as in other African colonies and, while Congolese were originally of necessity educated apart from Euro- peans, in the ten years immediately preceding the breakaway those who could profit from an academic primary or secondary education were quite freely admitted into schools which had been primarily designed for Europeans. It was what we might term these 'aca- demically emancipated' Congolese who both made the creation of universities in the Congo itself a necessity and who also insisted on their right to attend a Belgian university – though at first it was only the Catholic University of Louvain which opened its doors.[1] Some 450 Congolese students were being educated on government bur- saries either at the Belgian universities or at some equivalent Belgian higher institution during the university session of 1960–1. But it was then far too late.

It was the coming of the Second World War which thrust the Belgian Congo economically into such a position of world impor-

[1] The fault lay primarily with the universities themselves, whose rigorous conditions of admission were applied as ruthlessly to whites as to Congolese. At this time, for example, both Latin and Greek were necessary to study law or medicine. Administrative changes had soon to be made, even for whites.

tance (thereby highlighting its problems) as to force the pace of emancipation well beyond that envisaged by the most advanced and enlightened minds within Belgium itself. Indeed, the war marks the beginning, as well as being the cause, of transition throughout the whole of the African continent. For there was scarcely an area that was not affected in some measure by it. There was heavy fighting in Abyssinia. Great battles were fought in North Africa. Freetown Harbour in Sierra Leone became one of the vital strategic posts for the Allies. Air bases all along the West and East African coasts became essential to air-fighter supply as the Mediterranean was closed to shipping. Huge expeditionary forces were raised everywhere. In short, Africa became a mighty reservoir from which to draw both men and raw materials essential to the all-out war effort.

The Belgian Congo was particularly affected in that not only were her rich deposits of uranium invaluable, but also her rubber output became of increasing importance and had to be intensified after the loss of Malaya. In consequence she attracted to herself thousands of scientists and technicians. European personnel were needed to command her armies who fought in Egypt, in the Middle East, and in Burma. Thousands of natives were brought in from the bush to join the various expeditionary forces and for the first time they made contact with 'evolved' Africans, as did thousands of others who flocked to the large towns to earn good money in the various industrial plants. In 1939, for example, Leopoldville had a population of 40,000. By 1945 it had grown to 100,000 and by 1960 was over 300,000. Very soon Congolese soldiers on duty or on exercises with troops in Nigeria, in Ghana, in Sierra Leone, were comparing their way of life with that elsewhere in Africa, and workmen in the Congo itself were clamouring to be organised on some such trade union basis as were the whites with whom they came into daily contact.

The impetus given to industrial output was continued in the immediate post-war period, and in some sectors intensified. The Congo became the leading African producer of cobalt, diamonds, tin, tungsten, and zinc materials, and the second biggest producer of copper. Secondary industries dependent on the processing of these raw materials more than doubled their production and hydro-electric developments were fully utilised and extended in the service of a booming industry. The Belgians, already worried about the possible consequences of the continued mass exodus from the bush into the industrial sectors, yet equally anxious not to lose the advantages the industrial momentum had given them, had to give immediate attention to the pressing needs of the Congolese.

In January 1946 the then Minister for the Colonies, Robert Godding, directed the Governor-General to institute a proper organisation of Congolese labour to prepare them for the future exercise of their democratic rights in industrial relations. Trade unions were to be created. And there was to be workers' representation from the shop-floor upwards on a basis of works councils (composed of African workers and their employer or his representative), local committees (comprising delegates from the works councils and trade unions, meeting under the chairmanship of the territorial administrator), regional committees (presided over by the district commissioner with delegates from administration, employers, and employees), and a provincial committee similarly constituted as the regional committees but chaired by the provincial commissioner (the provincial governor's deputy).

In 1947, following the principles laid down in the Charter of the United Nations, Belgium's trustee territories of Ruanda-Urundi were put under her 'tutelage' – the only difference in administration being that henceforward Belgium must admit authorised commissions of inquiry into these territories and submit to the United Nations periodic accounts of her stewardship. The same year saw the departure of a fact-finding commission of the Senate to the Congo, the publication of its lengthy report, and a determined effort to integrate the bush Congolese who had flocked to the towns into specifically determined communities. Some ten years later, by a decree of 26 March 1957, this was followed up by the creation of two distinct types of urban unit, the *commune* with its own burgomaster assisted by a municipal council elected by universal suffrage, and the *ville*, for example Leopoldville, with the same administrative structure but being a federation of *communes* within the same urban area. By 1947, also, the first Congolese were joining the government and provincial councils and the first official state schools were being opened – to the understandable dismay of the missionary orders who so far had enjoyed a virtual monopoly in all forms of Congolese education.

The fact-finding commission's report of 1947 led to the formulation of a ten-year plan for the future development of the Congo which was put into operation in 1950. It began by readily acknowledging the important role of the Congolese in all spheres of activity in the country and stressed that, while every effort must be made to develop the Congo still further, this could only be done by improving education and so making the Congolese increasingly capable of assuming greater responsibilities. The plan called for further large-scale investment (50 billion francs), half of which should come from private industry and half from the government.[1] The river systems must be further developed, harbour installations improved, modern roads built, and highways laid down to connect the east with the west from Kivu to the Congo. Improvements in transportation, electric-power services, and hygiene were also called for. In a serious attempt to halt the steady and undiminishing exodus from rural areas to the towns it was recommended that urgent attention be given to improving the lot of the tenant farmer by providing him with living conditions equal to those in towns and by extensive education in the use of fertilisers and mechanised equipment. Plans for education aimed at a target of 900 nursery schools, 3,600 first-cycle primary schools, 5,400 second-cycle primary schools, 280 post-primary schools for boys, 263 post-primary schools for girls, 450 apprenticeship centres, 121 secondary schools (of which 40 were to be teacher-training colleges), 41 professional schools, 12 domestic science schools, and two universities. In short, colonists and natives, with strong financial backing, were now going to work closely together as never before and colonists and Congolese in the now foreseeable future were together to rejoice in complete independence from the motherland. What, then, went wrong?

It is easy to say that the Belgians had remained for too long too wedded to their paternalistic policy; that they had not attempted to extend the education of the Congolese beyond mere literacy until their hands were forced; that they had neglected to train doctors, nurses, and skilled workers of all kinds from among the Congolese population; that they had deliberately reserved all key positions for the Europeans; that good government is not the same as self-government. These are only half-truths and like all half-truths misleading. The real causes of the final débâcle lie much deeper, are much more subtle and difficult of interpretation, and go back to the very characteristics of the Belgians themselves, to their strengths and

[1] Investments came from the Congo itself, Belgium, Switzerland, the United States, and the International Bank for Reconstruction and Development.

weaknesses, paradoxically to everything which through the centuries has made the Belgian the sincere democrat he is.

We must first of all remember how antagonistic the Belgians were to Leopold's desire to open up Africa, and how again and again they attempted to repudiate and sabotage his efforts. The Belgian has always been a home-loving person, and even today he is not a great traveller and rarely strays from a few favourite haunts inside Europe and within reach of his home base. All kinds of inducements (mainly financial gain) had to be held out to the first colonists and it took a long time for the colonising spirit to develop. When it did, it brought a distinct cleavage in attitude and outlook between home politicians and the *colons*. The *colons* grew into their colony, became genuinely a part of it, and inescapably came to have an entirely different view on and approach to the problems the home government was called upon to resolve in the post-war period. Indeed, the home government, until after 1945, was as little interested in Congolese affairs as the average Belgian. Very few Belgians either cared or knew about what went on in the Congo unless they had relatives there, and what information they gleaned was scrappy and often unreliable. To the ordinary Belgian man-in-the-street the Congo was some sort of Caliban's land and the *colon* an opportunist who had found means of getting rich quick and from time to time appeared in his native country to flaunt his riches and make invidious comparisons between his easy way of life and that of his more humdrum kin back at home. There was tremendous surprise registered, for example, at the time of the 1958 World Exhibition at how civilised and well educated so many of the natives of Caliban's land turned out to be. And then with typical illogicality, forgetting he was only seeing the élite of the Congolese in Belgium, the average home-staying Belgian wanted to know why the *colons* were not giving the Congolese more civic rights and more responsibility more speedily and expeditiously! The *colons* felt a real sense of grievance, knowing they were the only real experts on Congolese affairs, and therefore came much to resent the tardy efforts of post-war governments to effect changes which could have repercussions *they* and not the home-based government would have to deal with.

At the same time, however, though growing apart from the homeland and taking full root in the Congo as they had been encouraged to, the *colons* remained essentially Belgian in their fundamental outlook and basic ideals. Belgium itself had prospered by good government from a sound middle-class bourgeoisie, and even the socialists were at heart bourgeois. Throughout the decades the constant aim in Belgium had been to strengthen the bourgeoisie by recruiting to it all who had ability, and the school system had been carefully devised to enable the poorest in the land to rise by his own efforts and so play a full part in an affluent bourgeois society. The *colons* adopted the same principle in the Congo. The growth and development of the big mining companies (such as the *Union Minière*), while inevitably leading to the tearing-away of thousands of natives from their tribal backgrounds and to concentrating them in urban areas nearer the mines, led equally to a tremendous improvement in social conditions, to sensible and modern town-planning, to the provision of a large variety of schools for the Congolese population to enable them also to 'get on in the world'. These schools' programmes had been encouraged by successive socialist and Liberal governments and from 1945 onwards the numbers of *évolués* (well-educated Congolese living in the large towns and away from their tribal attachments) had risen rapidly.

In theory the *évolués* should have turned themselves into sound Congolese bourgeois types and should have worked in complete harmony with the Europeans. In practice they did this – but only for so long as the Congo was able to remain in peaceful isolation from the rest of the continent and from African anti-colonialism. And when this island of bourgeois respectability had its ideals challenged from without, the *évolués* soon grasped the ambiguous nature of their position. They lived in two worlds, the one of their traditional Bantu culture and the other of Western civilisation, and, while they had a foot in each, they now belonged to neither. Moreover, they came to feel increasingly like the dog in the fable: well-fed, well-groomed, well cared for – but with a collar round its neck. In 1956 the Congolese were demanding a Congolese nation composed of Africans *and* Europeans and a thirty-year timetable for political, social, and economic emancipation in the Congo. By 1959 they were demanding independence for 1961.

Finally we have to acknowledge that the deep-rooted political, religious, and linguistic antagonisms of the Belgians also played a not inconspicuous part in furthering the débâcle. Within Belgium itself these various rivalries have often bred a healthy and competitive spirit which in the long run has been of service to the nation as a whole. But to bring these rivalries to the Congo was inviting trouble.

How could the Congolese be expected to grasp the complexities and subtleties involved? What did it matter to him whether the European spoke French or Flemish? What did it matter to him whether the missions were Catholic or Protestant – except that by sheer strength of numbers the Catholic missions tended to serve him better? What was there very wrong about having official state schools alongside the Catholic variety? And why bring politics into these issues? Why should the socialists be generally against the Catholics and the Flemings usually for them? Why tie up linguistic problems with both religion and politics? To say the least, it was confusing.

From 1945 onwards the socialists, strongly backed by the *Ligue de l'Enseignement* (the progressive and active socialist teachers' association), repeatedly challenged the hold of the Catholic missionaries on the educational programmes of the Congo and agitated for more official state schools and a more neutral and non-European approach to education as a whole. They failed to remember that Leopold II would never have had state backing for the educational programmes he envisaged in the early days of his colonial adventure. He had to turn to the missionaries. Moreover, the missionaries at the time were probably the only people who could make some impression on the tribal African. The socialists failed to accept that a tradition of subsidised Catholic education had inescapably been established and that that tradition – like all good and healthy traditions – could not be lightly abandoned. The Catholic monopoly was broken, as we have seen, by the opening of official state schools in 1947 when subsidies were for the first time also granted to Protestant missions, which elected to run properly organised and inspected school services. In 1954 a direct clash occurred between the Catholic missions and the Liberal–socialist government over educational policy in the Congo. The then Minister for the Colonies, Auguste Buisseret, claimed in a debate on 15 June in Parliament that he was pushing ahead with establishing further official state schools at the urgent request of the *évolués*! So the Congolese were now to be dragged into the white man's factions to enable this or that politician to prove his point. All this was not lost on the Congolese. They too could be anti-clerical. They too could be anti-government. In a word, once Belgian solidarity broke in the Congo, then the very foundations of the system of government envisaged were swept away.

In 1956, when the Congolese trade union movement had been in existence for almost ten years, demands were made for equal pay for equal work. This was conveniently shelved and not implemented until some three years later. In 1956 Patrice Lumumba founded a Congolese National Movement to match the *Abako* (association of the Lower Congo), created one year earlier by Joseph Kasavubu.[1] Both organisations had the blessings of the government and their political leanings were encouraged by the Minister for the Colonies, Maurice van Hemelrijck, who was at the time actively considering a plan submitted to him by Joseph van Bilsen of the Colonial University in Antwerp for the gradual phasing-out of Belgian control and its replacement by Congolese administrators over a period of thirty years. In 1958 an All-African People's Congress was called in Accra and van Hemelrijck gave Lumumba permission to attend along with two of the committee members of his National Movement. Lumumba became a permanent member of the organisation set up at the Accra conference and on his return to Leopoldville told a large meeting he called that he had pledged his movement to the unanimous view propounded at Accra that no African country should be a dependent territory after 1961.

Mounting tension naturally followed this heady pronouncement and the word 'Independence' was bandied about with all the fervour of a tribal fetish word. Political groups now began to spring up throughout the Congo, significantly seeking no attachment to, and no affiliation with, any Belgian political groupings. Lumumba's National Movement grew in strength and drew to it adherents from the *Abako*. In Belgium in 1958 the Social Christians replaced Van Acker's socialist government and the new Minister for the Colonies, Léo Petillon, changed the title to that of Ministry of the Belgian Congo and Ruanda-Urundi, announced a policy of decolonisation, appointed a parliamentary commission to formulate a policy for the emancipation of the Congo, and in so doing effectively removed from the Belgian authorities in the Congo any effective executive power, since every decision taken by them was to be subject to examination by the commission. Rumour and counter-rumour that independence was imminent ran round the Congo.

On 4 January 1959 Kasavubu called a mass meeting of his party in the Kalumu *commune* of Leopoldville. It was banned. Supporters of the *Abako* who had gathered in large numbers to hear the burgo-

---

[1] Both Lumumba and Kasavubu were typical *évolués*. The former was a post office clerk and the latter a clerk in the finance department of the government of the Congo.

master of the *commune*, M. Pinzi, give a report on his recent visit to Brussels, in their disappointment became wildly excited and clamoured for independence. Other Congolese joined in the mass hysteria. The police were called and unwisely used firearms to disperse the crowd, Kasavubu meanwhile calling for calm. Incensed by the police measures the Congolese started attacking all the public buildings they came to (churches, schools, hospitals, and social centres) and the Europeans, seriously fearing for their lives, mistakenly called in the army. The rioting lasted two days. Some fifty Congolese and the same number of Europeans were killed, and some 300 Africans injured. The stunned *colons* were completely bewildered at the turn of events. That this should happen to them! They naturally blamed the home government for its too liberalising measures and sought immediately to assert some sort of authority by imprisoning the luckless Kasavubu and his associates. Van Hemelrijck recognised the injustice of this but had to move warily.[1] He released them two months later and had them secretly flown to Brussels out of immediate harm's way. They were not held as prisoners there, but were required to study Belgian institutions to equip themselves for their future responsibilities in the Congo.

Within ten days of the rioting proposed programmes for the gradual attainment of self-rule were published. King Baudouin made his speech promising independence. Plans were announced for the holding of elections by universal suffrage for the constitution of *communal* and territorial councils, and these councils were then to elect provincial councils early in 1960. Van Hemelrijck, now hopelessly discredited among the *colons* for his liberalising approach, resigned in September 1959 and was replaced by Auguste de Schrijver. The Governor-General, Henri Cornélis, also offered his resignation, but no suitable replacement could be found and he was asked to stay on. Kasavubu and his associates returned to Leopoldville in May to a tumultuous reception. *Abako* extremists now began stirring up the Congolese with demands for immediate independence and Kasavubu threatened that unless this was promised the *Abako* would boycott the elections which had now been fixed for December. Meanwhile, a Round Table Conference had been called for January 1960 in Brussels, with the avowed object of working out ways and means of speeding up the granting of independence via the local

---

[1] He had replaced Pétillon in Eyskens' *new* 1958 Cabinet. See Appendix 2.

elections and the establishment of the provincial councils to the setting-up of two legislative assemblies, if possible, before the end of 1960. It was assumed that this first Parliament might be expected to last four years and so have time to draw up a constitution. Courageously King Baudouin now decided that he must himself again visit the Congo and he left on 17 December 1959, accompanied by Auguste de Schrijver, to hold frank talks with the main Congolese party leaders. He was well received and toured all the provinces, including Ruanda-Urundi, before returning a fortnight later to announce in a broadcast to the Belgian people that all with whom he talked eagerly desired a large measure of provincial autonomy. In these ways he was skilful in preparing a favourable climate of opinion, at home and abroad, for the success of the forthcoming conference.

Delegates assembled in Brussels on 20 January 1960, having been selected by the Governor-General primarily on the results of the December elections. The conference had its tragical and farcical sides and to say the least of it was tempestuous, the Belgians, however, remaining cool and firm and insisting that correct and constitutional procedures be followed. Kasavubu demanded independence by March and wished the conference to frame a constitution which would be binding on the Belgian government. When the Belgian delegates rightly refused, he stalked out and was not seen again. Lumumba was a week late in arriving because he had been sentenced to six months' imprisonment in Stanleyville for inciting riots there the preceding October. The conference would not continue without his presence. He arrived dramatically to display the manacle wounds on his wrists. Moise Tshombe, representing Katanga, stood for a federal structure for the Congo and insisted that it must remain linked with Belgium. Lumumba on the other hand, now the chief spokesman since Kasavubu had left, wanted complete independence by 1 June. The Belgians insisted on 1 August. A compromise was reached by choosing 30 June.

It would be tedious and not very profitable to discuss in detail the sixteen main resolutions agreed to by the conference. De Schrijver recommended a united Congo with decentralisation of public services and a large measure of autonomy at the provincial level, and this was accepted by all except Tshombe. King Baudouin was to remain Head of State until Independence Day. Elections were to be held in May and the new Head of State would be nominated by a joint session of the two legislative assemblies brought into being by these elections. This first Parliament would sit for no longer than four years, during which time it would draw up a constitution which would include future procedures to be adopted for electing the Head of State. As a purely interim measure, and to supervise the elections as well as maintain law and order in the delicate in-between period, Walter Ganshof van der Meersch, Professor of Law in the University of Brussels and Attorney-General to the Supreme Appeal Court, was to be sent to the Congo as Resident Minister. Belgium assured technical aid and capital investment for the Congo and the Congolese in turn gave guarantees respecting the safety and position of Belgians remaining in the Congo. The whole was submitted to the Belgian deputies and Senate, and was accepted in March and May 1960 as the *Loi Fondamentale.*

A second conference was called in Brussels between 26 April and 16 May to plan for future economic, financial, and social matters and also to discuss the position of Ruanda-Urundi, which would have to be administered for the time being by the United Nations. The first conference was officially closed on 21 February with a speech to the delegates from King Baudouin.

In the Congo, however, and particularly as the time for the elections approached, all kinds of party manoeuvring went on accompanied by riots and disturbances everywhere. Belgian authority was repeatedly defied and army reinforcements had to be flown in to cope with the situation. Party leaders dismissed one another from the *Abako* without any apparent effect and Lumumba was denounced to his party as being in league with the communists (an accusation which in the light of subsequent events was probably true). When the results of the elections were made known, however, it was clear that Lumumba's Congolese National Movement, together with its associated smaller parties, had gained an overall majority, though it could only claim 30 per cent of the seats in the Lower House. The *Abako*, of course, were its strong rivals. Many stormy discussions followed between Lumumba and Ganshof van der Meersch, after which Lumumba demanded the immediate withdrawal of Belgian troops and tried to flout the agreements of the Round Table Conference in order himself to become the first Head of State. Katanga, under Tshombe's leadership, was now threatening to secede. The *Abako* were announcing the formation of an independent government in Leopoldville. It needed all Ganshof van der Meersch's skill, patience, and firmness to bring about necessary reconciliations and a compromise whereby Kasavubu became Head of State with Lumumba as Prime Minister. Joseph Ileo was elected President of the Senate. On 24 June 1960 Kasavubu was officially confirmed in his position by both Houses and at once issued an invitation to King Baudouin to attend celebrations for Independence Day.

Hardly were the celebrations over, however, than the grim farce took a more sinister turn. On 1 July Lumumba requested membership of the United Nations and received full support in a letter from the Belgian government dated 5 July. On 7 July the Security Council of the United Nations accepted the application. Almost immediately the Congolese army mutinied and both Russian and Czech assistance and munitions were available through Ghana. Lumumba demanded immediate withdrawal of Belgian troops from the Congo at the very moment that Belgium was having to pour in additional troops to protect the very lives and property of her nationals. On 12 July Lumumba made a formal appeal to the United Nations to curb this Belgian violation of the Congo's sovereign rights. The Belgian troops were peremptorily ordered out on 19 July and United Nations forces moved in to restore order and keep the peace.

Profiting from the general disorder Tshombe quietly took over Katanga on 11 July, held on to the Belgian troops who were stationed there, and requested all Belgian technicians to stay put. Tshombe knew perfectly well what he was about. A member of the ruling family of the Lunda tribe, he had been educated at a secondary Methodist missionary school and had inherited from his father at the age of thirty-three a highly flourishing business concern. He soon ran through his inheritance, was declared bankrupt, and was rescued by the Belgian owners of the *Union Minière*. From that time onwards he was one with them and (in extreme African nationalist eyes) committed the unforgivable sin of understanding and getting on well with the Belgian industrialists and using them for the good of his country—Katanga. He was intelligent and politically astute, and saw well before independence that a tight federation of the various states, with power virtually centred on Leopoldville, could never work. He wanted a loose confederation, and while he at no time refused to give of Katanga's tremendous wealth to help the rest of the Congo, he was not going to see that wealth frittered away. Having declared Katanga independent because the rest of the Congo was in a state of anarchy, he maintained comparative peace and prosperity there and sought, in reality, to keep it as a political nucleus on which he hoped a peaceful loosely-built confederation might yet be built.

On 5 September Kasavubu dismissed Lumumba and appointed Joseph Ileo, President of the Senate, as Prime Minister in his stead. And while this quarrel was going on General Joseph-Désiré Mobutu, commanding the Congolese army since the mutiny, on 22 November seized control, expelled the Soviet and Czech embassies, and broke off relations with Ghana on the grounds of unwarranted interference in Congolese affairs. A fortnight later similar treatment for the same reasons was meted to the ambassador of the United Arab Republic and his staff, the Cairo government taking reprisals by nationalising all Belgian assets in Egypt. Lumumba fled to Stanleyville, where he was captured and jailed on the orders of Mobutu. For a time Kasavubu and Mobutu together maintained an uncertain authority, though Tshombe refused to recognise the claims of either to power. The announcement on 10 February 1961 that Lumumba had escaped from imprisonment in Elisabethville, the capital of Katanga, followed by news of his assassination by tribesmen three days later turned public opinion against Kasavubu. The situation was again explosive, the Security Council of the United Nations now deeming it necessary to authorise the use of force by United Nations troops to prevent war and to urge the immediate withdrawal of all Belgian and other foreign military and para-military personnel. Tshombe, who depended so much on Belgians and other Europeans for officering his troops (still engaged in ejecting pro-Lumumba factions from northern Katanga), was the first Congolese to reject the resolution. Kasavubu and Mobutu quickly supported him and the result was a military alliance signed between Tshombe, Ileo, and Albert Kalonji, the leader of south Kasai, Ileo going so far as to declare that Katanga could no longer be deemed secessionist.

This truce did not last long. A new government with Cyrille Adoula as Prime Minister was formed in July 1961, Adoula declaring that he would immediately end Katangan secession. In August United Nations forces tried to disarm Tshombe's forces and met with a severe rebuffal. Tshombe agreed finally to meet Dag Hammarskjöld in Northern Rhodesia but, as we know, the meeting never took place since Hammarskjöld's plane crashed. In November the Security Council passed a further resolution calling for an immediate end to Katangan secession and Tshombe prepared for all-out war. Bitter fighting resulted. Elisabethville was captured on

5 December and on 18 December came a cease-fire when Tshombe agreed to go to Leopoldville to negotiate with Adoula. Throughout 1962 the talks dragged on, with U Thant begging the United States, Great Britain, France, and Belgium to bring economic pressure on Tshombe to force him to come to terms. At the end of the year signs that United Nations forces might again take military action led Tshombe to declare a 'scorched earth' policy, but by mid-January 1963 political realism at last prevailed and Tshombe offered the U.N. troops unhampered passage, and promised all assistance with integrating Katanga into the federation of the Congo. Ileo was appointed Minister Resident in Elisabethville. The Congolese government was reorganised to include for the first time Ministers from Katanga. Tshombe retired to Europe to self-imposed exile.

By June 1964 the last of the U.N. forces had left the Congo, but the country was in such an appalling economic plight that Kasavubu could think of nobody to clear up the mess, if not Tshombe with his important Belgian industrialist connections. In July 1964 Tshombe had responded to the invitation and become Prime Minister. That he failed was no fault of his own. He had immediately to face a pro-Lumumba uprising which led to the loss of Stanleyville. Appeals for aid to the United States were answered, but he got no support at all from Nigeria, Senegal, Liberia, or Ethiopia, and in desperation he tried to strengthen his position by recruiting mercenaries in South Africa, which earned him a boycott by the Organisation for African Unity. He recaptured Stanleyville in November with the aid of Belgian paratroops and the rebels finally retreated, white mercenaries now remorselessly destroying any further serious opposition.

In February 1965 Tshombe visited Brussels and there brought off his one important economic *coup* by persuading the Belgian government to hand over the shares (to a total value of 300 million dollars) of companies operating in the Congo on a basis of reasonable compensation. Elections were held between 18 and 30 March and Tshombe's newly-launched personal political party, the Congolese National Convention, secured a clear majority only to find the results challenged on the grounds of alleged political corruption. Voting had to be repeated in three provinces and he lost ground. Kasavubu, who never really trusted Tshombe, now profited from the situation by declaring that the time was not ripe for government by one party. In the manoeuvring that ensued Tshombe's following in Parliament was reduced to a majority of thirteen and on 13 October Kasavubu seized the opportunity to dismiss him and replace him by another Katangan, Evariste Kimba. Tshombe left for exile in Spain. The situation deteriorated and finally on 25 November Kasavubu was deposed in a bloodless *coup* led by Mobutu, who proclaimed himself President and announced elections for February 1966.

The Presidency of General Mobutu was gladly accepted as providing greater stability for the country after the years-old struggle between Tshombe and Kasavubu. Tshombe, however, still retained much sympathy throughout the Congo and, military dictatorship or not, fears were expressed that he might, even now in exile, be in league with the Belgians and planning a comeback. Reports abounded that he was busily recruiting mercenaries in Spain for such an eventuality. Accordingly, on 19 May he was expelled from the Congolese Parliament by a vote of 96 to 3. In September it was announced that he would be tried for high treason in his absence. In March 1967 a military court sentenced him to death on charges that he had organised rebellion against President Mobutu, had attempted to set up an independent state of Katanga, had hired mercenaries to fight against the government, and had issued illegal currency for Katanga. In June 1967 Tshombe left by chartered plane to fly from Ibiza to Majorca for a holiday. His plane was highjacked and the crew forced at gun-point to land him in Algeria, from where the Congolese government demanded his extradition. Nothing happened and Tshombe languished in gaol until his death from a heart attack on 30 June 1969.

So ends the sorry story. Belgium has since been criticised in some quarters for granting independence to the Congo before she was ready for it. It has been argued that Belgium's negligence to train a sufficient number of élites to be ready to fill the important administrative and governmental posts was bound to lead to a lack of political experience on the part of the Congolese leaders, and that the timing was all wrong in that independence was granted at a moment of serious economic difficulties in the Congo. It has even been suggested that Belgium wanted it that way and wanted independence to fail so that she could take over again. That is an unworthy and unwarranted accusation. For despite all her faults Belgium has always wished the Congo well. She may have been tardy and (sometimes in some quarters) loath to implement desirable reforms immediately, but even then she had constantly in mind the ultimate interests and well-being of the Congolese. What she did do was to allow herself to be jockeyed into an untenable position, but that is not criminal. She was subjected to all kinds of pressures both from within the United Nations, from the newly independent African countries, and not least from her own Socialist Party. She was worried by this constant criticism, for she was proud of her record in the Congo so far and knew that record would stand up to fair scrutiny.

World opinion had considered her a model colonial power when in 1924 she had been given the trusteeship of Ruanda-Urundi. She had striven hard to live up to that reputation and had grown in the process to think of herself as a model character in all her international dealings. Now her self-confidence was badly shaken and in consequence she had weakly acceded to most of the Congolese demands at the Round Table Conference when she should have been firm and dynamic in purpose. Yet what other could she do? It is perfectly certain that the temper of the Belgian people at that time would bitterly have opposed any attempt to continue to rule in the Congo by force. As to the economic situation, the damage was already done. Foreign investment had ceased to flow into the Congo from the moment of the January rioting of 1959. All in all Belgium may take what comfort she can from the thought that she met the challenge honestly when it came. She may also pertinently ask (again for her comfort) how much better, in the long run, have most of the newly independent countries in Africa fared.

Appendices

The Belgian Royal Family

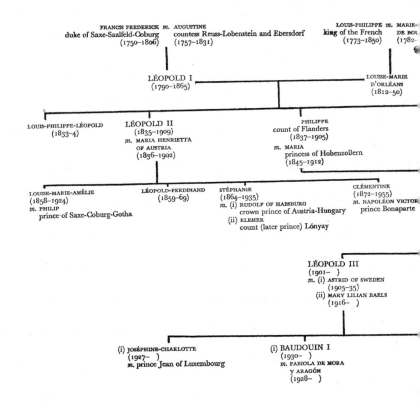

FRANCIS FREDERICK *m.* AUGUSTINE
duke of Saxe-Saalfeld-Coburg   countess Reuss-Lobenstein and Ebersdorf
(1750–1806)   (1757–1831)

LOUIS-PHILIPPE *m.* MARIE-
king of the French   DE BOU
(1773–1850)   (1782–

LÉOPOLD I
(1790–1865)

LOUISE-MARIE
D'ORLÉANS
(1812–50)

LOUIS-PHILIPPE-LÉOPOLD
(1833–4)

LÉOPOLD II
(1835–1909)
m. MARIA HENRIETTA
OF AUSTRIA
(1836–1902)

PHILIPPE
count of Flanders
(1837–1905)
m. MARIA
princess of Hohenzollern
(1845–1912)

LOUISE-MARIE-AMÉLIE
(1858–1924)
m. PHILIP
prince of Saxe-Coburg-Gotha

LÉOPOLD-FERDINAND
(1859–69)

STÉPHANIE
(1864–1935)
m. (i) RUDOLF OF HABSBURG
crown prince of Austria-Hungary
(ii) ELEMER
count (later prince) Lónyay

CLÉMENTINE
(1872–1955)
m. NAPOLÉON VICTOR
prince Bonaparte

LÉOPOLD III
(1901–)
m. (i) ASTRID OF SWEDEN
(1905–35)
(ii) MARY LILIAN BAELS
(1916–)

(i) JOSÉPHINE-CHARLOTTE
(1927–)
m. prince Jean of Luxembourg

(i) BAUDOUIN I
(1930–)
m. FABIOLA DE MORA
Y ARAGÓN
(1928–)

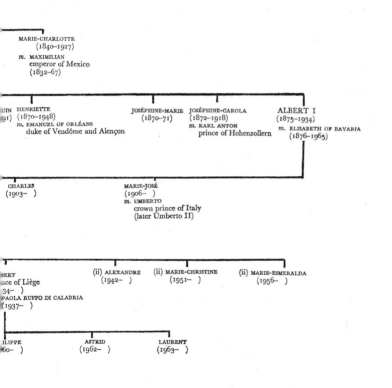

MARIE-CHARLOTTE
(1840–1927)
m. MAXIMILIAN
emperor of Mexico
(1832–67)

UIN   HENRIETTE   JOSÉPHINE-MARIE   JOSÉPHINE-CAROLA   ALBERT I
91)   (1870–1948)   (1870–71)   (1872–1918)   (1875–1934)
       m. EMANUEL OF ORLÉANS   m. KARL ANTON   m. ELISABETH OF BAVARIA
          duke of Vendôme and Alençon   prince of Hohenzollern   (1876–1965)

CHARLES   MARIE-JOSÉ
(1903–)   (1906–)
                              m. UMBERTO
                                 crown prince of Italy
                                 (later Umberto II)

BERT   (ii) ALEXANDRE   (ii) MARIE-CHRISTINE   (ii) MARIE-ESMERALDA
ace of Liège   (1942–)   (1951–)   (1956–)
34–)
PAOLA RUFFO DI CALABRIA
(1937–)

ILIPPE   ASTRID   LAURENT
60–)   (1962–)   (1963–)

Appendix 2

List of Governments from 1830 to the present

1830–40	Catholic–Liberal alliance
1840–45	*Pierre Nothomb* (moderate Catholic)
1845–47	Compromise government, mainly Catholic-based
1847–52	*Charles Rogier* (Liberal)
1852–57	Coalition government with Catholics predominant
1857–68	*Charles Rogier* as nominal head, with *Frère-Orban* in *de facto* control
1868–70	*Frère-Orban* (Liberal)
1870–78	*Anethan* and *Jules Malou* (Catholic right wing)
1878–84	Second Liberal ministry of *Frère-Orban*
1884–1919	Catholics in undisputed control
1919–39	Various Catholic–Liberal coalition governments leading to tripartite government with socialist representation
1939–44	*Pierlot* (Catholic) forms a Catholic–Liberal coalition and carries his government into exile
1944–45	*Pierlot*'s coalition consisting of PSC, PSB, Liberals, and communists (who withdraw in November 1944)
1945 (5½ months)	*Van Acker*'s coalition – representation as with Pierlot
1945–46	*Van Acker*. PSB, Liberal, communist
1946 (15 days)	*Spaak*. All PSB
1946 (4 months)	*Van Acker*. PSB, Liberal, communist
1946–47	*Huysmans*. As above.
1947–49	*Spaak*. PSC, PSB
1949–50	*Eyskens*. PSC, Liberal
1950 (2 months)	*Duvieusart*. All PSC
1950–52	*Pholien*. All PSC
1952–54	*Van Houtte*. All PSC
1954–58	*Van Acker*. PSB, Liberal

1958 (4 months)	*Eyskens.* All PSC
1958–60	*Eyskens.* PSC, Liberal
1960–61	*Eyskens.* As above
1961–65	*Lefèvre.* PSC, PSB
1965–66	*Harmel.* As above
1966–68	*Vanden Boeynants.* PSC, PLP
1968–	*Eyskens.* PSC, PSB

PSB *Parti Socialiste Belge* (Socialists)
PSC *Parti Social Chrétien* (Catholics)
PLP *Parti de la Liberté et du Progrès* (Liberals)

For Further Reading

Anonymous. *La Patrie Belge*: Bruxelles, 1905
    Belgique, La Relation Officielle des Evénements, 1939–1940: London, 1941
Bernard, Henri. *Par La Paix Armée vers La Guerre Totale*: Bruxelles, 1951
Bronne, Carlo. *Léopold I et son Temps*: Bruxelles, 1942
Charriaut, Henri. *Belgique, Terre d'Héroisme*: Paris, 1915
Dechesne, Laurent. *Histoire Economique et Sociale de la Belgique*: Paris/Liège, 1932
Delsinne, Léon. *Le Parti Ouvrier Belge*: Bruxelles, 1955
Jaspar, Marcel-Henri. *Souvenirs sans Retouche*: Paris, 1968
Lichtervelde, Louis de. *Léopold II*: Bruxelles, 1949
Mallinson, Vernon. *Power and Politics in Belgian Education*: London, 1963
    Modern Belgian Literature (1830–1960): London, 1966
Michiels et Laude. *Notre Colonie*: Bruxelles, 1951
Pirenne, Henri. *Histoire de Belgique* (seven volumes): Bruxelles, 1902–32. This is an indispensable and standard work
Spaak, Paul-Henri. *Combats Inachevés*: Paris, 1969
Stinglhamber et Dresse. *Léopold II au Travail*: Bruxelles, 1945
Thonissen, J. J. *La Constitution Belge Annotée*: Bruxelles, 1879

The following newspaper files have also been consulted:

    La Dernière Heure (Liberal)
    Le Drapeau Rouge (communist)
    La Libre Belgique (Catholic–conservative)
    Le Peuple (Walloon – left wing)
    Le Soir (independent)

Index

Printed in Great Britain by Western Printing Services Ltd, Bristol